An OPUS book

SHAKESPEARE

OPUS General Editors

Keith Thomas
Alan Ryan
Peter Medawar

OPUS books provide concise, original, and authoritative introductions to a wide range of subjects in the humanities and sciences. They are written by experts for the general reader as well as for students.

Shakespeare

A Writer's Progress

PHILIP EDWARDS

Oxford   New York

OXFORD UNIVERSITY PRESS

1986

Oxford University Press, Walton Street, Oxford OX2 6DP
Oxford New York Toronto
Delhi Bombay Calcutta Madras Karachi
Kuala Lumpur Singapore Hong Kong Tokyo
Nairobi Dar es Salaam Cape Town
Melbourne Auckland
and associated companies in
Beirut Berlin Ibadan Nicosia

Oxford is a trade mark of Oxford University Press

British Library Cataloguing in Publication Data
Edwards, Philip
Shakespeare: a writer's progress.—(OPUS)
1. Shakespeare, William—Criticism and interpretation
I. Title II. Series
822.3'5 PR2976
ISBN 0-19-219184-5

Library of Congress Cataloging in Publication Data
Edwards, Philip
Shakespeare: a writer's progress.—(OPUS)
Bibliography: p. Includes index.
1. Shakespeare, William, 1564-1616—Criticism and
interpretation.
I. Title. II. Series.
PR2976.E28 1986 822.3'3 85-15552
ISBN 0-19-219184-5

Printed in Great Britain
at the University Press, Oxford
by David Stanford
Printer to the University

Preface

It is the purpose of this book to give a general account of all Shakespeare's writings, prefaced by a sketch of his life. The risks of attempting to compress Shakespeare into two hundred pages are obvious enough, but perhaps the loss of detail will be forgiven in the interests of trying to see Shakespeare whole. This book stresses the inter-relationship of all he wrote, poems, sonnets, comedies, histories, tragedies. His work is a unity, and the meaning of each part is enlarged by recognizing that unity. Muriel Bradbrook once spoke of 'the modifying and shaping power which his work as a whole seems to exert upon each of its parts'. The meaning of *The Two Gentlemen of Verona* is not complete until *The Tempest* has been written.

The brief account of Shakespeare's life with which the book opens is particularly concerned with the choices open to Shakespeare as a writer at the end of the sixteenth century, and I suggest that in assessing his commitment to the theatre we should look at the different kind of evidence provided by the sonnets, the great length of many of his plays, and the enigmatic countenance of his extraordinary last plays. The second chapter treats the community of theme which binds Shakespeare's writings together, concentrating on family, sexual, and social relationships. The third chapter is mainly about the non-dramatic verse, especially the sonnets, with a consideration of some attitudes to language expressed or implied in the plays.

The chapters which follow discuss the plays. Accepting that all classifications and divisions are temporary and provisional, I have used the familiar groupings of comedy, history, and tragedy, but I have added the category of tragicomedy, in which I include the middle or 'dark' comedies and the late 'romances'. This grouping of the middle and late comedies is essential to my argument. I believe it helps us to understand what preoccupied Shakespeare in his final plays, and how those plays include, comment on, and round off the arguments and transactions of the earlier works. The chapter on the tragedies is shaped by a concept of tragic commitment and its two faces of love and violence.

The main object of this book is to provide something of use to the playgoer and student, young or old, who is moving forward to a fuller knowledge and understanding of Shakespeare's work. For that reason I have included a great deal that will appear familiar and obvious to those who know their Shakespeare well. At the same time, I offer this as my personal view and estimate of what Shakespeare has written, and I hope it will interest those who do not need the more introductory material.

The quotations from Shakespeare's works are not taken from any one modern edition, and I accept responsibility for their form. They are, however, keyed to the act, scene, and line numbering of the Riverside Shakespeare (1974), textual editor G. Blakemore Evans.

I acknowledge with gratitude a period of study-leave given by the University of Liverpool (assisted by a grant from the Leverhulme Trust), and also the hospitality of the Huntington Library, California, and New College, Oxford, where much of this book was written.

Finally, I should like to dedicate this small work to the Shakespearians of the University of Liverpool past and present, beginning with Bradley and Walter Raleigh, and including among many others Peter Ure and Ernest Schanzer, both of whom died in mid-career, and at this time my colleagues Kenneth Muir and Ann Thompson, to whom I owe so much.

Liverpool   PHILIP EDWARDS
1985

Contents

1 A career in the theatre   1
2 Relationship   27
3 Poems and poetry   55
4 Comedy   83
5 History   104
6 Tragedy   126
7 Tragicomedy   160
   Epilogue   182

   A note on Shakespeare criticism   185
   A chronology of the plays and poems 196
   Index   199

1

A career in the theatre

Beginnings

It is doubtful whether Shakespeare's parents could read or write. There were no schools in the villages near Stratford-upon-Avon where they spent their childhood, and they both signed all documents with their marks. John Shakespeare was an enterprising man, however. The son of a tenant farmer at Snitterfield, he had left the land, learned the glover's trade at Stratford, married the daughter of the farmer who owned his father's farm, and become very active in the affairs of the newly constituted Borough of Stratford-upon-Avon. Considering the work he had to do in the many offices he held as chamberlain, alderman, justice of the peace, and bailiff—the highest office in the borough—it seems unlikely that he had not in time learned to read. If he had, he clearly found it easier to affix his glover's mark to a document than to try to sign his name. By becoming bailiff in 1568 John Shakespeare became entitled to the coveted status of gentleman, and appears to have applied for his coat of arms. He and his wife Mary (formerly Arden) had eight children born between 1558 and 1580; of the four girls only one survived beyond infancy. William Shakespeare, the eldest of the boys, was born in 1564, the year in which Galileo and Christopher Marlowe were also born, and the year in which Calvin and Michelangelo died.

Shakespeare certainly had his schooling, though there is no documentary evidence of it. The school at Stratford was one of the many ancient schools 're-founded' by King Edward VI. Whereas Ben Jonson left moving tribute to Camden, his master at Westminster School—

> most reverend head, to whom I owe
> All that I am, all that I know—

the masters at Stratford grammar school in Shakespeare's time, Walter Roche, Simon Hunt, Thomas Jenkins, have to be content with the indirect tribute of Shakespeare's works. The second of these masters has been assumed to be the Simon Hunt who went to the college for English Catholics at Douai, became a Jesuit, and died in Rome. The master who succeeded Jenkins in 1579 was John Cottam, whose brother was executed as a seminary priest in London in 1582. It is possible that resistance to the Reformation was in some ways evident at school, as it may have been, as we shall see, at home.* Jonson said of Shakespeare that he had 'small Latin and less Greek', but that means much more than most of us have. It is not in any case Shakespeare's facility in writing Latin or the extent of his reading in Roman and Greek authors which is important. In his Latin-based education, the constant emphasis on the structure of language and the arts of language, on the analysis of expression, on the development of an argument, on logic, on debate and on oratory, provided a major foundation not only for the declamations in the history-plays but the wit-combats in the comedies and the passion or cunning in the arguments of Isabella or Iachimo. He was presumably introduced to Roman comedy by reading Terence and Plautus. Of the poets, it is Ovid whose influence is most clearly seen in the plays, especially *Titus Andronicus*. The new English Bible, in its 'Geneva' or 'Bishops' version, was probably the most important English element in Shakespeare's education.

The great mystery of Shakespeare's boyhood is not about his schooling but about what happened to his father. Here in 1577 is one of the most prominent of Stratford's citizens and the most active in its affairs, Alderman Shakespeare, suddenly withdrawing from attendance at meetings of the council, and never returning, although they kept his place open until 1586. He mortgaged his wife's estates and there are several indications of financial embarrassment. He was summoned to Westminster in 1580 to appear at the Queen's Bench and give surety for his maintenance of the Queen's peace. He did not appear, and suffered fines of £40. In 1591, during a nation-wide drive to secure conformity, John Shakespeare's name was returned as one of forty-one people not attending church. Some of these were open Catholics who paid their fines, some had been excommunicated, some were in ill health, and of nine, including John Shakespeare, the first return remarked: 'It is said that these come not to church

---

*Since this was written, the view that Shakespeare had a Catholic upbringing and that John Cottam had a decisive influence on his life has been strongly urged by E. A. J. Honigmann in *Shakespeare: The 'Lost Years'* (Manchester University Press, 1985).

for fear of process for debt,' and the second return: 'They are thought to forbear the church for debt.' Many have held the view that in making these recusancy returns John Shakespeare's former associates, who had given several tokens of their feeling for him, were trying to cover up their colleague's religious scruples by the pretence that he was afraid of being arrested for debt if he went to church. The inference would be that it was his conscience that prevented him from continuing to take part in the work of a Borough council which was inextricably bound up with the maintenance of the official practices of the Church of England, and that the evidence of financial embarrassment points to an attempt to reduce his vulnerability to crippling recusancy fines. Scholarly biographers show sturdy contempt for the theory that it was religion and not business troubles that darkened John Shakespeare's later years. One shakes his head at biographers who are tempted 'by the notion of a religious romance in the drab life of a town councillor'; another says: 'These interpretations have a romantic appeal, but John Shakespeare was a tradesman, not an ideologue.' (So much for Bunyan!) But it is becoming more difficult to make away with the Catholic 'spiritual testament' reported to have been discovered in the rafters of the Shakespeares' house in Henley Street in 1757. The manuscript has disappeared, but striking support for its authenticity has come during this century in the discovery that the testament follows a formula for such confessions of faith drawn up by Cardinal Borromeo and very widely circulated, and, secondly, that there was an English version current almost identical in wording with the Henley Street testament which Malone transcribed. No doubt John Shakespeare's name—and that of his patron saint, St Winifred—were inserted at the appropriate places by whoever provided him with the document. The presumption is strong that John Shakespeare retained an allegiance to the old faith and that in middle life his conscience dictated that he cease from compromise. He withdrew from the council when William Shakespeare was 12 years old. What would have been the effect on the children of the father's obstinate course during these years when hostility to recusants was so marked can only be imagined, as can the effect on Shakespeare of being brought up in a household where religious debate must have been a continuous presence.

Those who have tried to prove from the plays that Shakespeare was a Catholic have laboured in vain. Late in the seventeenth century Richard Davies said: 'He died a papist.' It may be so; perhaps a return to his father's faith towards the end of his life? But no deduction can be made about his doctrinal or ecclesiastical allegiance from the plays. They are steeped in very generalized Christian sentiment, but there is a surprising absence of specifically Christian doctrine in them, Catholic or Protestant. The Sermon on the Mount is everywhere, but only very rarely indeed is there, as in *Measure for Measure*, any direct reference to the atonement and redemption through Christ. The idea of salvation and damnation, I shall argue, is central to an understanding of the tragedies, but the nature of the world beyond this world, the demands that it makes on one, and the means to reach it, are presented not as something revealed but as a haunting and troubling mystery. There is a great deal of anxious religious questing and very little Christian conviction.

In plays written for Protestant audiences in a country where the reformed religion was the only one tolerated you would not expect any personal unorthodoxy to be openly expressed, but I can find nothing in the plays to suggest that Shakespeare lived as a convinced Catholic or a convinced Anglican either. As for his sympathies, the most telling evidence is not in how he portrays friars, nor in his ignorance of the confidentiality of the confessional, nor the anti-papal tone of *King John*, nor the sympathetic treatment of Katharine of Aragon in *Henry VIII*, but in that single line of Sonnet 73, 'Bare ruined choirs where late the sweet birds sang.' If that line, in context, does not express sadness about the course which the juggernaut of history had taken in England in the sixteenth century, poetry is a mere rhapsody of words.

John Shakespeare had made a good marriage. His son William's seems at best imprudent and was perhaps disastrous. At 18 years old he married Anne Hathaway, a woman of 26. Their first child, Susanna, was born five months after the wedding (baptized May 1583). Twins, Hamnet and Judith, were born in February 1585. Before he was 21 Shakespeare was the father of three young children, with a wife nearing 30. Orsino in *Twelfth Night* is not exactly an author figure, but it is hard not to suspect a certain authorial feeling in his advice to Viola: 'Let still the woman take / An elder than herself.' In *The Tempest* Prospero cautions Ferdinand about his relations with Miranda and warns him that, if he should 'break her virgin knot' before their wedding,

> No sweet aspersion shall the heavens let fall
> To make this contract grow; but barren hate,
> Sour-eyed disdain, and discord, shall bestrew
> The union of your bed with weeds so loathly
> That you shall hate it both.
>
> (IV. i. 18–22)

The constant bitterness in the plays and poems about the tyranny of sexual desire (which will be discussed in the next chapter) is not the sort of thing that arises from listening to other people's conversation.

London

There is a complete absence of information about Shakespeare between the birth of the twins in 1585 and the year 1592, when Robert Greene, making his celebrated attack on Shakespeare as an 'upstart crow', gives us unmistakable evidence that Shakespeare had established himself as a dramatist in the London theatre. It is not at once that even an upstart crow can gain a footing firm enough to arouse resentment like Greene's, and it is common sense to assume that by 1592 Shakespeare had for several years been an actor who was now making a name for himself by writing plays for his fellow-actors. Perhaps the important gap to fill in Shakespeare's life is between 1578, when he presumably left school at the age of 14, and the birth of the twins in 1585, rather than the seven years to 1592, most of which must have gone into his apprenticeship in the theatre.

The implications of Robert Greene's attack are important. Greene came from a family background very similar to Shakespeare's: his father was a Norwich saddler. But he had won his way to Cambridge and was Master of Arts. After travelling abroad he had settled into a squalid enough life as a writer in London, producing prose romances, pamphlets, and plays, until 1592 when in the year of his early death he wrote in gloomy remorse *Greene's Groatsworth of Wit, Bought with a Million of Repentance* (repenting among other things the six-year desertion of his wife). It is as a professional *writer* addressing his colleagues that he turns to attack the players for whom they have been writing: 'those puppets ... that spake from our mouths, those antics garnished in our colours.'

Yes, trust them not, for there is an upstart crow, beautified with our feathers, that with his *tiger's heart wrapped in a player's hide* supposes he is as well able to bombast out a blank verse as the best of you; and being an absolute *Johannes Factotum* is in his own conceit the only Shake-scene in a country.

Here is the indignation of the intellectual, the university man without office in Church or State, who has demeaned himself by condescending to grace the new public theatres with the fruits of his education, finding himself put out of even this mean business by the imitative efforts of the unlettered players.

The professional theatre was very young in Shakespeare's day and who was to provide its plays was an open question. The first public theatre was opened (just outside London's boundary) in 1576, when Shakespeare was a boy of 12. Two years before, this bewildering new breed of men, the 'common players', had a symbolic triumph in the granting of a licence under the Great Seal by the Queen to the Earl of Leicester's men to perform their plays in any city in England. In 1583 the Queen herself became the patron of a company of players. At the same time these men who were without identifiable profession or calling were liable to prosecution under the act against rogues and vagabonds, and there was continuous warfare against them by churchmen, moralists and above all by the authorities of the City of London. It is astonishing that the infant theatre survived at all; it flourished because the demand by the audience could not be extinguished, and because the audience included the Court of Queen Elizabeth, who was herself happy to encourage the professional companies as a cheap and reliable source for the entertainment which she and the greater nobility were pleased to call for when occasion demanded.

It is noticeable that the playwrights who dominated the London theatre in Shakespeare's apprentice days were, socially speaking, a homogeneous group. Lyly, a gentleman, had been above the rough and tumble of the open stages. But Marlowe, a Cambridge graduate, was, like Greene and Shakespeare, the son of a respectable tradesman in a provincial city—a Canterbury shoemaker. Thomas Kyd was the son of a scrivener with a grammar-school and not a university education (Merchant Taylors). A later non-university recruit was Ben Jonson, whose father, a man of education, died before he was born; his mother then married a bricklayer and he was 'brought up poorly'.

The two dramatists who most influenced the young Shakespeare were the oddly assorted couple who between them more or less invented Elizabethan tragedy, and who might have been found in 1591 or thereabouts 'writing in one chamber' and serving the same patron: the tempestuous and reckless Christopher Marlowe and the staid, timorous, cautious Thomas Kyd. (By 1594 these two, with Greene, were dead; all three men died in their thirties.) With the great uncertainty about the dates of plays in the late 1580s and early 1590s, one must be very careful in talking about influence. There may well have been reciprocal influence between Marlowe and Shakespeare. If *Tamburlaine* helped to produce *Richard III*, *Henry VI* may have helped to produce *Edward II*; and *Edward II* certainly influenced *Richard II*. But there is no doubt that the work of Marlowe and Kyd was of immense importance in Shakespeare's development. He incorporates them, competes with them, quarrels with them. He accepted the antithetical structures which each created to accommodate his idea of tragedy: the soaring career of the individualist Marlovian hero to the boundaries of the human imagination—and back; and the web of conflicting aspirations of Kyd's *Spanish Tragedy*, where men and women tread the circuits printed out by an indifferent deity. He accepted the structures and denied the premises. Where Tamburlaine is beauty, Richard III is ugliness; where Faustus is a scholar, Macbeth is a soldier; where Hieronimo is tied, Hamlet is free. Although the plays of Lyly and Peele had considerable influence on Shakespearian comedy—and as late as *The Winter's Tale* Peele's *Old Wives Tale* was running in Shakespeare's mind—there are no voices dominating Shakespeare's comedies in the way that the voices of Marlowe and Kyd are ever-present voices in his histories and tragedies: voices like the voice of the rival poet in the sonnets, which cannot be discounted, which force admiration and which must be disputed.

Which of the actors' companies Shakespeare worked with and wrote for in the years before the plague of 1592 to 1594 changed the whole face of the London theatre is difficult to discern. The history of the companies themselves—Queen's, Strange's, Pembroke's, Admiral's—is tangled and obscure. More serious than our ignorance of his company affiliations is the difficulty of knowing which were his earliest plays. That the *Henry VI* plays were a great success by 1592 is apparent from three separate sources: Greene's parody of a line in *3 Henry VI*, 'O tiger's heart wrapped in a woman's hide!', Nashe's enthusiastic description of the effect of the death of Talbot on English audiences (see below, p. 104, and Henslowe's record of many performances of 'harey the vj' at his theatre, the Rose, on Bankside south of the Thames from March to June 1592. Apart from this we have no information about the dates and order of composition of the earliest of the surviving plays, nor about the extent to which he worked in collaboration with other playwrights. At some point he was one of the team that worked on the unlucky play *Sir Thomas More* (and the three pages in the manuscript that are generally accepted as Shakespeare's are the only specimen of his handwriting we possess, apart from signatures). Collaboration was standard practice; in his major period Shakespeare was very unusual in not partaking in it. In his later years he collaborated. *Pericles Prince of Tyre, Henry VIII*, and *The Two Noble Kinsmen* are all of joint authorship. It would be very surprising if Shakespeare had not in his earliest days been accustomed to work as contributor and collaborator as well as sole author. Of the plays collected in the First Folio, opinion that *1 Henry VI* and *Titus Andronicus* are of composite authorship has declined; but it certainly would not be in any way unusual if Peele *did* have a share in the early scenes of *Titus*.

Early work

The best way to try to assess the early work of Shakespeare is to take stock of him when he is 30, when in 1594 with the formation of the Lord Chamberlain's company with himself as one of the leading sharers we enter a new phase of his career in the theatre. If we look back at what he had achieved by that time, we must be impressed at the ambitiousness of his whole endeavour. In the realm of the history-play, the idea of writing a sequence of four plays on the Wars of the Roses was bold, imaginative, and original. Marlowe had written two plays on an obscure Levantine potentate. But here is English history, dramatized and moralized for English audiences as it had never been before. Shakespeare did not invent the English-history-play but he transformed it, and no one had conceived it in the epic terms of a major sequence like the first 'tetralogy'. In the first scene of the first play, as the great nobles of England assemble round the coffin of the dead King Henry V, it is clear that the actor-son of the Stratford glover is a new presence in the English theatre. No wonder Greene was shocked. But in a way *Titus Andronicus* is more breath-taking. If ever there was a play which a young man wrote to show people what he could do, it is this. Here is an extraordinary experiment in the theatre of cruelty painted on a vast canvas of invented happenings in imperial Rome. It is more than possible that Shakespeare thought the whole thing up himself, even if he built it with bricks made from Ovid and Seneca. There is certainly no extant source. It is demonstrable that in his earlier plays Shakespeare relied less heavily on sources than he did in his middle and late career; the long-current notion that he began as an adapter of other men's work is not tenable. Whether or not the attempt to clothe extremes of cruelty and suffering in poetic richness succeeds or not is a matter of opinion, but *Titus Andronicus* is a formidable work and its faults are those of a young poet determined to be heard.

However bold and striking Shakespeare's first ventures in tragedy and history were, his actual achievement is more assured in comedy than in the other genres. No one would call the second part of *Henry VI* brilliant as one calls *The Comedy of Errors* and *Love's Labour's Lost* brilliant. *The Two Gentlemen of Verona* is (I shall argue) an underestimated play, and it is certainly a very *thoughtful* work, in which Shakespeare began to try out ideas that came to fruition in *A Midsummer Night's Dream* and *As You Like It*. What impresses us about these early comedies is not only the control and assurance of the writing but the distinctiveness of the design and tone of each play. Each is a different experiment in what can be done. There are no sources for these plays as Lodge's romance was a source for *As You Like It* and Greene's for *The Winter's Tale*. Shakespeare appropriated snippets from everywhere with the skill of the lifelong kleptomaniac that he became, from Plautus, from a hellenistic romance, from an Italian novella, from the *commedia dell' arte*, from native English comedy, but considered as a whole each play has only one source and that is Shakespeare's creative imagination.

A choice of direction

The courtly setting of *Love's Labour's Lost*, its satire on affectations in literature and language, its gentle mockery of the
conventions of the theatre, may well suggest a more cultivated
audience than the audience for which *The Taming of the Shrew*
was written. That such a literary and sophisticated piece should
be among Shakespeare's earliest plays provokes questions about
the direction of his literary ambitions. It is notable that, in the
apology which he felt he should make for his share in the
publication of the *Groatsworth of Wit*, Henry Chettle spoke of
Shakespeare in these terms:

... myself have seen his demeanour no less civil than he excellent in the
quality he professes. Besides, divers of worship have reported his
uprightness of dealing, which argues his honesty, and his facetious grace
in writing, that approves his art.

(Kind Heart's Dream, 1592)

It obviously impressed Chettle that Shakespeare was well known
among people who were above him in social rank, people 'of
worship', who liked him enough to resent the terms of Greene's
attack and to speak up on his behalf.

Now, although to live by one's pen has always been a matter of
great difficulty, in Elizabethan times it was quite impossible. To
be a writer you had to be something else as well: one of the landed
gentry, an official in Ireland, a Fellow of a college, a churchman,
or an actor. The alternative was to find patrons, as (just at this
time) Samuel Daniel was doing, living as a pensioner of, succes-
sively, Sir Edward Dymoke, the Countess of Pembroke, Fulke
Greville, and Lord Mountjoy. There was very little money in
writing plays. The big money in the theatre went to Philip
Henslowe, who owned theatres, and his son-in-law Edward
Alleyn, the great actor. It is not to be supposed that it was only
because in 1592 the plague closed the theatres for two long years
that Shakespeare wrote and published his two major narrative
poems, *Venus and Adonis* and *The Rape of Lucrece*, with their
dedication to the Earl of Southampton. Looking back over his
career, we tend to think of him kicking his heels while the theatres
were shut, filling in the time with writing poems to earn some
bread and butter. But it is not so clear that in 1592 Shakespeare

was so irrevocably committed to a career in the theatre as his exclusive profession. Ben Jonson did his very best to free himself from dependence on a public theatre which he disdained, and he sought, as Dekker rudely put it in 1601, to 'screw and wriggle himself into great men's familiarity'. He won the patronage of many of the flattered nobility and the monarch himself, though he was never able to 'leave the loathèd stage' (his words) entirely. The plague years of 1592 to 1594 may conceivably have precipitated a decision brewing in Shakespeare's mind for years to lessen his dependence on the theatre as the source of his livelihood and to widen his scope as a writer. Chettle's 'divers of worship' may have been the original audience for *Love's Labour's Lost*, and the phrase may be an indication of the beginnings of Shakespeare's search for patronage. But it is evident that, in offering his *Venus and Adonis* in 1593 to Henry Wriothesley (pronounced Risley), third Earl of Southampton, Shakespeare was making a cautious approach to someone he didn't know well.

Right Honourable, I know not how I shall offend in dedicating my unpolished lines to your Lordship, nor how the world will censure me for choosing so strong a prop to support so weak a burden. Only if your Honour seem but pleased, I account myself highly praised, and vow to take advantage of all idle hours till I have honoured you with some graver labour. But if the first heir of my invention prove deformed, I shall be sorry it had so noble a godfather, and never after ear so barren a land for fear it yield me still so bad a harvest. I leave it to your honourable survey, and your Honour to your heart's content, which I wish may always answer your own wish, and the world's hopeful expectation.

> Your Honour's in all duty,
> William Shakespeare.

The person to whom this deferential epistle was written was just emerging from his teens. An orphan, he was the ward of the Lord Treasurer, Lord Burghley, who wished him to marry his granddaughter, Elizabeth de Vere. One of the most definite facts of Shakespeare's life, apart from what parish registers record, is that this dedication led to a warm friendship between Shakespeare and Southampton. The dedication to the latter of *The Rape of Lucrece* in the following year runs as follows:

The love I dedicate to your Lordship is without end: whereof this pamphlet without beginning is but a superfluous moiety. The warrant I have of your honourable disposition, not the worth of my untutored lines, makes it assured of acceptance. What I have done is yours, what I have to do is yours, being part in all I have, devoted yours. Were my worth greater, my duty would show greater; meantime, as it is, it is bound to your lordship, to whom I wish long life still lengthened with all happiness.

Your Lordship's in all duty,
William Shakespeare.

The difference in the tone of the two dedications is astonishing, and so is the closeness of the friendship publicly claimed by Shakespeare in the second. The question inevitably arises whether this love 'without end' which Shakespeare professes for Southampton is the same as the love which the poet expresses for his youthful patron in the sonnets. We know from comments made on Shakespeare's work by Francis Meres that the sonnets had been circulating in manuscript during the 1590s. 'The sweet witty soul of Ovid lives in mellifluous and honey-tongued Shakespeare; witness his *Venus and Adonis*, his *Lucrece*, his sugared sonnets among his private friends, etc.' (*Palladis Tamia*, 1598). Sidney's great sequence *Astrophil and Stella* was published (five years after Sidney's death) in 1591. A whole spate of sequences followed, by Constable, Daniel, Drayton, Spenser, and others. Shakespeare's sonnets were not printed until 1609, with the publisher, Thomas Thorpe, providing the enigmatic dedication to 'Mr. W. H.' as 'the onlie begetter of these insuing sonnets'. (Versions of two of the sonnets had been printed in Jaggard's *The Passionate Pilgrim* in 1599.) It is unlikely that Shakespeare himself authorized Thorpe's publication.

That Southampton is the young man of the sonnets, the 'lovely boy' who is the subject of the first 126 of them, is a reasonable assumption; no one else fits the position better. Whether he is or not, the sonnets, though they are neither autobiography nor an autobiographical novel, have an immense amount to tell us about Shakespeare himself, about patronage, about his view of himself as a poet, and about his career in the theatre. To say so is to take a risk, the risk that when we meet Shakespeare in heaven and ask him about the young man and the dark woman and the rival poet he will burst into laughter and say he invented the whole thing one weekend in Stratford. The risk is worth taking. Inferences from documents can be far more dangerously insecure than inferences made with all proper allowance from the writings that came from Shakespeare's pen. We can agree that it is inconceivable that the sonnets are or were ever intended to be an exact poetic record of the course of Shakespeare's relationship with an aristocratic young patron and a sexually rapacious dark-haired woman. It is inconceivable that the sonnets as a whole should have been written for and sent to the ostensible recipients. (These matters are discussed in Chapter 3.) But that there is a solid core of autobiography in the sonnets, in the events referred to, the relationships described, the emotions expressed, seems to me beyond dispute. It may not be their most important or interesting feature, but it can hardly be argued away.

Two states of mind which recur and stand out in the sonnets are a painful, querulous sense of the poet's inferiority and an abiding conviction, overcoming all self-doubting, of the worth of his own poetry.

'Fortune reigns in gifts of the world, not in the lineaments of nature,' said Rosalind. It is Fortune that has allotted to the poet his humble social status and so denied him the respect the world would have shown him had he been born to an ancient and honourable family and large acres. It is because of the lottery of birth that he is no better a man than he now is. In Sonnet 29 he is 'in disgrace with Fortune and men's eyes': the second disgrace follows the first. What by 'nature' he might have been is immaterial; he is 'made lame' by Fortune's spite (37). Touchstone 'railed on Fortune in good terms', and so does the poet.

> O for my sake do you with Fortune chide,
> The guilty goddess of my harmful deeds,
> That did not better for my life provide
> Than public means which public manners breeds.
> Thence comes it that my name receives a brand,
> And almost thence my nature is subdued
> To what it works in, like the dyer's hand.

(111)

By his 'harmful deeds' he does not mean crimes. He means the behaviour and the way of life of an upstart crow of an actor, behaviour that does him harm with the people by whom he would like to be accepted. His 'means' are not an income from lands or even trade, but the 'public' means of the greasy pence which the groundlings pay to see *Henry VI*. So how can his 'manners'—his conduct in general—not be as coarse as the 'means' which support him? It is notable how the poet claims that his *nature* is obscured by his condition. He is like Guiderius or Arviragus in *Cymbeline*, a prince's son chafing in the incongruous circumstances of life which Fortune has provided for him. His nature is 'almost' subdued to the condition of his circumstances. Almost but not quite.

It may be hard to accept that Shakespeare, who seems to *us* to be well on the way to his pinnacle as one of the world's very greatest writers, should be resentful of the environment which generated, moulded, and brought forth his work. But it surely is the case. Even Shakespeare envied others.

> Wishing me like to one more rich in hope,
> Featured like him, like him with friends possessed,
> Desiring this man's art, and that man's scope,
> With what I most enjoy contented least ...
>
> (29)

In Sonnet 66, a sudden anger gives vitality to a rather conventional complaint ('Tired with all these, for restful death I cry'):

> And art made tongue-tied by authority,
> And folly, doctor-like, controlling skill.

What made Shakespeare write these lines? What had he been stopped from saying? *Who* is the fool 'controlling' (i.e. restraining, restricting) his work? Is it censorship? or is it the players who have the power to say yea or nay to what he writes? It could be either, or both.

It is impossible to date the sonnets. They may have had their genesis in a sequence written to Southampton in 1593–4, urging him to marry, promising him the immortality of verse, recording the growth of their affection, and in the ensuing years they may have been worked over, added to, and developed in such a way that the 'real-life' content was considerably diminished. If this is so, sonnets like 29, 66, and 111 may have been written before Shakespeare was securely in the position in the theatre which gave so much more freedom to his art, as a sharer in the Lord Chamberlain's company. In the mid-1590s he abandoned altogether the publication of non-dramatic verse (and perhaps the writing of it too) except for the single poem 'The Phoenix and the Turtle'. There is no evidence of any further effort to secure a patron. Why did he turn away from all other literary activity and devote himself so single-mindedly to writing for the theatre? I suggest the answer may be found in *Timon of Athens*, in the contemptuous portrayal of the obsequious and venal poet, the loftiness of whose moral preachments is carefully calculated for its efficacy in extracting cash from Timon. It is impossible to think that Shakespeare did not receive presents from Southampton. Nicholas Rowe, who wrote the first biography of Shakespeare in 1709, said 'my Lord Southampton, at one time, gave him a thousand pounds, to enable him to go through with a purchase which he heard he had a mind to'. This is a hundred years on, and the sum is legendary, but there must be some truth in the story. In 1594 Shakespeare may well have decided that the 'control' of his art by 'authority' in the theatre was a lesser evil than the 'control' which the need to please patrons and dependence on their munificence would certainly exert on his art. He may have seen stretching ahead of him a lifetime of beseeching and acknowledging favours and writing unctuous 'country house' poems, and said no. The price of acceptance by the great was the acceptance of one's inferiority. 'I ensconce me here, / Within the knowledge of mine own desert.' In Sonnet 49, with a bold equivocation (see p. 63), he recognized his desert as something which is both decided by the social superiors he consorts with and also decided by his consciousness of his own merit. The debate in *Troilus and Cressida* between Ulysses and Achilles (III. iii) on whether a man's worth is established by what others think of him, or whether there are absolute standards, is considerably deepened by the perplexities of self-valuation shown in the sonnets.

The sonnets are not about love but about a poet in love. The self, now grovelling now proud, that tries to ascertain its true identity and relationship is the self of a poet. A constant theme is the time-honoured and conventional assertion that these love-poems will outgo the ravages of time and the vicissitudes of constancy and still remain when all around is waste.

> Not marble nor the gilded monuments
> Of princes shall outlive this powerful rhyme.
>
> (55)

This sort of thing comes quite easily to a poet of Shakespeare's talent, and seems incongruous in a man so indifferent to the preservation of his writings. As one reads more deeply into the sonnets, one begins to get the sense that the exclamatory promise of enduring life in verse is being transmuted into a less material concept (see p. 64). Poetry (inspired by love) is the spiritual centre of his life. Writing is the activity that justifies existence. The survival of poetry becomes detached from questions of fame and reputation. What lives on is poetry not persons. If anything lives on, that is; because in the plays of his last years, especially *The Tempest*, Shakespeare is still pondering the relative insubstantiality of writing and of living.

> Now my charms are all o'erthrown,
> And what strength I have's mine own,
> Which is most faint.

(Epilogue, 1–3)

Why Shakespeare after 1594 wrote only plays, and cared so little about the preservation of those plays, remains a mystery, but in thinking about it, it is important not to forget the evidence within the sonnets.

The middle years

Apart from very brief intervals, there was no playing at the public theatres in London between the summer of 1592 and the autumn of 1594. At Christmas 1594 Shakespeare was one of the three payees of the newly formed Lord Chamberlain's men for performance at Court. The others were William Kempe and Richard Burbage. They were the nucleus of the most successful, prosperous, and stable theatrical company in Elizabethan, Jacobean, and Caroline times. Shakespeare wrote for no other company than this, in which he was a 'sharer', and, when they had their own theatre, a 'householder' or joint owner of the property.

The assurance of Shakespeare's art in these energetic years from 1594 to 1599 when he had become to some extent his own master is apparent from simply listing the plays. After the exploratory *King John* he wrote the second major sequence of history-plays, *Richard II*, the two parts of *Henry IV*, and *Henry V*. In tragedy there was just the one play, *Romeo and Juliet*, against a remarkable series of outstanding comedies, *A Midsummer Night's Dream, The Merchant of Venice, Much Ado About Nothing, As You Like It*. Francis Meres reverently listed twelve of his plays in his *Palladis Tamia* of 1598 as evidence of his view that 'As Plautus and Seneca are accounted the best for comedy and tragedy among the Latins, so Shakespeare among the English is the most excellent in both kinds for the stage.' His list included the enigmatic 'Love's Labour's Won', whose existence as a published play (though it has totally disappeared) was surprisingly confirmed by its appearance in a bookseller's list discovered in 1957.

It was while he was writing these masterpieces and to a considerable extent because he was writing these masterpieces that Shakespeare grew prosperous. This was rather a misfortune, because his prosperity has excited contempt in every generation since Pope wrote in 1737 that Shakespeare

> For gain, not glory, wing'd his roving flight,
> And grew Immortal in his own despight.
>
> (*Epistle to Augustus*, 71–2)

Pope must have his little joke. But it is a characteristic that human beings share with dogs to soil every monument they pass. Much lesser men than Pope have continued to greet with glee the recorded financial dealings of Shakespeare, taking them as evidence that the man who by some accident wrote *Hamlet* and *King Lear* was essentially a grasping and covetous man of property on the make.

Though Shakespeare must have spent a great deal of his time in London—and there is evidence of his residing in Bishopsgate, Southwark, and Cripplegate—it is quite clear that he continued to think of himself as a Stratford man. In 1597, the year after the death of his only son, Hamnet, he bought New Place, a fine house (the second largest in Stratford) opposite the Guild Chapel. In documents he is described as William Shakespeare of Stratford-upon-Avon, gentleman. In 1598 Abraham Sturley of Stratford referred to him as 'our countryman Mr Shaksper'. Sturley had heard he wanted to buy land at Shottery, and was writing to another Stratfordian, Richard Quiney, who was in London. Quiney, hoping to see Shakespeare in London and borrow £30 from him, wrote him a letter addressed 'To my loving good friend and countryman Mr. Wm. Shackespere' (which, probably never delivered, is the sole surviving sample of the poet's correspondence).

After ten years work as an actor and a writer, Shakespeare had re-established the family's position in Stratford which his father had achieved before the decline in 1577, and it is commonly assumed (though there is no documentary evidence) that he was responsible for renewing the claim for a grant of arms which it would seem was made, though not pursued, by his father in his prosperous days. The grant, by Garter King-of-Arms, was referred to scornfully by York Herald in 1602 as an example of the abuse of such conferments. 'Shakespeare yᵉ Player', he wrote under a sketch of the well-known arms. The poet of the sonnets did not speak idly of the 'disgrace' in 'men's eyes' of being a common player.

In the year 1599 the Lord Chamberlain's men built their own theatre, the Globe, on the south bank of the Thames. Shakespeare had not yet written the superb last comedy of his middle period, *Twelfth Night*; possibly the experimental citizen comedy *The Merry Wives of Windsor* was still to come, though it may have been written as early as 1597. But the move to the Globe marks the beginning of the great period of Shakespeare's tragedies, with *Julius Caesar* and then *Hamlet*. For eight or nine years after *Twelfth Night* the only plays which the Folio classes as comedies were *All's Well That Ends Well* and *Measure for Measure*. These two are often grouped with *Troilus and Cressida* as 'problem plays', but are better described as tragicomedies. With *Julius Caesar*, Shakespeare began the creative collaboration with North's translation of Plutarch continued in *Antony and Cleopatra* and *Coriolanus*; the fictional extravagance of *Titus Andronicus* is replaced by a controlled and sculpted dramatization of one of the most famous incidents of world history, the assassination of Julius Caesar. *Hamlet* is of a very different lineage. Shakespeare rewrote an earlier play, now lost, possibly by Thomas Kyd, based on a peculiarly barbaric nordic story. The earlier *Hamlet* was, with *The Spanish Tragedy*, the most celebrated example of the Elizabethan revenge-play, much of whose blood, Nashe scornfully remarked, came by transfusion from Seneca. With such a parentage, Shakespeare's *Hamlet* is wholly different in tone from *Julius Caesar*, yet the two plays have the closest links as studies in a particular kind of tragic commitment (see pp. 132–6).

In February 1601 the Chamberlain's men were unluckily and unwittingly involved in Essex's abortive rebellion by being paid to re-enact the old play of *Richard II* the day before the rising. They were so obviously innocent of any complicity in the plot itself that they suffered no penalty. Southampton was involved, however, and was condemned to death, though the sentence was commuted. The Queen understood the intentions of the conspirators in reviving this play of deposition and commented bitterly to the antiquarian Lambarde, 'I am Richard II, know ye not that? ... He that will forget God will also forget his benefactors; this tragedy was played forty times in open streets and houses.'

When James succeeded to the throne in 1603 he appropriated to the patronage of members of the royal family all the major London acting companies, the leading company, Shakespeare's, becoming the King's men. Shakespeare and his colleagues were called on a great deal more for Court appearances than had been the custom in Elizabeth's days. It is also notable that in *Macbeth* Shakespeare pays a number of tributes to the Scottish king. Shakespeare was not given to flattery and it may be allowed that references to touching for the king's evil, to demonology, and to Banquo's successors hardly spoil a good record. But the topicality of *Macbeth* raises the question how far any of Shakespeare's plays were 'occasional' or specially commissioned. Legend has it that *The Merry Wives of Windsor* was a response to Queen Elizabeth's desire to see Sir John in love, and attempts to link the play with celebrations of the Order of the Garter are of long standing. *A Midsummer Night's Dream* may well have been written to celebrate a noble wedding. This play contains the one clear reference in Shakespeare's plays to the Queen, the 'fair vestal, throned by the west' (ii. i. 158). (I assume the reference to Elizabeth at the end of *Henry VIII* is by Fletcher.) There is a rare and unfortunate mention of contemporary events in a Chorus in *Henry V* wishing Essex success in Ireland in 1599. Both *Troilus and Cressida* and *Love's Labour's Lost* have been thought to be too esoteric in their appeal to have been written for the public theatre, and it is not implausible that they were designed for a private audience, perhaps at the Inns of Court. There is little hard fact in all this, but in general it is obvious that Shakespeare was not accustomed to produce plays to grace public occasions, and that topical references within them are remarkable for their sparseness. It is not on the surface that Shakespeare's plays reflect his age.

The tragedies and the stage

It is quite impossible to make a brief comment here on the achievement of the astonishing period of Shakespeare's career, roughly 1604 to 1608, when he wrote *Othello, King Lear, Macbeth, Antony and Cleopatra, Coriolanus,* and (perhaps unfinished) *Timon of Athens.* But, since we have been talking of audiences, it is worth raising at this point the major question of whom ultimately Shakespeare was writing these extraordinary plays for. That Shakespeare chose the role of theatre-poet rather than that of kept-poet in 1594 is clear enough, and I have also suggested that this choice accompanied an alteration in his views on literary immortality. How far then is the stage of the Globe, which is his immediate platform, also his final platform? and how far is the pleasure of the Globe audience the arbiter of what he writes?

There is interesting evidence that there was a circle of admirers in Shakespeare's day who found a significance in his plays which, it is implied, was unlikely to be appreciated in stage performance. The perplexing epistle to the reader which is found only in some copies of the Quarto of *Troilus and Cressida* (1609) claims that the play was 'never staled with the stage, never clapper-clawed with the palms of the vulgar'. Whatever the authority of this disdainful remark, we have an implication here which supports the comments of Gabriel Harvey, who, speaking admiringly of *Hamlet,* wrote of its special appeal to 'the wiser sort'. The writer of the epistle knows that intellectuals are given to despising the fare of the public theatres, but he insists that Shakespeare is an exception.

This author's comedies . . . are so framed to the life that they serve for the most common commentaries of all the actions of our lives, showing such a dexterity and power of wit that the most displeased with plays are pleased with his comedies.

It is a truism that Shakespeare wrote on all levels, to please the less discerning as well as the more discerning of his audience. In saying this we follow one 'An. Sc.' who remarked in 1604: 'Faith, it should please all, like Prince Hamlet.' But this does not solve one very perplexing problem. If Shakespeare wrote with the theatre audience uppermost in his mind, why is it that nearly all his tragedies were far too long to be performed in full on his stage? The average length of Elizabethan plays was under 2,500 lines, allowing two to two-and-a-half hours playing time. Only three or four of Shakespeare's plays are within that limit and, while the early and middle comedies are generally under 3,000 lines, most of the histories and tragedies are well over the 3,000-line mark. Of the tragedies, only *Titus Andronicus*, *Julius Caesar*, *Timon of Athens*, and *Macbeth* are under 3,000 lines. *Richard III*, *Hamlet*, *Othello*, *Antony and Cleopatra*, and *Cymbeline* are all immensely long plays, over 3,500 lines each. The only other dramatist who persistently wrote overlength plays was Ben Jonson. Jonson most certainly regarded his plays as literature to be read and pondered, and he carefully published the full texts as literary texts. 'Words, above action,' he proclaimed in the Prologue to *Cynthia's Revels*, and he established a first for English playwrights by publishing a collection of his plays, poems, and masques as his 'Works' in 1616: *The Workes of Beniamin Jonson*, in folio with a beautiful engraved title-page. Shakespeare did not initiate or oversee the publication of any of his plays. It is doubtful that any of the twelve 'good' quartos published in his lifetime has the guarantee of his personal supervision even if in some cases Shakespeare may have consented to their publication. Shakespeare's colleagues over many years, John Heminges and Henry Condell, presenting his works to the public after his death, wrote:

It had been a thing, we confess, worthy to have been wished, that the author himself had lived to have set forth, and overseen his own writings. But since it hath been ordained otherwise, and he by death departed from that right, we pray you do not envy his friends the office of their care and pain to have collected and published them.

If Shakespeare had after his retirement from the stage been intending to follow Jonson's example and publish his works, it does not appear that he had begun collecting and preparing the manuscripts.

Quite regularly and knowingly Shakespeare must have brought

along to the playhouse manuscripts of plays which were too long to be acted in their entirety. There is little evidence that he played a major part in cutting them down to a length suitable for normal performance. For some plays, two distinct versions exist. Some people hold that the Folio text of *King Lear* was prepared by Shakespeare to replace the longer version preserved in the Quarto publication. I cannot credit this; many of the Folio changes suggest playhouse incomprehension of or impatience with Shakespeare's design. With *Hamlet* it is possible to be more definite. The Quarto version published in 1604 must have been based on Shakespeare's original manuscript and cannot as a whole have been intended for performance as it stood. The Folio version is shorter, and seems to represent a stage in the play's history when the manuscript was being got ready for performance, but it is still far from being short enough for normal production limits. Some of the cuts and alterations may indeed be Shakespeare's, but others cannot conceivably have been made by him and must have originated in the playhouse. The final acting version of *Hamlet*, whoever prepared it, has disappeared; and the same has to be said as regards many if not most of Shakespeare's plays. With *Macbeth*, however, it may be the other way round. The surviving text, of 2,500 lines, may be the acting version of a longer play which is no longer extant. We don't know what we're missing.

My strong impression is that, in his later years at least, Shakespeare did not spend much time in the theatre tailoring his plays to the needs of performance. If he had cared deeply about the acted versions of what he wrote, surely more of them would have been preserved. But then, if he had cared deeply enough about the longer versions, would he not have taken greater care to preserve them as well?

I can see only one solution to this problem. Everything that Shakespeare wrote, he wrote in terms of the stage, always thinking of the form it would take and the effect it would have when given life by actors in performance. At the same time, those long, brilliant, unwieldy texts which have come down to us witness to an ideal theatre in Shakespeare's imagination. He wrote for himself perhaps. If the players of Shakespeare's day were in the habit of truncating and altering play-texts to suit their own convenience without too much concern for what the author might think, even if the author were Shakespeare, we may come to think that the full noon of a play was for the author the completed written text, and that performance was the afternoon light. The matter goes deeper than the mutilation of a text. It is in the very nature of the performance of a Shakespearian tragedy that, as it brings his art to life and releases the possibilities latent in the text, it also necessarily—by the choices made by the actors and the stamp of their personality and the limits of their capacities as well as the unavoidable cuts—excludes and shuts off whole regions of the text's potential. Yet when his plays are *not* on the stage they are inert and shadowy, incomplete and unfulfilled. They require the life of the theatre, and the theatre, in Shakespeare's own day and ever since, is bound to some extent to filter out some of their strength.

The paradox seems to me essentially Shakespearian: the play, like man's life as Sonnet 73 puts it, is consumed by that which nourishes it. He wrote his plays for himself, he wrote them for his audience in the theatre, and he wrote them for an audience beyond the theatre. For all these audiences he composed texts expressly fashioned for performance, knowing that the stage could never fully carry its burden. He does not believe in his plays as literary texts and has no wish to preserve them as such; but nor does he believe that what he writes is to have its full and sufficient incarnation in any stage performance. He brought along to the theatre plays which belong to an ideal theatre, and he gave them to his fellow-actors to do with them what they would or what they could. What was preserved and handed on was not of *his* providing. The configuration of the young Shakespeare's literary ambitions becomes blurred in middle age. However wrong the first line of Pope's couplet may be, perhaps there is some truth in the second: 'And grew Immortal in his own despight.'

Last years

To attribute to Shakespeare strong feelings about the fleeting and impermanent nature of theatrical art is after all a natural consequence of heeding what he himself reiterates in his last plays, particularly *The Winter's Tale* and *The Tempest* (see Chapter 7, pp. 167–81). These last plays, written between roughly 1608 and 1613, show an abrupt and disconcerting change in the direction of his art. It has become customary to call *Pericles, Cymbeline, The Winter's Tale*, and *The Tempest* 'the Romances', but in this book they are classed as tragicomedies. People used to say that they indicated a sort of conversion in Shakespeare after the darkness of the 'tragic period' to a new serenity and calm; this became more difficult after a famous essay by Lytton Strachey who said he found not serenity but boredom punctuated by occasional fierceness and a delight in pure poetry. In the mid-twentieth century the plays were very generally accepted as symbolic representations of an optimistic transcendent view of existence. More prosaic explanations of the bizarre nature of these plays have been that Shakespeare was imitating the youthful Beaumont and Fletcher and that he was exploiting the resources of the more intimate indoor theatre of Blackfriars, which the King's men had leased in 1608. Whatever else he might have been doing, it seems certain that Shakespeare was making some rather radical enquiries into what drama was and what drama could do, and that he positively courted accusations of improbability. These experiments are the sort a man can afford to make when he has written *King Lear* and *Antony and Cleopatra.*

In both *Henry VIII* and *The Two Noble Kinsmen* Shakespeare collaborated with John Fletcher, who came to succeed him as the main dramatist for the King's men. The collaboration was not a great success. Fletcher was an excellent dramatist with an outstanding stage sense, but he was not inconvenienced by seriousness of mind. *The Two Noble Kinsmen* might have been better if left entirely to him; *Henry VIII* better if left entirely to Shakespeare. *Henry VIII* is a pageant-like play. The portrait of Katherine of Aragon, immensely dignified and courageous in her contest with the terrible Wolsey, is quite splendid, but the play shirks the responsibility of presenting a Henry VIII who could possibly account for what is shown happening to Katherine, and takes refuge in cowardly evasion. The play is not really to be classed with the great earlier sequences on English history.

If we date *The Two Noble Kinsmen* in 1613, Shakespeare might still have been under 50 when he made his farewell to the stage. There was almost certainly no sudden or final withdrawal to Stratford or severance from the King's men. As late as 1612 Shakespeare bought the Blackfriars gatehouse near to his company's new theatre. It was let to a tenant, but Shakespeare may well have thought of using it himself. The King's men were now regularly using both the 'private' Blackfriars theatre and the outdoor Globe. The old Globe, set on fire during a performance of *Henry VIII* in June 1613, was burned to the ground and had to be rebuilt.

Shakespeare had for some years been buying land and property in Stratford. The purchase of the Old Stratford freehold in 1602 gave him 120 acres (in the hands of a tenant farmer). In 1605 he paid £440 for a half-interest in the corn and hay tithes in the hamlets of Old Stratford, Welcombe, and Bishopton, bringing him an income of about £60 a year. In the great Stratford row of 1614 about the attempt to enclose the common fields at Welcombe, Shakespeare's name gets mentioned, but it is impossible to discern whether he was among those favouring the enclosure or those vehemently against it.

As for family matters, Shakespeare's brother Edmund, sixteen years his junior, became an actor in London, fathered an illegitimate child, and died in 1607, aged 27. His father had died in 1601, his mother in 1608. His daughter Susanna married Dr John Hall in 1607, and a granddaughter was born in 1608. His other daughter, Judith, married Thomas Quiney in February 1616; immediately after the wedding the husband was in serious trouble as the father of an illegitimate child who died, along with the mother, at the birth.

Shakespeare made his will in March 1616, not long before his death, dividing his possessions between his daughters and making gifts to Burbage, Heminges, and Condell among others. He bequeathed his sword to Thomas Combe, but there is no mention of books. The only reference to his wife is the odd bequest, inserted as an afterthought, of the second-best bed. She outlived her husband and died in 1623, aged 67. Shakespeare himself died in April 1616; he was buried in Holy Trinity Church on 25 April. The precise day of his death, like that of his birth, is not known. He was baptised on 26 April and buried on 25 April. He may have been just 52 when he died.

His great monument, the 'First Folio', his collected plays, appeared seven years later, in 1623, with the 'portrait' by Droeshout: *Mr William Shakespeares Comedies, Histories, & Tragedies: Published according to the True Originall Copies.* John Heminges and Henry Condell took the responsibility for the venture.

Eighteen of the plays were here published for the first time. *Pericles* and *The Two Noble Kinsmen* were not included. There was a long commendatory poem by Ben Jonson. Jonson's comments on Shakespeare were often critical; he 'wanted art' and 'sufflaminandus erat' (i.e. he didn't know when to stop). But he also said: 'I loved the man, and do honour his memory (on this side idolatry) as much as any.' The Folio elegy has its hesitations, but for its comment on the Stratford man whose work had delighted two English monarchs Jonson can have the last word.

> Sweet Swan of Avon! what a sight it were
>   To see thee in our waters yet appear,
> And make those flights upon the banks of Thames,
>   That so did take Eliza, and our James!

2

Relationship

To recognize the uniqueness of each of Shakespeare's plays is a primary and basic task. Every generalization is an infringement of a play's individuality, a weakening of its special quality and its meaning. The diversity of Shakespeare's plays is quite astonishing, even among those allied by subject or genre. It's not that Hamlet doesn't speak the same language as Coriolanus; he doesn't even breathe the same air. At the same time, one play constantly reminds us of others, and very often we have the feeling of one play building on another. Indefatigable experimenter though he was, never interested in writing the same play twice, it is nevertheless a single exploration of human experience that Shakespeare undertook in the rich variety of his thirty-eight plays. They are not, taken together, an aggregation: two, three, or four plays considered as a group will assert something that none of them taken alone asserts. The purpose of this chapter is to distinguish some threads, chiefly about personal relationships, which run in and out of Shakespeare's plays, linking them together and demonstrating that his life's work was a single organism of accumulating meaning, an 'intertissued robe of gold and pearl' (to use Henry V's words). We respect diversity, and the distinctiveness of each play, while at the same time we attend to their relationship one with another.

It is the more necessary to insist on the double objective of the part and the whole in a short book in which there is bound to be more emphasis on groups of plays than on the individual play. In grouping the plays I have accepted the time-honoured distinctions of the First Folio of comedy, history, and tragedy, and I have added tragicomedy. But no system of grouping Shakespeare's plays is more than a temporary convenience to ourselves. There are no real boundaries: as soon as we put up fences Shakespeare knocks them down. The histories *Richard II* and *Richard III* are indispensable components of Shakespearian tragedy; the Roman tragedies are critically important in studying Shakespeare's dramatic use of history. A play like *Cymbeline* seems to belong to every group we can think of, while *Troilus and*

Cressida belongs to none. Even the major distinction between comedy and tragedy has only a limited usefulness. Shakespeare's tragedy is continuous with his comedy, as is most evident in the last plays, where the one balances and responds to the other. If we use Northrop Frye's seasonal metaphor, we can say that, with tragedy moving towards winter and death and comedy moving towards spring and new life, each is an integral part of the same cycle. No comedy is ignorant of death, no tragedy unaware of love and regeneration. *The Comedy of Errors* begins in the intense negation of separated souls and the threat of death; it ends with the nativity (as it calls it) of joyful reunions. *Romeo and Juliet* and *King Lear* show love achieved and then destroyed.

Or we could say that Shakespearian tragedy and comedy are the different sides of the same medal. The happenings are not so very dissimilar, though their treatment is. Malvolio accoutred with cross-garters is in comedy; Coriolanus in the gown of humility is in tragedy. The banished Rosalind in *As You Like It* seems to grow into the personality of her adopted disguise; and so does the banished Edgar, as Poor Tom in *King Lear*. The recklessness which made Shakespeare put Shylock and his deadly bond into *The Merchant of Venice* and the Porter and his jests into *Macbeth* shows how well he recognized the affinity of the two primordial masks of drama. In moving between the unit of the single play and the achievement of Shakespeare's entire work, we need to be very flexible, always ready to modify or dissolve the groupings and categories which we establish.

The family

In *The Comedy of Errors* the individual's insistent need for relationship is imaged in the long and lonely search of a brother for his twin. Throughout the plays the ties of blood between brothers and sisters, parents and children, continue to be of paramount importance, surpassing sexual love and friendship. *Twelfth Night* begins with the grief of two women who have lost their brothers, Olivia and Viola. Sebastian, when he arrives, has to supply the double loss. His union as husband with Olivia is much more quizzically treated than his reunion as brother with Viola. The grimmest visions of sundering and hatred are antagonisms within the family. The bond which Iago breaks—

loyalty to his commanding officer—is comparatively slight; the bond which Macbeth breaks—to his king, kinsman, and guest— is more profound; but the bond which Claudius in *Hamlet* breaks is the deepest of all. He murders his own brother, to possess himself of his brother's wife and his brother's kingdom. The first human crime after man had disobeyed God was Cain's murder of his brother Abel, and this initial decomposition of human fellow- ship is several times alluded to in the play. Claudius says of his offence,

> it smells to heaven;
> It hath the primal eldest curse upon't,
> A brother's murder.
>
> (III. iii. 36–8)

As You Like It begins with a double example of brotherly hatred and rejection. Oliver deprives Orlando of his rights and tries to get him killed; Duke Frederick has usurped his own brother and banished him. *The Tempest* again makes a double use of fraternal betrayal; it was the treachery of a trusted brother that drove Prospero from his dukedom, and as soon as this brother is set down on Prospero's island he begins to incite Sebastian to do away with *his* brother and so get the kingdom of Naples. There is a savage enmity of brothers in both *Much Ado* and *King Lear*, though in both plays the iniquitous brother is a half-brother and illegitimate.

The isolation and apartness of Hamlet is marked by the absence of brother or sister; he differs in this from Laertes, and at the graveside in Act V he cannot comprehend Laertes' feelings for Ophelia. Hamlet is indeed all son: his relationships with his father and his mother are everything. The play too is 'all son'; there are no less than three of them, Hamlet, Laertes, Fortinbras, devoted to righting the wrongs of their fathers. Rebellion by a son against what his father expects of him is treated by Shakespeare in *Henry IV* as something not deep-seated, a kind of game that Prince Hal can stop playing when he wishes. He tells his father that he will

> in the closing of some glorious day
> Be bold to tell you that I am your son.
>
> (*1 Henry IV*, III. ii. 133–4)

All the same, *Henry IV* manifests the strain of conforming to the expectations of the father and also the risk to the free play of the spirit in accepting the burden of inheritance. Bertram in *All's Well* is a real rebel against what his dead father requires of him. Everyone tells him of his responsibility to conduct himself by his father's standards. The family honour is symbolized in the ring he wears, an heirloom

> Which were the greatest obloquy i' th' world
> In me to lose—

(IV. ii. 44–5)

and he gives it away to the girl he has seduced (or so he thinks). But he is forced to reaccept the unavoidable inheritance.

The relationship between son and mother is of vital importance in two tragedies, *Coriolanus* and *Hamlet*, and the treatment in the one is the antithesis of the other. Coriolanus's disaster comes from his fervent commitment to the ideals of Volumnia; Hamlet's disaster springs in part from his insistence that his mother should fulfil *his* ideals. In the relationship of a son with either father or mother, although the importance of the bond is often enough stressed, there is much pain and strain and little happiness. It is quite different with the relationship of father and daughter, to which Shakespeare gave extraordinary attention. The figure of the obtuse, overbearing, hectoring father, standing in the way of his daughter's sexual life, as it is portrayed in Capulet in *Romeo and Juliet*, Egeus in *A Midsummer Night's Dream*, or Polonius in *Hamlet*, develops into the titanic figure of King Lear, divorcing himself from his dearest daughter because she won't publicly profess her love for *him*. Lear is eventually to awake from the destruction of his old self to accept the presence and the love of the banished daughter, and his need of her. Cordelia's husband, the King of France, has been rather brusquely got out of the way by Shakespeare (IV. iii. 1–2) in order that nothing should obstruct the singleness of the attention of father and daughter to each other.

> When thou dost ask me blessing, I'll kneel down
> And ask of thee forgiveness.
>
> Upon such sacrifices, my Cordelia,
> The gods themselves throw incense.

(V. iii. 10–11, 20–1)

In the last plays, from *King Lear* onwards, the love between father and daughter becomes the redeeming element in life. Great pains are taken to emphasize that the love is non-sexual. In *Pericles* the hero seeks as a bride a woman whom he discovers to be living incestuously with her father. His final relationship with his own daughter Marina is schematically arranged as a pointed antithesis to this initial incestuous situation; at the very end of the play, after the deeply moving reunion of father and daughter, Pericles is united with his wife, and a husband is provided for Marina. In *The Winter's Tale* the contrast with an incestuous relationship is made obliquely, by altering the story of Greene's *Pandosto*, which is the source of the play. In *Pandosto* the king commits suicide on learning that the young woman he desires is in fact his daughter.

Lear banishes Cordelia, Pericles abandons Marina, Leontes orders the death of Perdita. Each father has to expiate this wilful severance, and in the end is admitted, perhaps only very briefly, to a relationship which transcends other relationships. The importance of the relationship, as a bond between the different generations, can be measured by the ferocity of the warfare between the generations in *King Lear*. Why has Gloucester protected the king? Because, he tells Lear's daughter,

> I would not see thy cruel nails
> Pluck out his poor old eyes, nor thy fierce sister
> In his anointed flesh rash boarish fangs.
>
> (III. vii. 56–8)

Goneril and Regan are indeed 'unnatural'; they defy the principle of existence by which human life holds together. Albany gives us a wonderful image of the daughters' attack on nature itself in persecuting their father.

> That nature which contemns its origin
> Cannot be bordered certain in itself.
> She that herself will sliver and disbranch
> From her material sap perforce must wither
> And come to deadly use.
>
> (IV. ii. 32–6)

The blinding of Gloucester, betrayed by his son Edmund into the hands of Cornwall and Regan, is the summation of the cruelty of this conflict between the generations within a family, which both is and signifies the ultimate breach in nature. Now, in play after play, Shakespeare brings back the rejected daughter to the penitent father, and in showing the awakening or reawakening of love between them suggests in the recognition of mutual need a kind of sustaining principle in life, when harmony between the old and the young is no bar to the freedom of the younger generation. 'Thou that beget'st him that did thee beget'—Pericles to Marina. So, all through *The Tempest*, wishing to repair the breach in nature caused when brother's hand was lifted against brother, Prospero works for the marriage of the daughter who had preserved him (I. ii. 152–3) with the son of his enemy. 'I have done nothing but in care of thee' (I. ii. 16).

Between *The Comedy of Errors*, ending with the reunion of a long-separated family, and *The Tempest*, Shakespeare's histories and tragedies and comedies have concentrated the expression of life-denying forces in the rupture of the bonds of the family, brother against brother, child against parent, parent against child; and in the maintenance or renewal or repair of these bonds they have expressed the sustaining energy of human society. While it is true to say that these family disruptions and reunions have immense symbolic resonance in conveying the destructive power of hate and the constructive power of love, Hamlet and Prince Hal and Coriolanus are sons and not symbols: the primal relationships of the family are the bedrock of the plays.

Sex, love, and friendship

The masque which Prospero organizes to celebrate the 'contract of true love' between Ferdinand and Miranda is full of invocations of general fertility from Iris, Juno, and Ceres, but Venus and Cupid have been prevented from attending:

> Here thought they to have done
> Some wanton charm upon this man and maid,
> Whose vows are that no bed-right shall be paid
> Till Hymen's torch be lighted.

> (IV. i. 94–7)

These vows of pre-marital abstinence had been sternly enforced by Prospero before the masque started, with warnings of all sorts of misery for the couple should they break them (see p. 5). It is usual for the earlier Shakespeare comedies to conclude with betrothal, and in *The Shrew*, *The Merchant*, and *Twelfth Night* Shakespeare altered his source to avoid having lovers in bed together before marriage. The last plays are insistent on preserving the virginity of young lovers. The matter is discussed in *The Winter's Tale* as well as *The Tempest*, and Marina's preservation of her stainless chastity in the brothel reads like something from the lives of the saints.

But the fact that Shakespeare so often bans sex between the lovers in his comedies, and closes the comedies before marriages are consummated, does not mean that sexual abstinence and celibacy are portrayed with any enthusiasm.

> For aye to be in shady cloister mewed,
> To live a barren sister all your life,
> Chanting faint hymns to the cold fruitless moon—
> Thrice blessed they that master so their blood
> To undergo such maiden pilgrimage;
> But earthlier happy is the rose distilled
> Than that which withering on the virgin thorn,
> Grows, lives, and dies in single blessedness.
> (Theseus in *A Midsummer Night's Dream*, I. i. 71–8)

The vows of the king and his nobles in *Love's Labour's Lost* to three years of celibacy are shown to be unnatural and impossible to observe. In *Measure for Measure* there are two outstanding portrayals of asceticism in Isabella and Angelo. Angelo's self-denial is self-regarding, and he quickly succumbs to the virginal radiance of Isabella, desiring her foully for the things that make her good (II. ii. 173–4). Isabella's purity is of a different sort. She has offered God her unpolluted body. Her chastity expresses itself fiercely, and perhaps it is the strength of the suppressed sexuality that arouses Angelo.

> Th' impression of keen whips I'd wear as rubies
> And strip myself to death as to a bed
> That longing have been sick for, ere I'd yield
> My body up to shame.
> (II. iv. 101–4)

Shakespeare neither derides nor blesses Isabella's dedication to virginity but it certainly has little appeal.

The reason Shakespeare keeps young lovers ardent in desire but prohibited from sexual congress is not the attractiveness of abstinence nor a question of morals. It is a question of protecting them, of wanting to hold them in the perpetual innocence and expectation of the figures on Keats's Grecian urn.

> More happy love, more happy, happy love!
> For ever warm and still to be enjoyed,
>   For ever panting, and for ever young—
> All breathing human passion far above,
>   That leaves a heart high-sorrowful and cloyed,
>   A burning forehead, and a parching tongue.

The 'wanton charms' that Venus might have forced on Ferdinand and Miranda are described in some detail in one of the last passages Shakespeare ever wrote, the wry address that Palamon makes to Venus in *The Two Noble Kinsmen* (v. i. 77–136). This is a Venus who has absolute power over mankind:

> thou that from eleven to ninety reign'st
> In mortal bosoms.

She is a huntress, and those whom she captures she deforms and makes ridiculous, as Circe did. She makes 'the fiercest tyrant' 'weep unto a girl', and 'the King / To be his subject's vassal'. 'Take to thy grace,' pleads Palamon,

> Me thy vowed soldier, who do bear thy yoke
> As 'twere a wreath of roses, *yet is heavier*
> *Than lead itself, stings more than nettles.*

The Two Noble Kinsmen is the story of Chaucer's *Knight's Tale*, about two bosom friends who fall in love with the same woman and thus turn from friendship to hostility. To set beside the discord which sexual desire arouses, the play gives three separate celebrations of perfect friendship between people of the same sex, not only Arcite and Palamon but Pirithous and Theseus (i. iii. 35–47) and Emilia and Flavina (i. iii. 59–82). Theseus has now chosen marriage, but Hippolyta says that the 'knot of love' between the two men was so strongly tied that it 'may be outworn, never undone', and she thinks Theseus cannot honestly say whether he loves her or Pirithous best. On hearing this, Emilia (soon to be the embarrassed object of two men's love) speaks of her childhood affection for the dead Flavina.

> But I
> And she I sigh and spoke of were things innocent,
> Loved for we did, and like the elements
> That know not what nor why yet do effect
> Rare issues by their operance, our souls
> Did so to one another.

'Loved for we did.' This seems to echo Montaigne's great essay 'On Friendship' (arguing its superiority to sexual love). 'If a man urge me to tell wherefore I loved him, I feel it cannot be expressed but by answering, Because it was he, because it was myself.'

The Winter's Tale offers us the same sort of contrast as *The Two Noble Kinsmen* does between the discord attending adult sexual love and the harmony of childhood friendship. Just before the eruption of Leontes' insane jealousy against him, Polixenes describes their intimacy in boyhood.

> What we changed
> Was innocence for innocence; we knew not
> The doctrine of ill-doing, nor dreamed
> That any did. Had we pursued that life,
> And our weak spirits ne'er been higher reared
> With stronger blood, we should have answered heaven
> Boldly 'Not guilty'; the imposition cleared
> Hereditary ours.

(I. ii. 68–75)

Shades of the prison-house begin to close about the growing boy. Progress into adult sexual life, the acquisition of 'stronger blood', is here described in terms of the Fall.

The Two Noble Kinsmen was Shakespeare's last play. *The Two Gentlemen of Verona* was one of his first. Those who are embarrassed by the crudity of the ending of that early play have perhaps not considered it carefully enough in the context of the rest of Shakespeare's writing. Proteus has deserted Julia because of an infatuation with Silvia, the beloved of his best friend Valentine, and he attempts to force her when she rejects his overtures. Valentine rescues her and not only forgives the ashamed and penitent Proteus but surrenders Silvia to him. 'There are, by this time,' said Quiller-Couch, '*no* gentlemen in Verona' (Cambridge edition (1921), p. xiv). Quiller-Couch went on to mention Montaigne's essay on friendship *and* the sonnets, but only to wonder whether this absurd 'literary convention' about the claims of friendship could be the cause of Shakespeare's 'crucial blunder' in this play. But the issues raised by the ending of this play were of lifelong importance to Shakespeare. Here is more of Montaigne's essay:

All things being by effect common between them: wills, thoughts, judgements, goods, wives, children, honour, and life; and their mutual agreement being no other than one soul in two bodies, according to the fit definition of Aristotle, they can neither lend or give ought to each other.

(Florio's translation, Everyman edition, i. 203–4)

Valentine makes an offer of sharing on Montaigne's lines, repudiating the sexual relationship as less important than friendship. But to make over a person in this way is hardly possible, let alone acceptable, and there is no hint of Shakespeare commending Valentine's impulsive gesture. He does, however, save him from facing the consequences of his curious idealism. The triangle of Valentine–Proteus–Silvia suddenly becomes quadrilateral as, on hearing Valentine's offer, the page swoons and turns out to be the faithful Julia in disguise. So the renewed friendship can remain while each has his proper sexual partner. This optimistic resolution will be seen to parallel the similar handling of the father–daughter relationship in the last plays, when, as in *Pericles* and *The Winter's Tale*, the reunited father and daughter are each provided with a spouse.

The sonnets rework in brilliant, extended, and searching form the basic story of *Two Gentlemen of Verona* and *The Two Noble Kinsmen*. The passionate affection of the poet for a young man, the hoped-for marriage of true minds, is disrupted by their sexual relations with the same woman. The physical intimacy with the woman, which the poet can't resist, is contrasted with the intimacy of souls which the poet attempts to reach with the young man. The poet's contempt for himself in cohabiting with the woman is generalized in the great sonnet on lust (129), 'Th' expense of spirit in a waste of shame'.

> Enjoyed no sooner but despised straight;
> Past reason hunted, and no sooner had,
> Past reason hated as a swallowed bait
> On purpose laid to make the taker mad.

The importance of these central lines is twofold. In the first place they relate the desire for sexual possession to the fatal passion for other types of *forbidden* acquisition. The standard 'complaint' against sexual love, as opposed to soul love, was that it was a repeated cycle of ardent desire expunged by satisfaction and not a steady undiminished glow. The whole quality of the relationship (it was held) changed when desire achieved its object. The parallel between desire for a woman and desire for political power emerges in the pattern of sententious images in *The Rape of Lucrece*, looking forward unmistakably to *Macbeth*.

> I have debated even in my soul
> What wrong, what shame, what sorrow I shall breed,
> But nothing can affection's course control
> Or stop the headlong fury of his speed.
> I know repentant tears ensue the deed,
>   Reproach, disdain, and deadly enmity—
>   Yet strive I to embrace mine infamy.

(498–504)

In *Macbeth*, the hero's terrified drive to the guilty orgasm of the murder is followed by not one shred of the glory he had hoped for from gaining the crown: 'Nought's had, all's spent', Lady Macbeth says, in words which maintain the sexual parallel. She had urged him to the murder by making it a test of Macbeth's virility.

>   Art thou afeard
> To be the same in thine own act and valour
> As thou art in desire?
>
>   Prithee peace!
> I dare do all that may become a man
>
> When you durst do it, then you were a man;
> And to be more than what you were, you would
> Be so much more the man.

(I. vii. 39–41, 45–6, 49–51)

In the second place, the passage from the sonnet on lust is important in its relation to *Measure for Measure*. Claudius' betrothed Juliet is with child. The couple have anticipated a proper church wedding but in Elizabethan eyes their formal betrothal before witnesses made their conduct forgivable at least, provided a church service was to follow. Love and procreation are sympathetically and warmly portrayed in these two, as against the cold chastity of Isabella, the rigidity of Angelo's use of the anti-sex laws, and the sordid syphilitic underworld of Vienna. Yet when Lucio asks Claudio, who is a victim of the anti-sex laws, why he is being taken to prison, he answers with the bait imagery of Sonnet 129.

> Our natures do pursue,
> Like rats that ravin down their proper bane,
> A thirsty evil, and when we drink we die.
>
> (I. ii. 128–30)

Even normal sexuality, when the partner is not a promiscuous nymphomaniac like the dark woman but a loved bride, seems to have become tainted with strong feelings of guilt.

In two of the major tragedies, *Hamlet* and *King Lear*, guilt and nausea about sex are indexes of troubled or unbalanced minds. There is more than moral indignation in Hamlet forcing his mother to listen to his vision of her intimacy with Claudius.

> Nay, but to live
> In the rank sweat of an enseamèd bed,
> Stewed in corruption, honeying and making love
> Over the nasty sty . . .
>
> (III. iv. 91–4)

When the mad Lear expounds his levelling theory of universal delinquency to the blind Gloucester (IV. vi), sex is the root of all evil. All people are united in the lust of their hearts if not in their secret deeds. 'Let copulation thrive!' he shouts—because for society to condemn it can be nothing but hypocrisy.

> None does offend, none I say, none; I'll able 'em.
> Take that of me, my friend, who have the power
> To seal th' accuser's lips.
>
> (IV. vi. 168–70)

The most violent image in the whole scene is of women's sexual organs as the sulphurous pit of hell.

> But to the girdle do the gods inherit,
> Beneath is all the fiend's—

There's hell, there's darkness, there is the sulphurous pit, burning, scalding, stench, consumption. Fie, fie, fie! pah, pah! Give me an ounce of civet. Good apothecary, sweeten my imagination. There's money for thee.

(IV. vi. 126–31)

There is similar imagery in Sonnet 144.

> I guess one angel in another's hell.
>   Yet this shall I ne'er know, but live in doubt
>   Till my bad angel fire my good one out.

'Fire' and 'burn' were the common colloquial terms for venereal infection, so that actual as well as moral disease is in Lear's mind.

Lear in his ravings cannot disconnect the ingratitude and cruelty of his daughters from the sexual acts which conceived them, even though they were 'got 'tween the lawful sheets'.

> Judicious punishment! 'twas this flesh begot
> Those pelican daughters.

(III. iv. 74–5)

He had said that to Poor Tom, who took the point: 'Pillicock sat on Pillicock hill.' Lear's perception that sexual intercourse, even when 'lawful', brings its revenges and punishments is deeply influenced by the moral and religious code of Poor Tom, whom he has hailed as his 'philosopher', and his 'learned Theban'. When he is not acting Poor Tom, Edgar has an extraordinarily severe moral view that his father's sufferings are directly related to the sexual licence which led to the birth of the illegitimate Edmund.

> The gods are just, and of our pleasant vices
> Make instruments to plague us:
> The dark and vicious place where thee he got
> Cost him his eyes.

(v. iii. 171–4)

Edgar's script for Poor Tom is of a ruined servingman who in his debonair days of elegance 'did the act of darkness' with his mistress. The act of darkness is in itself devilish; all references by Tom to darkness are to Satan and things satanic. He now spends his life fleeing from the pursuing fiends who destroyed him. Tom's wild philosophy is only a distorted extension of Edgar's simplistic and rigid world-view in which the devil tempts and God punishes. At the beginning of the play Gloucester chuckles as he recalls the 'good sport' that led to the birth of Edmund. 'Do you smell a fault?' he asks Kent. The smell is inescapable.

The perturbation in Shakespeare's plays and poems about the misery haunting sexual relations finds extreme expression in voices from his tragic period, Hamlet, Claudio, Lear, Edgar. Such disgust as they express seems to be linked to the yearning found in many places for an intimacy uncorrupted by the plague of sexual desire.

> What we changed
> Was innocence for innocence ...
>
> (*The Winter's Tale*, I. ii. 68–9)

> When thou dost ask me blessing, I'll kneel down
> And ask of thee forgiveness ...
>
> (*Lear*, v. iii. 10–11)

How far this element in Shakespeare's writings is associated with Europe's horror at the rapid spread of syphilis is hard to say. Three plays in particular dwell on venereal disease and the plain fact that sexual activity rots mankind as it increases it, namely *Measure for Measure*, *Timon of Athens*, and *Pericles Prince of Tyre*. 'Ay, she quickly pooped him; she made him roast-meat for worms,' says the brothel-owner in *Pericles* of one of his customers. (The grave-digger in *Hamlet* reminds us that 'we have many pocky corses nowadays that will scarce hold the laying in'.) *Measure for Measure* is full of gruesome humour about venereal disease. But it is Timon (whose problems have absolutely nothing to do with sex) who is most explicit on the physical corruption attending sex. He sees the whores who visit him as his most effective missionaries in his plan to destroy humanity:

> Consumptions sow
> In hollow bones of man, strike their sharp shins,
> And mar men's spurring.
>
>   Down with the nose,
> Down with it flat ...
>
>   Plague all,
> That your activity may defeat and quell
> The source of all erection.
>
> (IV. iii. 151–3, 157–8, 162–4)

It is a mistake to confuse the abounding creative fertility of Shakespeare's genius and his obvious contempt for all that is narrow-minded, prudential, puritanical, and strait-laced with a sort of jolly, easy-going indulgence about sexual activity. His tolerance does indeed soar above mealy-mouthed moral codes; and in bestowing life on such voluble, energetic, and earthy characters as the Nurse and Mercutio in *Romeo and Juliet*, Falstaff and Mistress Quickly, Touchstone, Pompey, and so on, he commends a kind of vitality with which, without his help, we might find it hard to sympathize. The rich humanity of Shakespeare's creativeness, and all his bawdiness, cannot, however, make away with the pervading unease in his works about sex, an unease which sometimes takes violent forms. But, as it is usual in Shakespeare to face everything with its opposite, there is also a powerful counter-movement. This is not to be found in the comedies, which are often only half-hearted in their applause for sexual love, but in *Venus and Adonis*, *Romeo and Juliet*, and *Antony and Cleopatra*. Each of these has a tragic ending, but each suggests the possibility of spiritual transformation through sexual love. In *Romeo and Juliet* the acceptance of the physical relationship as the very expression of love is an essential part of the play's beauty, power, and pathos. It is harder to see this in the comic fumblings of *Venus and Adonis*, but the masterly ending of that poem shows Adonis' distinction between love and lust to be prim and juvenile; his rejection of sexual love leads to his emasculation and death (see pp. 55–6). Venus mourning for the dead Adonis must have been in Shakespeare's mind when, years later, he created the final act of *Antony and Cleopatra*. Antony never fully accepts his relationship with Cleopatra. The deep sensual attraction she has for him is a bondage; he remains a Roman at the core and sees her as his destroyer, never more than partially recognizing what Octavius Caesar suddenly sees—that the sensual web in which she catches her lovers is a 'strong toil of grace'. Those 'lascivious wassails' which the world finds so gross are sanctified when 'such a twain can do't'; but Antony cannot so far escape from society's values as to accept his transfiguration: it is conferred on him posthumously in Cleopatra's ecstasy of adoration (see pp. 149–53).

Both the woman of the sonnets and Cleopatra are dark ladies, no longer young, of voracious sexual appetite. In the sonnets sexual congress with the dark woman is lust and expends the spirit in a waste of shame. *Antony and Cleopatra* rejects the either/ or of lust and love, as does, eventually, *Venus and Adonis*. The royal harlot Cleopatra is the person Shakespeare chose in whom to portray a richness in sexual love which has a mysterious though almost inaccessible power to redeem the spirit.

Society

As there is love and family relationship in every play of Shakespeare's, so also every play is concerned with the bigger community in which the characters live.

This community is often presented as a sharply defined geographical entity. Act IV of *Timon of Athens* opens with the hero leaving the walled city whose ingratitude has changed his life from love to hate. He looks back at the walls and curses those within. From now on the audience shares the viewpoint of the two exiles, Timon and the banished Alcibiades, gazing at their community—living behind the rear wall of the playing place— from the outside. Alcibiades brings an army against the city. The frightened citizens appear on the walls (presumably the upper stage) and plead with him not to destroy them. Society in this play is given a physical presence, a local habitation in the theatre. *Timon of Athens* has striking similarities with *Coriolanus*, and there is no play of Shakespeare in which the community is more stressed than *Coriolanus*. Communities are walled cities: Rome, Corioli, Antium. Coriolanus fights his way through the gates of Corioli (I. iv); he contemptuously turns his back on the Rome that has banished him, with his great cry 'There is a world elsewhere!' (III. ii); he approaches Antium (IV. iv); and finally prepares to set his army down 'before the walls of Rome' (V. iii). The city is a gated place needing protection from marauding armies as well as a body politic whose health depends on the reconcilement of its different elements. Coriolanus' tragedy is that he can only work within the one metaphor, of the community as a collection of creatures huddling within the walls, needing the protection of an army and a military leader.

The English or British nation is less easy to characterize in the theatre than Rome, but the tendency of speakers to insulate it by talking of the surrounding sea is of course common.

This fortress built by nature for herself
Against infection and the hand of war,
This happy breed of men, this little world,
This precious stone set in the silver sea
Which serves it in the office of a wall,
Or as a moat defensive to a house,
Against the envy of less happier lands,
This blessed plot, this earth, this realm, this England ...

(*Richard II*, II. i. 43–50)

This picture becomes even more strongly isolationist in the Queen's words in *Cymbeline* (III. i. 16–29), but that play, as we shall see, works to show such an image of the community as sterile and unacceptable.

A hero turning his back on a city that has rejected him is a potent image of alienation. Sometimes the hero wishes to escape but can't: 'Denmark's a prison.' Alternative ways of life are suggested by a change of place, and a difference in ethos and values is emphasized by journeying, on foot to the Forest of Arden, by boat to Bohemia, Cyprus, or Prospero's island. The island in *The Tempest* is the strangest of all Shakespeare's communities. It has no indigenous inhabitants. The witch Sycorax was banished there from Algiers and her misshapen son Caliban was born there. Prospero, exiled from Milan, was washed up on its shore with his infant daughter. A boatload of the ruling families of Milan and Naples and their attendants is lured to the island by Prospero's magic. So slender and skeletal a society, ostentatiously assembled and clearly labelled, is unique in Shakespeare. Good and evil, youth and age, civilization and barbarism, nature and nurture, ignorance and education, intellect and brute force, earth and spirit, mercy and malice, grapple in complex involvements to reveal each other's strength and weakness. It is an experimental social mix, stirred by Shakespeare and his creature Prospero.

Among more 'natural' societies, the Vienna of *Measure for Measure* stands out, its moral health being the play's main concern–though we might forget this at the end, when the resolution of personal problems obscures the fact that the social problems with which we began remain obstinately unresolved. The Scotland of *Macbeth* is another community given very clear definition. It asserts its identity under Duncan by defeating internal rebellion and foreign invasion. But then the victorious general himself plucks the heart out of the nation by regicide. The sufferings of Scotland are an external measurement of Macbeth's unnatural crime, running parallel with the mental suffering he inflicts on himself. It is impossible to think àbout the personal history of Macbeth without thinking of the fortunes of Scotland, and it is the same story in most of the tragedies. It is certainly so with *Hamlet*. *Hamlet* without the Prince of Denmark is indeed a nonsense, for the play is meaningless without the recognition that the fortunes of the State of Denmark, threatened by war from Fortinbras in the first scene and taken over without a battle by Fortinbras in the final scene, are quite central.

Two plays, one a comedy and one a tragedy, have a Venetian setting, and in both, *The Merchant of Venice* and *Othello*, 'Venice' signifies a prosperous, closely-knit, self-satisfied, and exclusive body of people relying for their finances and their security on aliens whom they do not admit to their inner circles. In Shylock the Jew and the black Othello, *in* Venetian society but not *of* it, Shakespeare provided his masterly studies of the alien in a Western world which was still to come into being. Our complicated responses to these great figures and the communities they live in may seem a special problem, but in fact almost every play shows friction between the community and nonconforming or unadmitted individuals whose presence questions its assumptions, subverts its values, and sometimes threatens its continuance, and our responses to these individuals are rarely univocal. 'Villains' like Iago, Don John, Edmund, Richard III are at the extreme end of a continuous line on which we have to place Shylock and Caliban, Thersites, Apemantus, Feste, and Lear's Fool. The *Henry IV* plays and *Henry V* are brilliant displays of the conflict between the establishment and nonconforming forces. Both the romantic defiance of Hotspur and the easy-going self-indulgence of Falstaff have to be destroyed if Prince Hal is to be secure as governor of the realm, and in *Henry V* he can only survive by blotting out not only potential rebels but the scurrilous marks of interrogation which Pistol, Bardolph, and Nym pose to his activities.

It is different in *King John*. The Bastard with his amused contempt for the pomposity, self-regard and hypocrisy of politicians and rulers is one of the most energetic of Shakespeare's cynics. But his subversiveness has to be welded on to the fabric of the establishment. Henry V is a strong king who can afford to suppress what he cannot incorporate. King John is a weak king who needs the strengthening realism of the Bastard—who quite literally saves the country. About the same time as *King John* Shakespeare wrote *Love's Labour's Lost*, and in Berowne created a figure who is the comedy version of the Bastard; a witty and intelligent observer whose consciousness of the self-deception and folly of those who run society never turns him into a non-joiner. Like the Bastard he moves from a detached scepticism to take over the organization of the community when the king and his little academe have run out of steam. On another level there is Touchstone, whose understanding of the ways of the world is a matter more for amusement than despair, and whose enthusiasm to press in among the country copulatives is contrasted with the isolation of Jaques, in whom the perception of folly does not encourage sociability.

In some plays, then, there is an enrichment of the community when it learns to incorporate its dissenting voices. Often enough there is a feeling of loss to the community when it suppresses the voices that challenge it. Sometimes the expulsion seems to be sheer gain. In every play the nexus is different because the problem of the coherence of society and the nonconforming individual is differently posed: Hamlet and Thersites are hardly comparable figures. But our understanding of the relationship between Shylock and the Venetians is considerably deepened when we see that it is a version of a relationship which is a recurring feature of Shakespeare's plays.

In the stories of societies disintegrating or painfully knitting themselves together, the figure of the ruler is of course of first importance—from Henry V masterfully obliterating all opposition to Prince Escalus vainly trying to stop the Montagues and Capulets fighting and King Lear dividing his kingdom. To say that Shakespeare's political thinking was 'right-wing' and authoritarian and that he believed in autocracy is not to say anything very useful, except that it is truer than to say he believed in parliamentary democracy. There is no doubt at all that the burden of his plays is that human society needs containment, control, and direction, that left to themselves human beings would soon destroy each other in the exercise of their natural

greed and aggressiveness. There are many prophecies of the
horrors of such anarchy, the most eloquent being the 'degree'
speech of Ulysses in *Troilus and Cressida* (I. iii. 75–137).

> Frights, changes, horrors,
> Divert and crack, rend and deracinate
> The unity and married calm of states
> Quite from their fixure...

> Each thing melts
> In mere oppugnancy...

> Then everything includes itself in power,
> Power into will, will into appetite,
> And appetite, an universal wolf,
> So doubly seconded with will and power,
> Must make perforce an universal prey
> And last eat up himself.

From the presentation of the anarchy and civil war that follow
the assassination in *Julius Caesar*, it seems clear that, whatever
the motives of Brutus and Cassius and whatever virtue they and
Shakespeare might see in republican Rome, Plutarch's view that
the Rome of the day needed the strong leadership of Caesar was
accepted by Shakespeare. That it was better to put up with the
unpalatable rule of a *de facto* monarch than invite civil strife and
disorder by challenging his authority is of course a constant
'lesson' of the English histories. Such quietism was standard in
the age, and was no doubt influenced not only by Tudor
propaganda but by the handed-down memory of the Wars of the
Roses of the previous century; it re-emerged with new anxiety in
Dryden after the recrudescence of civil war in the 1640s. Quietist
though he was, Shakespeare spent precious little time in his plays
applauding strong rulers. His history plays are grim studies in
ambition, aggression, cruelty, betrayal, and incompetence. The
few efficient governors in his plays, the people who show themselves capable of holding society together, are not a very appealing group: Henry IV, Henry V, Prospero, Julius Caesar, Henry
VIII. Society needs these figures, but they add little lustre to the
human race. It could hardly be otherwise; containing and controlling Caliban exacts a swingeing toll on the spirit.

In Shakespeare's plays the ideal ruler never appears; absence is one of his qualities. Along with his disabused vision of the exercise of power in practice goes a mystical idea of the true king, a messiah who is never out of people's minds but who is always waiting in the wings and never on the stage. This shadowy figure links human society with the divine. He is identified with his people and is their corporate expression. The only one of Shakespeare's English kings to perceive the sacredness and responsibilities of this great office was Richard II, who found it out too late. This idea of kingship informs the first scene of *Hamlet*, where apprehension for the future of the country is fused with the feeling of loss at the death of the old king and fear of the lurking spectre who resembles him. The king's name is his country's name; 'the majesty of buried Denmark' pregnantly refers to both king and country.

A belief in the need for authority is dyed deep into the fabric of Shakespeare's plays. But so also is a total distrust of authority. It is from this paradox that the mystical concept of kingship arises. No ordinary man is free from the accusation of the Sermon on the Mount: 'Judge not, that ye be not judged.' It is from the Sermon on the Mount that *Measure for Measure* takes its title, and it is the conviction that no man has the right to pass judgement on his fellow men that in the end paralyses firm government in the play.

> He who the sword of heaven will bear
> Should be as holy as severe . . .
>
> More nor less to others paying
> Than by self-offences weighing.
> (III. ii. 261–2, 265–6)

Unless there arise some sanctified figure to lead mankind, the whole elaborate edifice of authority is a fraud.

> Man, proud man,
> Dressed in a little brief authority,
> Most ignorant of what he's most assured—
> His glassy essence—like an angry ape
> Plays such fantastic tricks before high heaven
> As makes the angels weep.
> (II. ii. 117–22)

Isabella's words ring through the histories and tragedies. The contemptuous image of the ruler—a child in its finery, a chattering monkey—is found again in *King Lear*. In that play the thunder and lightning of the storm are 'dreadful summoners' revealing to Lear the imposture of those who pretend to a higher virtue. 'Robes and furred gowns' are worn to *hide* what's underneath.

> See how yond justice rails upon yond simple thief. Hark in thine ear: change places and, handy-dandy, which is the justice, which is the thief? Thou hast seen a farmer's dog bark at a beggar?—Ay, sir.—And the creature run from the cur? There thou mightst behold the great image of authority: a dog's obeyed in office.
>
> (IV. vi. 151–9)

It is as a consequence of such insight that Lear *welcomes* imprisonment as a rejection of the way of life that is bounded by the anxiety of 'who loses and who wins, who's in, who's out'. But the plays themselves tell us that society wouldn't continue to exist if it tried to base itself on insights like those of Isabella or Lear. The fundamental irony of More's *Utopia*, that only one form of social organization, which is totally unattainable, is rationally acceptable, is closely akin to what one is left with in trying to discern Shakespeare's politics.

The self

'He that should do his business might perceive that his first lesson is to know what he is, and what is convenient for him.' So said Montaigne. (Florio's translation, Everyman edition, i. 25.) The concept of a 'true self' is of immense importance in Shakespeare. The plays are journeys during which the self is discovered or unmade or recreated. The self is not a kind of private condition; it exists in activity and relationship. 'Being' emerges in 'doing'.

> If our virtues
> Did not go forth of us, 'twere all alike
> As if we had them not. Spirits are not finely touched
> But to fine issues.
>
> (*Measure for Measure*, I. i. 33–6)

This is Duke Vincentio talking to Angelo, as he begins his curious laboratory experiment on both the city and the deputy. He wants the pressure of new activity to reveal Angelo's true self.

> Hence shall we see
> If power change purpose, what our seemers be.
>
> (I. iii. 53–4)

Sad for Angelo! whom new experience forces to cry out 'What dost thou, or what art thou, Angelo?' (II. ii. 172).

It is in the tragedies, naturally, that we find the most violent shocks of not being able to recognize a changing self. 'Are you our daughter?' asks Lear in heavy humour. 'Does any here know me? This is not Lear. . . . Who is it that can tell me who I am?' (I. iv. 218–30). At this point he feels he knows perfectly well who he is; he is soon to ask the question in painful earnest. *King Lear* is unusual in the tragedies in its concentration on the reforming of the self, on coming to new understanding and new relationships. Othello and Coriolanus have no time to rebuild. They are both men whose being is defined in soldiering. Both men enter a perilous new dimension of life and eventually it is the whole self that breaks. 'Othello's occupation's gone!' Coriolanus sees the entire quality of his being, so carefully nurtured by his mother, threatened by the need to humble himself before the plebeians.

> Why did you wish me milder? Would you have me
> False to my nature? Rather say I play
> The man I am.
>
> I will not do't,
> Lest I surcease to honour mine own truth,
> And by my body's action teach my mind
> A most inherent baseness.
>
> (III. ii. 14–16, 120–3)

He cannot bend, so he breaks. He believes (wrongly) that he can create a new self. In banishment he

> forbade all names;
> He was a kind of nothing, titleless,
> Till he had forged himself a name i' th' fire
> Of burning Rome.
>
> (V. i. 12–15)

Namelessness was the condition of Richard II as well, who felt the loss of kingship as the abolition of his identity: 'for I must nothing be.'

> I have no name, no title,
> No, not that name was given me at the font
> But 'tis usurped. Alack the heavy day,
> That I have worn so many winters out
> And know not now what name to call myself.
>
> (IV. i. 255–9)

Nowhere in Shakespeare is the recognition of unfathomed depths in one's own nature more forcefully expressed than in the single line of Macbeth, soon after the murder of Duncan.

> To know my deed, 'twere best not know myself.
>
> (II. ii. 70)

The deed is so infamous that Macbeth dare not probe the infamy of the man who did it. He cannot live with the deed, recognizing with unwinking eyes the nature of the act and the nature of the perpetrator. He must cover up one or the other: cease to acknowledge either the deed or the guilty self. But he can't do this, and has to go on in the full knowledge of both; this is the 'torture of the mind' on which he lies.

The feeling of a dislocation of the self, putting an incomprehensible gap between past and present, is as frequent in comedy as tragedy. The sudden bewilderment of a person who has totally lost his bearings is one of the stock sources of laughter in the theatre. There can be no clearer demonstration of the kinship and the dissimiliarity between comedy and tragedy than in the treatment of the bewildered self.

> What, would you make me mad? Am not I Christopher Sly, old Sly's son of Burton-heath, by birth a pedlar, by education a cardmaker, by transmutation a bearherd, and now by present profession a tinker? Ask Marian Hacket, the fat alewife of Wincot, if she know me not.
>
> (*Shrew*, Induction, ii. 17–22)

The Lord's henchmen are insisting to Sly that he is really a proud nobleman. His struggle to preserve his identity grows fainter when he learns that there is a lady to go with his lordship. It is the same with Sebastian in *Twelfth Night* when he is mistaken for 'Cesario', his disguised twin-sister. He feels he is mad, or dreaming, but he is not prepared to fight against the gifts which comedy provides for the injured self: in this case, Olivia.

Let fancy still my sense in Lethe steep;
If it be thus to dream, still let me sleep.

(IV. i. 62–3)

It is *The Comedy of Errors*, of course, with its two sets of identical twins, that makes most capital out of situations of discontinuity. Mistaken for his Ephesian twin, Antipholus of Syracuse feels he is in a sinister town full of 'dark-working sorcerers that change the mind' if he is 'known unto these, and to myself disguised'. He and his servant try to fight their way out of this town of enchantment before the truth eventually comes out. Farcical though the situations are, the audience's laughter has an echo which is full of deep fears about the loss of assurance in one's sense of identity. It is very interesting that the laughter greeting Katherina's efforts to hold on to her identity in *The Taming of the Shrew* against the unremitting ploys of Petruchio to transform her into a Kate 'conformable to other household Kates' is in these days extremely uncertain, as though the conventions of comedy, dependent on the manners of the time, were wearing rather thin, and the more serious implications of breaking a woman's spirit, latent all the time, were showing through.

'To thine own self be true.' There are two difficulties about Polonius' injunction. One is that for many a self being true to it is too low an objective (and that is certainly true of the shallow and devious Polonius). The other is the problem of identifying the self, which can be as fluid as a blob of mercury. Once again *The Two Gentlemen of Verona* strikes the keynote in the carefully-named Proteus, especially in his soliloquy in Act II, Scene vi, when having fallen in love with Silvia he is conscious that to pursue his desires would be to betray Julia and Valentine, and his own honour. He argues in terms of being true to himself, but it is obvious that the difficulty lies in discovering the self to which one is to be true. He is a changed man, he says, because of the workings of love, which are not under his control. 'Love bade me swear and love bids me forswear.' To be true to Julia and to Valentine is to be true to a self that has passed away. If he keeps faith with *them* then 'I needs must lose myself'.

I cannot now prove constant to myself
Without some treachery used to Valentine.

(II. vi. 31–2)

Proteus' whole argument is selfish and sophisticated. But, dishonourable as he is, there is a core of honesty and realism in his uncertainty about a changing self.

A more famous self-justifying soliloquy is Prince Hal's in *1 Henry IV* (I. ii. 195–217), in which, after the planning of the Gad's Hill robbery, the prince dissociates himself from his companions but proposes not to have done with them just yet.

> I know you all, and will awhile uphold
> The unyoked humour of your idleness.

Hal justifies this procedure, which might seem hypocritical, by an argument which involves presenting himself to the world in different shapes as and when he chooses, and adopting those shapes in order to evoke certain responses from others. This flexibility of the self is not the same as the rapid costume-changes of that great actor Richard III as he manoeuvres himself into power, but it is not entirely dissimilar. Prince Hal inherits from his father the belief in the necessity of controlling the image which a royal person presents to the public; he does not need the lesson his father tries to give him on this matter, which is based on Ulysses' view that our nature is what other people think it is. To gain the throne the older Henry says he stole all courtesy from heaven and dressed himself in humility (unlike Coriolanus), avoided too much contact with the people and thus plucked allegiance from their hearts (*1 Henry IV*, III. ii. 39–55). His son goes further: the role seems to become the whole person. When his father dies and he becomes king, Hal says that he empties himself of his affections and assumes his father's spirits (*2 Henry IV*, v. ii. 123–33). To Falstaff he says 'Presume not that I am the thing I was. . . . I have turned away my former self' (v. v. 56, 58). His new kingly condition he images in terms of something detachable: 'This new and gorgeous garment, majesty,' he calls it, anticipating the synecdoche in *Henry V* when he reduces kingship to an 'intertissued robe of gold and pearl' worn to create 'awe and fear in other men'.

The self in Hal's eyes is something he can control and change, and by controlling it he can control the lives of others. The self is no mystery to him, and in that lies the fundamental difference between him as a hero and the next prince Shakespeare wrote about, Hamlet. Hamlet rather ostentatiously rejects the idea of the self as something that can be shown to the world like a garment. No outside of dress or behaviour 'can denote me truly'. 'I have that within which passes show' (I. ii. 85). But what is that inner self? The lack of definiteness of being (in a person sworn to revenge) can swing him into adopting a personality more readily than Hal himself, as when galvanized by the Player's emotion he briefly becomes a ranting stage-avenger. He always responds to the definiteness of others, the Player, Fortinbras, Horatio, Laertes. He knows that being is doing. The choice before him in 'To be or not to be' is the choice of accepting a nothingness of being in death or finding a definiteness of being in a resolute course of action. The very act of suicide, however, demands a certainty that he has not got, so that he is as powerless to accept non-being as he is to achieve being.

The capacity of disguise to release an aspect of personality which the sanctions of normal life suppress or restrain is possibly something that Shakespeare learned from Lyly, who in *Galathea* made a remarkable exploration of bisexuality in girls disguised as boys. Shakespeare did not choose to follow that line: Viola and Rosalind remain feminine. What Shakespeare does with Rosalind as Ganymede is to allow her to express that wonderful amused cynicism about love which actually strengthens her love as a woman for Orlando. The richest 'extension' of the self through disguise is undoubtedly in Edgar as Poor Tom. Edgar has a passion for disguise, and lives through it, ending as a medieval knight errant for the ritual of retribution against his half-brother. Perdita in *The Winter's Tale*, who has a passion for what is natural, the thing itself unhelped by art or artifice, feels her whole character changing because of the 'goddess-like' robes she wears at the sheep-shearing feast.

> Methinks I play as I have seen them do
> In Whitsun pastorals; sure this robe of mine
> Does change my disposition.

(IV. iv. 133–5)

It is surely the case that in *Measure for Measure* the Duke's 'performance' as a friar fulfils something within him that he could not fulfil as ruler and judge of his subjects. To prepare Claudio for the death which another judge has sentenced him to and to release others from the rigours of justice is more congenial than the impossible task of maintaining order in society.

Disguise, as with Duke Vincentio, is often used as a means of manipulating people. Shakespeare's plays are full of people stepping outside their proper personalities and deceiving others in order to bring about desired ends both good and bad. The good deceivers include Helena in *All's Well*, Paulina in *The Winter's Tale*, Prospero in *The Tempest*, Don Pedro in *Much Ado*, Kent and Edgar in *Lear*. The bad deceivers include Aaron in *Titus*, Richard III, Iago, Edmund, Iachimo in *Cymbeline*. Each of these contrives to establish an alternative reality and make others live in it. The damage to themselves as they act some part and assert the truth of some invented circumstance may be slight, but the effect on the selfhood of others may be disconcertingly great. The play-acting of Iago or Iachimo has as much power as the magic of Prospero to alter people's lives. *Much Ado About Nothing* is the most extraordinary play in this respect. The bad brother Don John tries to rewrite reality and scores an enormous success with Claudio's denunciation of his bride as a whore at the very altar. But the good brother Don Pedro has an equal delight in deceptions, and *his* great success is the plot which drives the sworn celibates Benedick and Beatrice towards marriage. *Much Ado* convincingly argues what flimsy and unstable beings we all are. What the self of Benedick or Beatrice is, whether it is *discovered* by Don Pedro's dissimulation or *created* by it, is hard to say. In tragedy as in comedy, the shape of selfhood seems provisional and malleable. Yet the concept of a 'self' is of primary importance, the distinguishing inner flame of personal identity which gives meaning and direction to one's life. The inaccessibility of the self, or its insecurity, is no evidence of its non-existence. If the idea of the self in Shakespeare were not of great magnitude, the repeated stories of its vicissitudes would not possess the power they have. To discover the self, to be true to it! A vain hope, but the only hope.

> What is your substance, whereof are you made,
> That millions of strange shadows on you tend?
>
> (Sonnet 53)

Poems and poetry

The narrative poems

Shakespeare's two ambitious long poems, separately published and carefully dedicated, are a pair as the comic and tragic masks are a pair. *Venus and Adonis* (1593) is light-hearted, erotic, irreverent, flippant even, until we reach the sombre ending. *The Rape of Lucrece* (1594) is solemn, heavy, and slow—so slow it sometimes seems to have stopped altogether. In the first a woman unsuccessfully tries to get a young man to have intercourse with her; in the second the man violently rapes the woman. The reluctant male and the reluctant female: a comic and a tragic subject. Both poems are concerned with the prolonged argument between love, desire, and physical sex which is continued in the sonnets, 'The Phoenix and the Turtle', and throughout the plays.

Venus and Adonis

Venus is one of those big matrons whom Rubens was soon to paint. She hoists Adonis off his horse, tucks him under her arm, and does her best to arouse him. The scramble and brawl is lightly and delicately painted in a whole series of superb images, mostly about birds. Venus is a famished eagle, a vulture; Adonis is a bird tangled in a net, 'a dive-dapper peering through a wave'. There is a grossness of sweating bodies in this farcical encounter:

> She sinketh down, still hanging by his neck,
> He on her belly falls, she on her back.
>
> (593–4)

But at the same time, and not in the least discordantly, his hand in hers is

> A lily prisoned in a gaol of snow,
> Or ivory in an alabaster band.
>
> (362–3)

Adonis pleads the separateness of love and sex, rehearsing the time-honoured distinction that real love is continuous whereas sexual desire terminates with satisfaction.

> Love comforteth like sunshine after rain,
> But lust's effect is tempest after sun.
>
> (799–800)

He escapes—

> Look how a bright star shooteth from the sky,
> So glides he in the night from Venus' eye—
>
> (815–16)

but he is savaged by the wild boar he's been hunting. As Venus phrases it,

> nuzzling in his flank, the loving swine
> Sheathed unaware the tusk in his soft groin.
>
> (1115–16)

He who refused intercourse is fiercely punished by a penetration that castrates and kills him.

Venus is transformed by his death, and the tone of the poem is transformed. The depth of the affection she now expresses qualifies our earlier view of her and shows the shallowness of Adonis' distinction between love and lust. She stoops to kiss the wounded place. There is no flippancy now.

> But he is dead, and never did he bless
> My youth with his, the more am I accurst.
>   With this she falleth in the place she stood,
>   And stains her face with his congealèd blood.
>
> (1119–22)

No doubt Adonis was right to refuse the 'tempest', but he achieved nothing. As in *Antony and Cleopatra*, the possibilities of spiritual union through sexual union only begin to be visible when it is too late (see pp. 41 and 151–3).

The Rape of Lucrece

It is worse than emptiness that Tarquin wins from the sexual act he brutally forces on Lucrece. Here is a union devoid of all possibility of communion. This long poem is full of 'sentences' moralizing on the one deed as it surveys it from every angle. Sometimes we feel we are listening to the Player King and Queen in *Hamlet*. Yet we also feel that Shakespearian tragedy is being

born in this slow labour. We have already seen Tarquin's lust for
Lucrece as an anticipation of Macbeth's lust for the crown of
Scotland. Tarquin knows the full dimension of what it is he is
about to do, as Macbeth does, but he urges himself forward just
the same. It is 'opportunity' that corrupts the tragic hero and
impels him to act, and Shakespeare (looking forward here to
Othello) suggests that virtue itself invites its own destruction
simply by existing.

> What virtue breeds iniquity devours.
> We have no good that we can say is ours
>   But ill-annexèd opportunity
>   Or kills his life, or else his quality.
>
> (872–5)

'The Phoenix and the Turtle'

'The Phoenix and the Turtle' was Shakespeare's contribution to
Robert Chester's *Love's Martyr* of 1601, where it appeared
alongside poems by Jonson, Chapman, and Marston. The general
theme is faithful love. Shakespeare took the opportunity of
celebrating the ideal of the communion that all lovers seek, even
though it is unfortunately no longer available.

> Love and constancy is dead,
> Phoenix and the turtle fled
> In a mutual flame from hence.
>
> (22–4)

Shakespeare cunningly suggests that the reason for the absence of
any more such lovers is that the love of the phoenix and the turtle
did not depend on sex.

> Leaving no posterity,
> 'Twas not their infirmity,
> It was married chastity.
>
> (59–61)

'The Phoenix and the Turtle' is a breath-takingly beautiful poem
that has no offspring itself in Shakespeare's work. The appropriate birds having been summoned, or in the case of the owl
banished—

> Foul precurrer of the fiend,
> Augur of the fever's end—
>
>   (6–7)

the anthem describes the union of two individuals in a series of paradoxes.

> Two distincts, division none:
> Number there in love was slain.
>
>   (27–8)

'Property' (that is, the sense of individuality and separateness) and reason are dumbfounded at this attack on them.

> Property was thus appalled
> That the self was not the same.
>
>   (37–8)

Reason surrenders, and cries:

> Love hath reason, reason none.
>
>   (47)

And we move to the lamenting rhythm of the Threnos.

> Beauty, truth, and rarity,
> Grace in all simplicity,
> Here enclosed in cinders lie.
>
>   (53–5)

The sonnets

The phoenix, of course, is supposed to rise again from its own ashes. But for the moment those ashes lie within an urn, and they have another threnody in Shakespeare's sonnets, written *in memoriam* to the idea of a unitary being compacted of two souls. They tell a strange story of a triangular relationship. In most of them the poet is writing to his patron, a young man much above him in social class. After the polite stages of urging him to marry and offering him poetic immortality, the poet begins to write of his passionate affection for this 'lovely boy', whose striking beauty combines that of both Adonis and Helen. 'But out alas, he was but one hour mine.' Their vastly different social origins and ways of life, the youth's inconstancy and misdemeanours, and his encouragement of rival poets, all make the relationship very uneasy; but the deepest complications are caused by a woman. However passionate and extreme the poet's love for the youth, it doesn't express itself in physical intimacy. His sexual relations are with the dark-haired, dark-complexioned woman to whom all the later sonnets (127–54) are addressed.

> Two loves I have, of comfort and despair,
> Which like two spirits do suggest me still;
> The better angel is a man right fair,
> The worser spirit a woman coloured ill.
>
> (144)

He hates himself for his subjugation to his own sexual desire for this woman, but there is worse when the woman deserts him—for the youth. The relationship with the youth is spread out over a period of years during which the poet himself is estranged; but Sonnets 115 to 125 record a great *redintegratio* of spiritualized love.

I have already recommended making the wager that there is a strong autobiographical element in the sonnets (see pp. 12–13). If, however, the basic 'story' is rooted in the events of Shakespeare's own life, it is certain that the sonnets grew as literature. For who is their real audience? Undoubtedly the 'private friends' among whom Meres said they circulated. Shakespeare looks beyond the two people to whom the poems were addressed, giving often enough one meaning to the 'recipient' and another to his friends. Many of the sonnets will have been part of the real-life flow of sonnets which at times brought Shakespeare near to poetic exhaustion (76, 103, 105); but there are others which seem (to say the least) a little inappropriate, and one cannot conceive any of the later sonnets being actually sent to or read by the dark woman: they are impossibly insulting. It may be that, as Shakespeare's relationship with the aristocratic friend and the promiscuous woman drew to an end, the sonnets which were directly associated with that relationship (sent or not sent) were added to in a meditative aftermath that may have stretched over many, many months. To keep adding to the sonnets and to arrange poems written at different times into thematically associated groups is hardly a matter of turning life into fiction; it is more a matter of prospecting deeper and deeper into the ultimate

significance of a relationship which in the first place was not I
think invented.

The result of all this is the greatest long poem Shakespeare
wrote and surely one of the greatest long poems ever written.
Agonizing over the 'real order' of the sonnets is a waste of time.
They are almost certainly in their proper order now. Though
there is a recognizable sequence of events in the poems, their
ordering belongs not to the calendar or to chronology but to
thought and feeling. And this ordering does not move to a
conclusion, either historical or philosophical; it denies a conclusion. If one reads the sonnets consecutively, the waywardness of
their contradictions and the inconclusiveness of their repeated
efforts to set a seal upon experience bring one as near to the
raggedness of life as art can reach. The complexity of emotions
and attitudes, unrivalled in English love-poetry, is achieved by
the positioning of the poems. The close-packed wealth of the
individual sonnet is multiplied beyond calculation by its mobile
relationship with neighbouring sonnets and with the whole sequence. The extreme coarseness of the 'will' sonnets (134–6) rubs
shoulders with the extreme spirituality of the final sonnets to the
young man. Self-disgust vies with injured pride, submissiveness
with indignation, accusation with forgiveness, hope with despair,
happiness with misery, admiration with contempt. To tamper
with the order of the sonnets is to lose many of the fine
juxtapositions by means of which the poems creatively quarrel
with each other. Sonnet 146, 'Poor soul the centre of my sinful
earth', tries out a traditional religious resolution of carnal wor-
ries; Sonnet 147 crashes in with 'My love is as a fever longing *still*'
(that is, always). Indeed, it seems that brutal intrusion is quite a
principle in the placing of the sonnets. Sonnet 20 is an unexpected
shock to the calm of its predecessors: it is the necessary, indispensable announcement of the *real* theme, concealed in the witty
explanation that the 'master–mistress' of his passion was first
intended for a woman:

> Till Nature as she wrought thee fell a-doting,
> And by addition me of thee defeated
> By adding one thing to my purpose nothing.
> > But since she pricked thee out for women's pleasure,
> > Mine be thy love, and thy love's use their treasure.

So the separation of love and sex is signalled. After this noisy interruption all is quiet again. In a similar way, 40 bursts in: 'Take all my loves, my love, yea take them all'; this time announcing the theme of the disastrous triangle—or tangle—with the dark woman. The great sonnet on lust (129), 'Th' expense of spirit in a waste of shame', is another sudden intervention in the midst of tranquil sonnets, quite altering their complexion with its intense light.

Not only is it best to read the sonnets in the 1609 order; it is essential to read them as a whole. It is as fruitless to read only a selection of sonnets as it is to read just the major soliloquies of one of the tragedies. The sonnets explain each other. So many people read perhaps the exclamatory sonnets on time in an anthology, 'Since brass, nor stone, nor earth, nor boundless sea', for example (65), and drift away not deeply moved. The sonnets come alive by statement and counter-statement. As a wave breaks one way, a powerful undertow pulls in the opposite direction. This process begins in the unit of the word by means of the pun, which is everywhere.

> So true a fool is love, that in your will,
> Though you do anything, he thinks no ill.
>
> (57)

A faithful fool or an absolute fool? From the single word we move to statement and counter-statement in the image and then in the individual sonnet. The individual sonnets within a group challenge and qualify each other, and group challenges group. In the sequence as a whole the principle holds good: the love for the youth is a balance between statements of scepticism and belief about the possibility of spiritual love coexisting with the frailty of the flesh, and the concept of love itself is a tug-of-war between the two spirits that 'suggest him still', embodied in fair youth and dark woman.

Statement and counter-statement often come about by pitting poetry against truth. There is plenty of that common convention that the true lover doesn't need the artifices of poetry but just speaks from the heart, or indeed remains silent; as is customary, this is an ironic procedure, for the poet needs the resources of his deeply valued craft for his appeal to unstudied spontaneity. 'My tongue-tied muse,' says Shakespeare in his eighty-fifth sonnet; 'I

think good thoughts while others write good words.' So! In 130,
'My mistress' eyes are nothing like the sun', Shakespeare makes
fun of this convention-that-attacks-convention, namely that the
plain words of the honest lover best describe true beauty, by
making the disavowment of poetic ornament convey a very
disagreeable impression of the beloved. Many times, the poet–
hero fears that the fatal facility of verse-writing is leading him to
betray his own best knowledge. This is beautifully shown in 35,
'No more be grieved at that which thou hast done', in which after
offering conventional excuses for the youth like 'Roses have
thorns and silver fountains mud', the poet turns with disgust
against his own glibness.

> All men make faults—and even I in this,
> Authórizing thy trespass with compare,
> Myself corrupting, salving thy amiss . . .

'Thus I will excuse you', says the poet of the guilty pair in 42, and
gives us the black humour that in fornicating with the youth the
woman is 'Suffering my friend for my sake to approve her'. We
must be prepared throughout the sonnets for unconvincing
stretches of rhetoric that are meant to be unconvincing. This
'failure' of the poet's art will chiefly be found in the final couplets,
which confidently attempt to resolve the problem at issue and
manifestly do not succeed (e.g. 34).

The power of the sonnets is often enough shown by the daring
of metaphor and simile: the harvest sheaves 'borne on the bier
with white and bristly beard' (12); the winter trees seen as 'bare
ruined choirs' (73); nativity 'crawls to maturity' and is therewith
'crowned' (60). Yet a sonnet will often make its point by insisting
on the inadequacy of comparison. There is an extraordinary
tentativeness about the sonnets (of which 'Shall I compare thee to
a summer's day?' is as it were a beginner's example). A turmoil of
conflicting thoughts will show up the insufficiency of what seemed
to be a promising image. I cannot stow you away and lock you up
as I lock my jewels up, says the poet in 48—but—do I in some
way own and possess you?—well, probably not—but you could
be 'stolen' from me—by my honesty in admitting that you are not
'mine'.

> Thee have I not locked up in any chest,
> Save where thou art not—though I feel thou art—

> Within the gentle closure of my breast,
> From whence at pleasure thou mayst come and part.
> And even thence thou wilt be stolen, I fear,
> For truth proves thievish for a prize so dear.

In the succeeding sonnet, 49, the images by their 'inadequacy' are constantly pulling the poem against its surface meaning. This is one of the many poems in which self-abasement wars with sullen assertiveness. (Shakespeare's poet is not the sort of person who doesn't need the reader's frequent forgiveness.) When you've had enough of me, he says, and pass me by without greeting me,

> Against that time do I ensconce me here
> Within the knowledge of mine own desert,
> And this my hand against myself uprear,
> To guard the lawful reasons on thy part.

Yes, yes, you'd do right!—he positively growls; I prepare my hiding-place, I know I'm worth nothing, I'll plead *your* case against myself. But the counter-movement is just as strong. By using the word 'ensconce' he is as much firmly protecting himself as he is skulking, and the hand upreared is as much an act of violence against the self as it is a legal asseveration for the opposing party.

'Such civil war is in my love and hate' (35). What the poet thinks of himself and what he thinks of the youth provide a continuing and complex oscillation in the sonnets as they jostle to assess the relationship and to define love. 'No longer mourn for me when I am dead', he says in 71, 'for I love you so' that I wouldn't want you to remember me 'if thinking on me then should make you woe'. You cannot decide whether he is being sarcastic, as some think, or whether this is the genuine surrender of all claims by a masochistic poet-lover. There is as much generosity in the sonnet as there is bitterness and complaint. But in the next sonnet, which directly continues the theme, as he foresees his death and the youth's response to it there is a new firmness in the renunciation of his rights; *really*, he says, I am not worth thinking about. Then follows one of the greatest poems Shakespeare or any poet ever wrote, 'That time of year thou mayst in me behold' (73). The thought of death is expanded to include the thought of growing old; dying becomes the universal tragic process of self-consumption, a process more of dignity than futility, as the poet compares himself with the dying season and compares the dying season with the ruined monuments of the ancient church. It is achievement that uses us up—'consumed with that which it was nourished by'—but at least there *is* achievement. So the couplet turns from the morbid post-mortem of 71 back to life. The prospect of death should 'make thy love more strong'. In the last of this wonderful group of sonnets (74) the poet returns to the contemplation of death with an entirely new strength. This poem he is writing is itself the distillation of the poet's spirit; this spirit-of-the-spirit was born from love; and this poem lives on whatever happens to its author. At the end he speaks of his body, dead:

> The worth of that is that which it contains,
> And that is this, and this with thee remains.

An unpoetic couplet? But it is as resonant as the rhetoric of some of the sonnets on time (e.g. 19) which promised the *young man* poetic immortality. The poet has stopped bothering about the young man in 74, as he has stopped bothering about himself. It is poetry that is the real worth of the speaker; a poetry generated by his relationship with the young man. The poet dies, expended, consumed; if the poetry lives on, what does it matter whether the young man mourns for his Will or not? If there is a resolution in the sonnets, it is in this poem; but the order of the sonnets does not permit such resolutions.

In two sonnets (37, 89) the poet pictures himself as a cripple limping along by the side of the splendid Adonis he's had the miraculous luck to be taken up by. The shame of his own 'deformity' is, however, a minor matter compared with the possibility of the corruption of this god-like beauty. The prolonged argument about the infection of beauty, running through poem after poem and quite central to the sonnets, is carried forward by the same self-cancelling procedure of statement and counter-statement which we have been observing. 'Lascivious grace', the oxymoron which begins the argument (40), is itself a self-cancelling paradox: 'Lascivious grace, in whom all ill well shows.' '*Well* shows'—does he mean that everything ill appears as if it were good, or that everything ill appears distinctly? The great series of Sonnets 92 to 96 probes this question, on the answer to which depends the continuance of the poet's affection. Sonnets 92

and 93 argue the appalling possibility that the young man is full
of falsehood and that, because of the radiance of his personality,
the poet would never be aware of his treachery.

> Whate'er thy thoughts or thy heart's workings be,
> Thy looks should nothing thence but sweetness tell.
> How like Eve's apple doth thy beauty grow
> If thy sweet virtue answer not thy show!
>
> (93)

'Eve's apple': humankind betrayed by the specious good. There
are two fears here. First, fear of the loss of moral discrimination,
fear of confounding right and wrong, good and evil. Secondly,
fear that the idea of purity in human life cannot be held fast to; if
it cannot, then the idea of purity of love is an illusion. This
concept of purity has nothing to do with indulging in or abstain-
ing from sexual relations; it is a quality of being that Shakespeare
is talking about, though the emblems of this quality are indeed
largely sexual. If the woman and the young man copulate, she will
infect him with venereal disease (144); it is not the act in itself but
the relationship that corrupts. It is bad enough to say that this
wonderful young man is actually so corrupt that the concept of
ideal love for him or anyone else crumbles and disintegrates. But
suppose one is quite unable to see that corruption? Then the
ultimate corruption will have come about—in the poet. The
guideposts of the conscience will have become indiscernible; there
are no knowable standards; all has become subjective and relative. Thus the two fears become one. Sin in the young man seems
like virtue. When he moves among objectionable people (67) you
stop objecting to them.

> Thou blind fool, Love, what dost thou to mine eyes,
> That they behold, and see not what they see?
>
> (137)

Since the young man sanctifies sin—or rather appears to
sanctify sin so that sin is no longer recognizable—there is no
possible course but that he should isolate himself from all
possible temptation,

> For sweetest things turn sourest by their deeds;
> Lilies that fester smell far worse than weeds.
>
> (94)

This couplet is the envoy of the most debated of all the sonnets, 94, 'They that have power to hurt and will do none'. It cannot be read by itself; it depends for its meaning on the sonnets that surround it.

> They that have power to hurt and will do none,
> That do not do the thing they most do show,
> Who, moving others, are themselves as stone,
> Unmovèd, cold, and to temptation slow—
> They rightly do inherit heaven's graces,
> And husband nature's riches from expense;
> They are the lords and owners of their faces,
> Others but stewards of their excellence.
> The summer's flower is to the summer sweet
> Though to itself it only live and die,
> But if that flower with base infection meet
> The basest weed outbraves his dignity.
> > For sweetest things turn sourest by their deeds;
> > Lilies that fester smell far worse than weeds.

Here again as the wave breaks in one direction the undertow pulls the other way. For only by abstemious aloofness, non-involvement, can beauty prevent its corruption which, because it is in a person so wonderful that the sin is imperceptible, drags with it everyone who admires or loves him. But, even as the poet praises those noble beings who keep themselves above the heat of involvement and passion, he fails; the images have turned against him. No one can like the austere, reserved, Angelo-like figure who is praised, nor this flower whose smirking, inactive self-sufficiency seems opposed to everything Shakespeare wrote in favour of relationship and action. The sonnet illustrates (purposely of course) the very confusion from which it is trying to get away. The magnetism of the young man makes it impossible to praise with any conviction his antitype, the person with the virtue we ought to try to emulate. So in the next sonnet, 95, the game on which everything depends is very nearly lost. The young man makes shame 'sweet and lovely'. 'Lascivious comments' on his delinquencies end up as praise.

> O what a mansion have those vices got
> Which for their habitation chose out thee,
> Where beauty's veil doth cover every blot
> And all things turn to fair that eyes can see.

After this series on 'lascivious grace' there are sonnets suggesting absence and the passage of time, and we move on to the group
beginning with the fanfare of 107 ('Not mine own fears nor the
prophetic soul'), which seeks to rescue love by 'the mutual
forgiveness of each vice'. That is to say, the poet acknowledges his
own frailty; his infidelity and inconstancy. Each of the pair must
acknowledge his 'trespass' (120); 'Mine ransoms yours, and yours
must ransom me'. The poet pictures the rediscovery of love as the
penitent's return to the soul's true home. He has made himself 'a
motley to the view'.

> Most true it is that I have looked on truth
> Askance and strangely.
>
> (110)

But all that is over. 'Now all is done, have what shall have no
end.' He has returned to 'my best of love', 'a god in love', 'next
my heaven the best'. (All this from 110.) The counter-statement
within these culminating sonnets of the young-man series is of a
new kind. On the one hand we have the sincere humanity of the
reciprocal recognition of limitation and frailty; but on the other
we have expressions of love that seem appropriate to a penitent
priest's fervent return to the mother church and the true object of
the soul's devotion. These two dimensions are both present in the
climactic Sonnet 116, 'Let me not to the marriage of true minds'.
True love survives the 'impediments' that have threatened separateness in so many earlier sonnets.

> Love is not love
> Which alters when it alteration finds.

The poet then moves from negatives to ecstatic affirmation.

> O no, it is an ever-fixed mark
> That looks on tempests and is never shaken;
> It is the star to every wandering bark,
> Whose worth's unknown, although his height be taken.
> Love's not Time's fool, though rosy lips and cheeks
> Within his bending sickle's compass come;
> Love alters not with his brief hours and weeks
> But bears it out even to the edge of doom.

As our eyes are led high up to the unmoving star and far away to

the edge of doom, we wonder where the young aristocrat has got
to. The ecstatic language is much like that of Ralegh in his 'Ocean
to Cynthia'—another long irresolute poem built on constant
contradictions and the sudden juxtaposition of differing perspec-
tives. There, at the height of the poet's enthusiasm, love no longer
depends on the fidelity of the loved one, nor her presence, nor
even her existence.

> A love obscured, but cannot be forgotten,
>   Too great and strong for Time's jaws to devour—
>
> From thee therefore that mover cannot move,
>   Because it is become thy cause of being.

But Ralegh cannot maintain the rapturous conviction that true
love survives the ending of an actual relationship. His poem
concludes with these words:

> Her love hath end: my woe must ever last.

Those noble sonnets of Shakespeare which are placed as the
conclusion of the series to the young man seem to me to be built
on the ruins of the love for the youth rather than to be a
rebuilding of that love. The poet's absence from the young man is
puzzlingly imaged in terms of an intellectual or spiritual journey:
'Gored mine own thoughts', 'Looked on Truth / Askance and
strangely' (110), 'I have frequent been with unknown minds'
(117). His new love is 'builded far from accident' (124). Sonnets
123 to 125, the last full sonnets of the young-man sequence, are
intolerably obscure and it may be that they hold in their depths
the explanation of Sonnets 107 to 116. Ostensibly, idealized love
is fully discovered by a return to the young man in a mutual
exchange of forgiveness. Yet there are strong hints that the poet is
not talking about the young man at all; that the discourse has
become allegorical and that the search for true love no longer has
a human object. Be that as it may, the 1609 order of the sonnets
will not give us any resting place here, worldly or other-worldly.
There is still the series to the dark woman to come, the most
painful of the sonnets, and not the less painful for being intermit-
tently jocular.

The variety of Shakespeare's sonnets is endless. There is the
simple happiness of

> So are you to my thoughts as food to life,
> Or as sweet-seasoned showers are to the ground,
>
> (75)

or the equally simple controlled scorn of 87 ('Farewell, thou art too dear for my possessing'), where the lines are urged on by their feminine endings to that wonderful conclusion:

> Thus have I had thee as a dream doth flatter,
> In sleep a king, but waking no such matter.

In Sonnet 90 the poet-hero is in a particularly black mood of childish self-pity. Sonnet 89 had ended 'For I must ne'er love him whom thou dost hate'. Sonnet 90 begins with a snarl that captures petulance to the life.

> Then hate me when thou wilt!—If ever, now—
> Now, while the world is bent my deeds to cross.

The mood can change completely during the course of a sonnet. In 29, for example, 'When in disgrace with Fortune and men's eyes', the poet moves from depression and self-distrust to the height (literally!) of happiness:

> Yet in these thoughts myself almost despising,
> Haply I think on thee, and then my state,
> Like to the lark at break of day arising
> From sullen earth, sings hymns at heaven's gate.

By no means every sonnet is a success. There are quite a few that are tired or weak. But taken as a whole (as they must be taken), it is hard to think of a richer poetic experience than the sonnets. They are not easy reading, but the reward for the kind of reading they demand and deserve is ample indeed.

Poems in the plays

There are a great many poems *within* Shakespeare's plays: songs and their music are an indispensable presence. What would *The Tempest* be without music? 'The isle is full of noises, sounds and sweet airs.' Is the reader of the plays then disfranchised, imagining music rather than hearing it? A further question arises: if music is indispensable, whose music are we talking about? Any music? Authentic Elizabethan, reconstructed Elizabethan, modern settings? Those who have listened to the songs in some productions might be excused for hurrying home to their texts and the pleasures of the imagination. There is no doubt that Shakespeare's plays need music for their full effect, but as with performance as a whole, better to have none than to have poor stuff.

There is of course a whole range of poems within the plays which are not meant to be sung: the sonnets in *Love's Labour's Lost*, the legends on the caskets in *The Merchant of Venice*, Hamlet's curious love-poem to Ophelia, the masque in *Cymbeline*, riddles, instructions, epitaphs. Many of these are jingles, meant to seem crude. Others are meant to stand out as a different kind of utterance and use a heavy beat and rhyme. The gnomic octosyllabics in *Measure for Measure* (III. ii) demand a specially emphatic pronunciation. We can't say how much of the doggerel of the Fool in *Lear* was chanted or sung. In two plays in particular a chanting that comes near to singing is required: for the Witches in *Macbeth*—

> Fillet of a fenny snake
> In the cauldron boil and bake—

and the dirge which the brothers say over the supposedly dead Fidele in *Cymbeline*, 'Fear no more the heat o' th' sun'—

> Golden lads and girls all must
> As chimney sweepers come to dust.

This last ranks in beauty with Ariel's threnody 'Full fathom five thy father lies'—which is also a lament for a death that hasn't happened.

It is the comedies which make most use of songs, and among the comedies *The Tempest*, *As You Like It*, and *Twelfth Night* are the most musical. As Ariel's music commands *The Tempest*, Feste's commands *Twelfth Night*, but where Ariel creates the atmosphere of his play, Feste is always ironically questioning his. He has too much knowledge altogether. Left alone at the end of the play, no longer needing the good favour of patrons and passers-by, he comes into his own with his cryptic wry song, 'When that I was and a little tiny boy':

> A great while ago the world begun,
>   With hey ho, the wind and the rain;
> But that's all one, our play is done,
>   And we'll strive to please you every day.

The Fool in *Lear* sings a snatch of the same song (III. ii).

Songs in the comedies provide an obvious thematic support. In *Measure for Measure* a page sings 'Take O take those lips away / That so sweetly were forsworn' for the deserted and lonely Mariana. In *Much Ado* the song 'Sigh no more, ladies' goes on to say 'Men were deceivers ever', a bull's-eye in a play where everyone is hoodwinking everyone else. In *As You Like It* 'Under the greenwood tree' and 'It was a lover and a lass' crystallize romantic exile and springtime love in a world without too much care.

Songs hardly surface in the histories, but in the tragedies their effect is profound. It is not so much now the beauty of the lyrics— many of the songs are simply versions of old and familiar pieces— but the dramatic use of song to create a special atmosphere. We have no words for the song the boy Lucius sings for Brutus in his tent the night before Philippi, but this music momentarily re-creates a life that disappeared with the resolution to kill Caesar. As the boy falls asleep over the strings of his instrument and Brutus turns to his book, the Ghost of Caesar enters to put an end to music and reading. Desdemona in her devastation and bewilder-ment finds that the old willow song will not go from her mind; here again as she sings the plaintive melody there is a moment of stillness before the storm. Ophelia's madness is largely made out of songs: old ballads and folk songs, sad songs, and improper songs she shouldn't have known, all of them pointing in to the central misery of a father killed and a lover gone.

Verse and prose in the plays

As well as the normal blank verse and prose of Shakespeare's plays there is also rhyme, usually in the form of rhyming couplets in the earlier plays, comedies especially. In the later plays rhymed couplets are used for special purposes, as for the inset 'Murder of Gonzago' play in *Hamlet*, or for the moral saws with which the Duke in *Othello* tries to soothe Brabantio (who sarcastically returns them). It is less clear in the early plays what governs Shakespeare's moves into and out of rhyme; sometimes it just seems to be as the mood takes him. More complicated rhyme-schemes are occasionally found. Richard II pronounces a complete sestet (ababcc) in reply to Aumerle's question 'Why looks your grace so pale?' at III. ii. 75. Lysander and Helena argue with each other in sestets in *A Midsummer Night's Dream* (III. ii. 122). At their first meeting (I. v. 48), Romeo and Juliet's exchange of words is in the form of a shared sonnet, ending in a kiss. Romeo has the first quatrain, Juliet the second; the third, like the couplet, is divided between them.

Shakespeare is not always happy in his prose; it can be lack-lustre, cumbrous, and convoluted. His greatest achievements are in the language he created for characters of comedy like Benedick and Beatrice, Rosalind in *As You Like It*, Falstaff in the *Henry IV* plays, and clowns early and late like Launce in *The Two Gentlemen* and Autolycus in *The Winter's Tale*. Yet *The Merry Wives of Windsor*, wholly in prose until the last scene, is the least interesting of the comedies. Prose becomes specially effective in contrast with verse, scene against scene or speaker against speaker, as in *As You Like It, Much Ado*, or *1 Henry IV*. Even so, as with the alternation of rhyme and blank verse, it is not always clear what motivates the change between verse and prose. While Rosalind's prose seems appropriate when she is voicing the reductive common sense of Ganymede, it is hard to see why the whole play, which starts off entirely in prose, suddenly shifts into blank verse at the end of the second scene. One thinks of Jaques as a prose character, and he is sensitive enough to leave abruptly when Orlando enters with 'Good day and happiness, dear Rosalind'— 'Nay then God b'wi'you, an you talk in blank verse'; but Jaques has his first scene entirely in verse. It is easier to work out a rationale for Iago's verse and prose, though even with him the choice seems at times arbitrary. The cynical Iago who companions Roderigo is a master of contemptuous prose, but the Iago who confides his plans and desires to the audience speaks in verse (see the change at I. iii. 383). It is a different kind of verse, of course, from the studied rhetoric with which he destroys Othello's peace of mind in Act III, Scene iii. Othello does not speak prose until Iago's poison has worked on him (IV. i. 32). In *Hamlet*, the Prince's rapid staccato prose in the nunnery scene (III.i) is in very sharp contrast to the measured verse of Ophelia's speech on his exit: 'O what a noble mind is here o'erthrown.' The distinction between the equilibrium of the minds of the two of them is not as clear and simple as Ophelia perceives it, but for the moment verse is orderliness of mind and prose disorder. *Troilus and Cressida* makes very effective use of the interplay of verse and prose. At the very opening, Troilus's rhapsodic verse has to battle against the reductiveness of Pandarus's prose, and the same thing happens in the consummation scene (III. ii). For example:

TROILUS.   O gentle Pandar,
From Cupid's shoulder pluck his painted wings
And fly with me to Cressid.
PANDARUS. Walk here i' th' orchard, I'll bring her straight.

(13–16)

The play's debate about valuation and truth is partly set out by the alternation of verse and prose. 'I speak no more than truth,' protests Pandarus. 'Thou dost not speak so much,' rejoins Troilus.

The question of 'style'

Anyone who sets out to analyse and categorize Shakespeare's blank verse soon finds himself in the rueful position of Sir Thomas Wyatt's lover in 'Whoso list to hunt':

I leave off therefore
Since in a net I seek to hold the wind.

Shakespeare's dramatic verse is 'wild for to hold'; untameable and in the end indescribable. Every reader can feel a difference between Shakespeare's early, middle, and late styles; can discern, that is to say, the movement from the more expansive rhetorical patternings to be found in the early comedies and histories to the compressed, elliptical daring of the final plays. But as soon as one begins to try a definition of *Shakespeare's* style at any one period, the difficulty makes itself felt. The style belongs to the characters. One can occasionally speak of the style of a single play: each of the Roman plays, for example, has its pronounced style, *Julius Caesar*, *Coriolanus*, and *Antony and Cleopatra*, though not one of them resembles another. Homogeneity is more noticeable in the earlier plays and disappears altogether in the late romances. *Cymbeline*, for example, is stylistically a mingled yarn. The first of the scenes in Rome (I. iv) is in an intense and brilliant prose utterly uncharacteristic of the rest of the play. It is as though Shakespeare were collaborating with—another Shakespeare. The essence of Shakespearian style is ventriloquism: the protean power of giving individuality of language to his characters. Even in a play like *Julius Caesar*, which does have a recognizably uniform style, Brutus is distinguished from all other characters by the way he speaks (see below, p. 81). The style is the man. Though bishops, dukes, and princes in the histories are often indistinguishable, main characters like Richard II, Hotspur, and Falstaff are given an absolute difference in their speaking styles; and the separateness of the world each lives in is created by linguistic singularity.

A special Shakespearian gift shared by many characters is a brilliance of descriptive recreation. The most famous of these set-pieces is presented to us not as observation or recollection of a real scene but as imaginative fiction, as Edgar reports to his blind father what he pretends to be looking at from the imagined Dover cliff (*King Lear*, IV. vi. 11–24). Most of these triumphs of descriptive writing, as in *King Lear*, have an important dramatic function. The dream of Clarence in *Richard III* is a prolepsis of his own death, already organized by his brother, and as an index of the guilt of his haunted imagination anticipates what Richard himself will be unable to escape from.

> O Lord methought what pain it was to drown!
> What dreadful noise of waters in my ears!
> What sights of ugly deaths within my eyes!
> Methoughts I saw a thousand fearful wrecks,
> A thousand men that fishes gnawed upon,
> Wedges of gold, great anchors, heaps of pearl,
> Inestimable stones, unvalued jewels,
> All scattered in the bottom of the sea.
> Some lay in dead men's skulls, and in the holes
> Where eyes did once inhabit, there were crept
> (As 'twere in scorn of eyes) reflecting gems
> That wooed the slimy bottom of the deep,
> And mocked the dead bones that lay scattered by.

> ... Then came wandering by
> A shadow like an angel, with bright hair
> Dabbled in blood, and he shrieked out aloud,
> 'Clarence is come—false, fleeting, perjured Clarence,
> That stabbed me in the field by Tewkesbury ...'
>
> (I. iv. 21–33, 52–6)

In *The Shrew*, Biondello's virtuoso prose-poem on Petruchio's arrival on horseback at his wedding describes something that could hardly be staged, but, even if it were possible, description betters performance in concentrating on the dishonouring effect of Petruchio's appearance. Gertrude's vivid and very detailed account of the drowning of Ophelia in *Hamlet* again gives the audience a sense of witnessing something that could not be staged. It is a particularly interesting use of narrative. Gertrude moves into impersonality as she describes the scene, for she could not possibly have watched the slow death she describes without intervening. The madness of Ophelia, her drowning and her funeral, are of the deepest importance in the play, and each is brought to the fore in a special way. Her death by water, strewn with flowers and crazily singing hymns, is put into the glass case of Gertrude's trance-like report.

Yet at times it seems that a sheer joy in the power of words to bring a scene alive before one's eyes made it impossible for Shakespeare to resist word-painting for its own sake. The descriptions of the animals in *Venus and Adonis* are obviously prize pieces. The horse is

> Round-hoofed, short-jointed, fetlocks shag and long,
> Broad breast, full eye, small head and nostril wide,
> High crest, short ears, straight legs and passing strong.
>
> (295–7)

There is also a hare, 'poor Wat' (679–708), and a snail (1033–6). It's more a question of delight than of showing-off, and it is the same delight that led to the brilliant but gratuitous picture of the apothecary and his shop where Romeo buys poison (v. i. 37–49), and to Hubert's account of the effect of the news of the death of Arthur in *King John*.

> I saw a smith stand with his hammer, thus,
> The whilst his iron did on the anvil cool,

> With open mouth swallowing a tailor's news,
> Who with his shears and measure in his hand,
> Standing on slippers which his nimble haste
> Had falsely thrust upon contrary feet,
> Told of a many thousand warlike French
> That were embattailèd and ranked in Kent.
> Another lean unwashed artificer
> Cuts off his tale and talks of Arthur's death.
>
> (IV. ii. 193–202)

Metaphor

Metaphor dominates the language of all the plays, growing more bold and complex in the later tragedies and tragicomedies. Probably the best way to study Shakespearian metaphor is to read *Macbeth* again. Even if one's favourite metaphors might come from other plays (perhaps Cleopatra's description of Antony, 'his delights were dolphin-like'), the density of figurative language in that short play is unique. There best of all can one see what Shakespeare achieved by presenting a concept, a quality, an abstraction, in terms of what is visual, physical, familiar. It is a kind of electricity, two thunder clouds moving towards each other and generating lightning as the associations of one word are suddenly merged with those of another—the blanket of the dark, the belt of rule, the milk of human kindness, life's fitful fever, this bank and shoal of time, pity like a naked new-born babe, a tale told by an idiot, his silver skin laced with his golden blood. The systematic study of Shakesperian metaphor is still in its early stages in spite of all the attention that has been given to 'imagery' in recent years (see 'A Note on Shakespeare Criticism', p. 187). As general description is not very helpful, here are one or two characteristic examples of metaphor at work.

> His coward lips did from their colour fly.
>
> (*Julius Caesar*, I. ii. 122)

This image depends on the pun in 'colour', which is a military flag as well as a hue or tint. Caesar's lips lost their colour through illness, but this because of a language game becomes cowardice for Cassius: his lips are soldiers running away from the colours. The pallor of a sick man's face also lies behind Hamlet's image in his 'To be or not to be' soliloquy:

> And thus the native hue of resolution
> Is sicklied o'er with the pale cast of thought.

'Resolution' here has a human face, normally ruddy but now wan and pale through illness; its loss of power is a sick man's loss of power. The disease which makes it pale is thought (which can mean melancholy but here probably means meditation). There is also present, in 'o'er ... cast' a suggestion of the sun's 'golden face' being 'stained' with clouds, as in Sonnet 33:

> Anon permit the basest clouds to ride
> With ugly rack on his celestial face.

So the weakening of resolution is both a healthy man sickening and the sun being clouded over.

In *Much Ado* (v. i), Leonato refuses consolation unless it comes from someone who has suffered like himself. From such a person he would 'gather patience' when he heard him

> Patch grief with proverbs, make misfortune drunk
> With candle-wasters.

This is very compressed and fast-moving. Grief overcome by proverbs is like ragged breeches being repaired, and then it is fuddled and drugged by the sayings of learned men who read far into the night, whose advice 'smells of the lamp', as we say. Oddly, these rather unworldly scholars must have fleetingly become late-night revellers—another kind of candle-waster—for Shakespeare to promote the peculiar notion that moral saws make misfortune 'drunk'.

Henry IV was a solemn fellow and it is to be hoped that Warwick and Surrey did not laugh when in his lecture on the vicissitude of things he said:

> And other times to see
> The beachy girdle of the ocean
> Too wide for Neptune's hips.
> *(2 Henry IV*, III. i. 49–51)

The king is trying to say that sometimes the sea withdraws from the land, and that you can tell this by an expanse of beach left where the sea used to come. The personification of this geographical event is ludicrous; not all Shakespeare's images are successful.

However, the king makes up for this with a Herbert-like sally
when, brooding over the crime of seizing the throne, he says:

> all the soil of the achievement goes
> With me into the earth.
>
> (IV. v. 190–1)

The figurative soil disappears when it combines with the real soil
of the grave.

Finally, a description of Hector, fighting in his last battle:

> And there the strawy Greeks, ripe for his edge,
> Fall down before him like a mower's swath.
>
> (*Troilus and Cressida*, v. v. 24–5)

The comparison here is much more conventional than in the
images we have been looking at. The Greeks tumble before
Hector's sword as though he were a mower with his scythe
reaping ripe corn. The originality is in the extraordinary way it is
put. 'The strawy Greeks'—men of straw—are 'ripe for his edge';
they stand there ready and waiting for Hector to kill them. So
very often, and constantly in the sonnets, it is not extravagant
novelty that creates the power of the Shakespearian metaphor but
the energetic refuelling of a commonplace comparison.

The poet as ventriloquist

Shakespeare's linguistic exuberance and the abounding fertility of
his vocabulary are particularly Elizabethan. Like all his contemporaries, Sidney, Nashe, Marlowe, Jonson, Marston, Dekker, he
exults in England's linguistic gold-rush. But at the same time, his
plays are full of his consciousness of the danger of these cascades
of words which it seems to take so little effort to produce. It is
perhaps the ease with which he as master-ventriloquist is able to
provide the appropriate language for murderers, virgins, princes,
Romans, usurpers, grave-diggers, in every kind of situation in
which he personally was *not*, that makes distrust of language so
prominent in the plays. It is not unexpected that plain blunt men
of action would be wary of talkers. There is Bolingbroke impatiently and disgustedly listening to Richard II spinning webs of
words before actually surrendering the crown. There is Lewis the
Dauphin in *King John* listening to the Bastard's powerful warning

of the dangers awaiting him. He knows it is all words; the Bastard is a 'brabbler'. He will not attend to him. 'Let the tongue of war / Plead for our interest and our being here' (v. ii. 164–5). Deeds not words. But the matter goes much further than the scorn of doers for talkers. In the balcony scene, Juliet longs to hear the words that will tell her that Romeo loves her, but words only seem to lead away from the truth she wants.

JULIET. Dost thou love me? I know thou wilt say ay,
  And I will take thy word, yet if thou swear'st
  Thou mayst prove false.

ROMEO. Lady, by yonder blessed moon I vow,
  That tips with silver all these fruit-tree tops—
JULIET. O swear not by the moon, th' inconstant moon,
  That monthly changes in her circled orb,
  Lest that thy love prove likewise variable.
ROMEO. What shall I swear by?
JULIET.   Do not swear at all;
  Or if thou wilt, swear by thy gracious self,
  Which is the god of my idolatry,
  And I'll believe thee.
ROMEO.   If my heart's dear love—
JULIET. Well, do not swear. Although I joy in thee,
  I have no joy of this contract tonight.

                  (II. ii. 90–2, 107–17)

In *King Lear*, Cordelia listens with disgust to her sisters' ornate professions of total love for their father, which she knows to be entirely false. Her reaction is not to speak at all when her turn comes; for her disgust is with words as well as with sisters. If words can sound so well and be so empty of truth, what value is there in using them? But the consequences of silence prove tragic indeed. You can't dispense with the treason of words.

        Angels are bright still, though the brightest fell.
        Though all things foul would wear the brows of grace,
        Yet grace must still look so.

                  (*Macbeth*, IV. iii. 22–4)

There is no manner of utterance that cannot be simulated; it is not just affected rhetoric that the false heart coins. Plain speech can be a contrivance, as Cornwall shrewdly recognizes in the

altercation between Oswald and the disguised Kent (*Lear,* II. ii.
95–104). It is a nice irony. Kent is fearless for the truth, as he has
demonstrated, and here he cannot stand the fawning insincerity
of Oswald; but his own speech, according with his role of rough
blunt fellow, is an assumed garb. All speech is under suspicion.
There is no way of knowing the heart from words any more than
from the face. 'Yet grace must still look so.' There is nothing that
truth can do except use words as best it can. It has to wear the
same clothes that deceit wears. Shakespeare's liars are the true
craftsmen of language; they know how to make it work. Honest
people have no special gift for speaking truthfully. Even those
who have not the slightest wish to deceive others are found
deceiving themselves with language and protecting themselves
with a cloak of unreality. Two plays in particular bring to the fore
the incapacity of language to convey unvarnished truth, *Love's
Labour's Lost* and *Hamlet.* In the former, Berowne's voluble
common-sense speeches seem a guarantee of an authentic link
between the heart and the tongue, but love makes him *write* as
affectedly as anyone else, and in the great fifth act he takes quite
some time, in the stony presence of the women they are wooing,
to reach a sobriety of language. He forswears 'three-piled hyper-
boles, spruce affectation' in a positive spate of rhetoric; only at
the very end do circumstances force him to 'honest plain words'.
Love's Labour's Lost is a play about linguistic excess of all kinds;
its satire on current affectations and fashions in Armado and
Holofernes mustn't obscure its larger debate—the whole question
of decorum in speech, the unending search for a language that is a
true and adequate response to self, situation, and society.

In *Hamlet* we have those among the Court Party, Claudius,
Polonius, and Laertes, whose rotund and periphrastic style of
moral generalities stands at a considerable distance from the facts
of their conduct, as even Laertes' affectionate sister recognizes:
she fears it is possible that he 'recks not his own rede'. Into this
comfortable world of words Hamlet inserts his curt punning
ripostes: 'Not so, my lord, I am too much i' th' sun.' In his antic
disposition he refuses to meet the confident circumlocutions of his
opponents with anything but teasing ambiguities. 'I am but mad
north-north-west; when the wind is southerly I know a hawk
from a handsaw.' This refusal to speak anything but riddles,
which alarm his hearers by their possible import as much as they

exasperate them by their absurdity, is not only part of Hamlet's grim battle with the king and his allies; it is part of his battle with himself. He distrusts every conviction and every form of speech such conviction may emerge in. He torments himself as well as Ophelia with his speeches in the nunnery scene, which circle in mockery about the possibility of his love, her constancy, his own contemptibility. The antic disposition is a strategy against Claudius and a defence against having to make statements. He can mock even scepticism in his teasing 'confession' of *Weltschmerz* to Rosencrantz and Guildenstern in the speech 'What a piece of work is a man!' (II. ii. 303–9). Hamlet knows what in himself he has to guard against, being carried away by hysterical rant as he is after the Player's Hecuba speech. 'What an ass am I', that 'must like a whore unpack my heart with words.' To Horatio, whose words are always so measured and prudent, he expresses his longing to be like him; but in the closet scene with Gertrude words again betray him into excess. 'Suit the action to the word, the word to the action.' In his advice to the players, Hamlet expresses the perfect marriage in which the balance between word and action is achieved by each helping the other to find itself. Control of language and control of self would go together. But discordance between thought, word, and deed is the upshot of the play.

Hamlet veers between 'wild and whirling words' and a withdrawal into the non-statement of riddle, pun, and irony. His fellow-intellectual Brutus in *Julius Caesar* is much more confident that he can master speech and master others with speech. Even in the quarrel scene with Cassius he speaks in measured and premeditated phrases. Yet he is in fact much more a prisoner of language than Hamlet. We see him at the beginning of Act II, Scene i trapped by an orator's analogies of adder and serpent's egg into believing he has proved the necessity of assassinating Caesar. Later in the same scene he is again pulled down by his own similes, when he talks about the assassination in the unhappy metaphor of the butcher's shop. 'Let's carve him as a dish fit for the gods . . .' After killing Caesar, his logic persuades him that he has done Caesar a benefit. At the funeral oration the measured balance of the clauses hideously simplifies the gravity and complexity of the issues involved. There is always a fatal gulf between the controlled speeches and the events they refer to. The eloquence of Brutus is no index of his understanding of himself or his situation.

One imagines that Shakespeare was nearer to his creature Hamlet than to Brutus: one whose acute sensitivity to language led not to confidence in words but to increasing suspicion of their loyalty.

4
Comapped Comedy[*]

'Improbable fictions'

The original audience of Shakespearian comedy is Christopher Sly. He is taken up from his sordid life by an aristocrat with a penchant for practical jokes who, insisting that Sly is really a lord, provides a play for his entertainment.

> Your honour's players, hearing your amendment,
> Are come to play a pleasant comedy;
> For so your doctors hold it very meet,
> Seeing too much sadness hath congealed your blood,
> And melancholy is the nurse of frenzy;
> Therefore they thought it good you hear a play,
> And frame your mind to mirth and merriment,
> Which bars a thousand harms, and lengthens life.
>
> (Induction, ii. 129–36)

Sly agrees to see it 'and let the world slip'. The play is *The Taming of the Shrew*, a fantasy of male domination.

Sly's benefactor has the right approach. Shakespearian comedy is a therapy. Its relevance to life is that it does you good. 'Let the world slip!' It is a matter of being taken out of ourselves. Of course 'being taken out of ourselves' sounds as though it could be distinctly uncomfortable. What happens is that we in the audience are taken out of ourselves in a comfortable way by watching characters being taken out of themselves often in a very uncomfortable way. The idea of 'holiday' is widely used in describing the atmosphere of a Shakespearian comedy, but we should be wary of applying it to the characters of the plays, who may well not think of what happens to *them* as a holiday, and reserve it for ourselves in the audience, who are allowed an hour or two off from the treadmill to join the extraordinary fantasies of life in Illyria or the forest of Arden.

By traditional definition stemming from Aristotle, comedy treats of the urban scene and everyday life. Not so Shakespearian

---

[*]This chapter deals with the comedies written up to 1601. The later comedies are discussed in Chapter 7, *Tragicomedy*.

comedy, which prefers courts and country places, with nonsensical plots, and situations very remote from ordinary existence. Truth is stranger than fiction and there are many remarkable instances in real life of twins being united in adult life after being separated since infancy, but it is not in the least the aim of Shakespearian comedy to reproduce a semblance of 'this working-day world'. It is a never-never-land. *The Merry Wives of Windsor* is indeed urban and bourgeois, but its jolly, business-like matrons Mistress Ford and Mistress Page make us long to return quickly to the shipwrecked Viola disguised as a eunuch at Duke Orsino's court. There is a strong citizen element in *The Taming of the Shrew*, in which Baptista drives hard financial bargains with the suitors for his daughters' hands, and Petruchio, for whom marriage and money are synonymous, moulds his eccentric bride into what befits a middle-class household. *The Comedy of Errors*, being of Roman origin, is about merchants and citizens and their wives, their homes and their servants. But Shakespeare chose not to develop this citizen strain, preferring the possibilities of the unrealistic pastoral and courtly romance he adumbrated in *The Two Gentlemen of Verona*. Economic realities, while they do not disappear, generally remain at a tactful distance. The bold fusion of these realities with romance makes *The Merchant of Venice* a very special case.

The sea-girt quality of merchant life in *The Merchant of Venice*, as in *The Comedy of Errors*, might appear simple realism for an Elizabethan living in London, but it is in fact an assertion of freedom from the constraints of verisimilitude. In a Shakespearian comedy you can generally travel from one inland town to another by sea; Padua, Verona, and Milan all seem to be ports. Eventually Bohemia has its sea-coast. Real geography is unimportant; the sea is all-important. The powerful symbolism of the sea dominates the late romances, and is already a strong presence in the earlier comedies, especially the two shipwreck twin-seeking plays, *The Comedy of Errors* and *Twelfth Night*. It is out of no ordinary ocean that Antonio's argosies, whose loss at sea has been the sole cause of the crisis of *The Merchant of Venice*, reappear and 'are richly come to harbour suddenly'. By his use of the sea Shakespeare shows us he will not be subject to the tyranny of the possible.

In their titles the comedies disclaim any serious intent. 'As You

Like It', 'Twelfth Night, or What You Will', 'A Midsummer Night's Dream', 'Much Ado About Nothing'. Constantly the plays mock themselves by breaking illusion. 'If this were played upon a stage now,' says Fabian in *Twelfth Night*, 'I could condemn it as an improbable fiction' (III. iv. 127). In *A Midsummer Night's Dream* the solemn efforts of the mechanicals to make their play real but not too real are Shakespeare's parody of his own contrivances, particularly in the stage representation of moonlight.

> This lanthorn doth the hornèd moon present,
> Myself the man i' th' moon do seem to be.
>
> (v. i. 244–5)

That is the best the mechanicals can do. As for Shakespeare, having expressly stated in the opening lines of the play that it is four nights to the new moon (so that the nights must be virtually moonless), he outrageously turns the moon full on for the adventures in the wood, using his verbal magic for *his* 'lanthorn'. It is in *A Midsummer Night's Dream* that Shakespeare gives to Theseus the brilliant and dismissive description of poetic imagination, comparing it with the 'shaping fantasies' of lovers and madmen. The 'poet's pen' 'gives to airy nothings, / A local habitation and a name' (v. i. 4–22).

These bland deprecatory gestures of Shakespeare don't deceive us. There is too much artistry in these 'airy nothings', too much irony in the use of these throwaway titles for us to accept his dismissals at their face value. These light-hearted entertainments have a way of touching the deepest chords of our experience. We don't want to be heavy-handed about this, or mistake the comedies for guide-books on conduct, but there is no doubt at all that the dramatist's benign and indulgent smile at the way of the world sometimes looks suspiciously like a wicked mephistophelean grin.

Delight and laughter

In talking of the structure and make-up of Shakespearian comedies we could take a hint from Sir Philip Sidney (who had seen none of them). Writing his *Apology for Poetry* in the early 1580s, he reprimanded the English comedy of his time for concentrating on laughter instead of delight. Repeating the traditional view that the source of laughter was ridicule, he spoke of it as a 'scornful tickling'. We laugh at mischances and deformity. But 'delight hath a joy in it'. We are delighted by the happiness of others, whereas we laugh at their misfortunes. Delight and laughter are contraries; 'for delight we scarcely do but in things that have a conveniency to ourselves or to the general nature; laughter almost ever cometh of things most disproportioned to ourselves and nature'. Sidney admitted, however, that 'laughter may come with delight' even though it is not bred by delight. Three centuries later than Sidney, Baudelaire made a very similar discrimination in his brilliant essay on comedy of 1855. Laughter, he said, which comes from a man's idea of his own superiority, is 'one of the clearest marks of Satan in man'. Laughter is scorn, and 'we must be careful to distinguish between joy and laughter'. 'Joy is a unity.' Baudelaire's joy is Sidney's delight.

The motive force of Shakespearian comedy is most certainly not the scorn of satire. Whoever felt scornful of Sir Andrew Aguecheek? Or felt that the mockery of the lovers in, say, *Love's Labour's Lost* or *As You Like It* was scornful? It is the satirist himself who is in the dock: Jaques in *As You Like It*, who would do (says Duke Senior) 'mischievous foul sin in chiding sin'. The motive force of Shakespearian comedy is delight, in the movement of the characters from separation to union, from discord to harmony, from severance to integration. For reasons that we shall look at, you could not have this progress without laughter, yet delight is primary and laughter consequential.

But laughter there certainly is. Its source is not primarily in the wit of the conversation as in Congreve and Wilde. With some notable exceptions, like Rosalind and Touchstone, Benedick and Beatrice, much of the jesting now seems laborious and distinctly unfunny. There *is* some scornful laughter, at the discomfiture of the self-important Malvolio or the disappointed suitors Aragon and Morocco in *The Merchant*. But unkind laughter, like the patrician laughter at the uneducated such as Dogberry or Bully Bottom, has a way of dissolving into sympathy for the victim, as it certainly does for the half-educated Armado in *Love's Labour's Lost* (who is one of the very few characters to be mocked for affectation—the chief crime in Restoration comedy). We have to face it, however, that, though it is not scornful, the chief cause of laughter in Shakespeare's comedies is indeed people's discomfiture: the bafflement and fear caused by mistaken identity in *Errors*, the practical joke played on Benedick and Beatrice, the confusion of the lovers in the *Dream*, the vexatious state of Katherina in *The Shrew*. Laughter, which arises in us because of the collapse of our expectations, has its source in the defeated expectations of the persons of the play. Their bewilderment is our amusement. Their bewilderment, however, is an essential component of delight, since the movement from separation to union is almost universally through bewilderment. Delight requires transformation; transformation causes bewilderment; bewilderment evokes laughter.

The initial stage of separation needs little documentation. Shakespeare's comedies usually start with unhappiness. In *As You Like It*, dispossession and disinheritance for both the hero and the heroine: Orlando is hardly used and his life is threatened by his brother Oliver; Rosalind is banished by the uncle who deposed her father. In *A Midsummer Night's Dream*, Hermia is under threat of death or perpetual celibacy if she doesn't marry a man she hates. In *Twelfth Night*, a shipwrecked sister is mourning a missing brother. In *The Comedy of Errors*, a father is under sentence of death in a foreign town where his son also searches for the other half of a broken family.

Bewilderment as a purgatorial experience is brilliantly shown in *A Midsummer Night's Dream*. The threatened lovers and their followers escape from a hostile court to the wood near Athens only to become the victims of the fairy king's ill-directed kindness. The incomprehensible switch of Lysander's and Demetrius's affection from Hermia to Helena is frightening for the women and funny for the audience. The confusions increase wildly before Oberon and Puck are able to bring things under control and make relationships better than they were to begin with. Only one other play so strikingly marks this central phase of the action with a move to the wild or pastoral setting that somehow we think of as an indispensable in Shakespearian comedy, and that is *As You Like It*, where we shift to the forest of Arden and then, with all problems solved, head back to court. It is the weight of these two great plays, combined with the pattern of the late romances, that makes us think of the green place as standard. It is a powerfully symbolic accompaniment to the changes of fortune and relationship that we witness, but, while bewilderment is never absent, the green setting is optional. Nevertheless, place is always important in the comedies, more important than in the tragedies. For the Syracusans in *The Comedy of Errors*, Ephesus is charged with a sinister enchantment capable of changing the inner core of being. 'There's none but witches do inhabit here.' The forest in *The Two Gentlemen* where Valentine joins the outlaws and Proteus attempts rape is an early use of the wild place as the proper setting for extremes of behaviour, emotion, and insight; the way to the heath in *King Lear* is long but direct. The action of *The Merchant of Venice* ricochets between the Rialto of Shylock and the Belmont of Portia. Here the tragedy-comparison would be the constant switches in *Antony and Cleopatra* between Rome and Egypt: the values associated with one place constantly challenge the values of the other. When they meet in the court of law, Portia of Belmont defeats Shylock of Venice, and the final scene is in a moonlit Belmont.

The stratification of *The Merchant*, which thus has a thematic value, also illustrates a structural principle of the earlier comedies. In the first three scenes of *A Midsummer Night's Dream* there is no sequence in the action: we are introduced to three separate sets of characters and their problems: the Athenian aristocrats, the Athenian workmen, the fairy Court. The Athenian aristocracy divides into two components: Theseus and Hippolyta (and attendants), and the four young lovers. The subtle linking of these four elements as we move from city to woodland and back is the secret of the play's brilliance. There is a similar procedure in *Twelfth Night*. The first scene (almost literally) strikes a keynote, with music for the love-sick Orsino; then we have Viola and the captain on the sea-coast; then Sir Toby Belch, Maria, and Sir Andrew; then Viola disguised as a page; then Olivia, Feste, Malvolio. The comedy is an elaborately plaited rope, with each strand separately introduced. Or it is a polyphonic music blending the voices of separate choirs.

Transformation

Bewilderment, we said, accompanies transformation. All drama deals with change, but the changeability of the person in Shakespearian comedy is surely remarkable. Sometimes it is voluntary, like Viola's decision to change herself to Cesario; this causes an involuntary change in Olivia's life. Katherina in *The Shrew* is forced by Petruchio's relentless programme to contract her whole nature into a wary submissiveness. Benedick and Beatrice are induced by Don Pedro's practical joke to surrender their sworn commitment to single life. The conversion of brother Oliver in *As You Like It* from wickedness to goodness after being rescued by Orlando is psychologically more reasonable than many of the transformations. The least reasonable is the transformation of the self-confident weaver and amateur actor Nick Bottom into a monster with an ass's head, as part of Oberon's scheme to tame his stubborn queen. 'Bless thee Bottom,' cries Peter Quince, 'bless thee; thou art translated.' Translated indeed; for Titania waking is under Oberon's spell to love whatever she sees.

> I pray thee gentle mortal sing again,
> Mine ear is much enamoured of thy note;
> So is mine eye enthrallèd to thy shape,
> And thy fair virtue's force perforce doth move me
> On the first view to say, to swear, I love thee.
>
> (III. i. 137–41)

So Bully Bottom ascends to the bed of the fairy queen. A jocular version perhaps of the mystic's central experience of melting into communion with celestial beings.

I have had a most rare vision. I have had a dream, past the wit of man to say what dream it was. Man is but an ass if he go about to expound this dream. Methought I was—there is no man can tell what. Methought I was, and methought I had—but man is but a patched fool if he will offer to say what methought I had . . . I will get Peter Quince to write a ballad of this dream. It shall be called Bottom's dream, because it hath no bottom.

> (IV. i. 204–16)

The transformation of Bottom, a triumph of comic invention and hilarious on the stage, is a central point in Shakespearian comedy. In every play we find the firmness of the sense of personal identity begin to tremble and dissolve. Sometimes it's nightmare, as it is for Katherina, and for Antipholus in *Errors*. Sometimes it is a blessed dream, as it is for Sebastian in *Twelfth Night*, suddenly awarded a new past and a beautiful wife, and as it is for Bully

Bottom. In Chapter 2 we saw that comedy was as concerned as tragedy with the instability of the all-important sense of selfhood and personality. In voluntary disguise or under pressure the very nature of the characters changes before our eyes. As often as not the origin of the transformation is love.

Love as madness

It is a spell put on her by Oberon in spite that changes Titania to the ridiculous indignity of being besotted on Bottom with his ass's head. But the potency of the juice of the flower love-in-idleness, whose origin Oberon describes in such detail and with such ceremony (II. i. 148–72), is comedy's way of explaining the irrational infatuations and obsessions which love promotes in its victims. It was Cupid's shaft (narrowly missing Queen Elizabeth) which gave the flower its power. As Bottom says, 'Reason and love keep little company together nowadays.' Love's omnipotence, for the good or ill of those whom it enslaves, is the subject of the comedies.

> Love's a mighty lord,
> And hath so humbled me as I confess
> There is no woe to his correction,
> Nor to his service no such joy on earth.

So speaks Valentine in *The Two Gentlemen* (II. iv. 136–9), a resister who has been forced to acknowledge the power of love. There are many such resisters. The King in *Love's Labour's Lost* sets up his 'little Academe' to pursue learning for three years with the rigorous exclusion of the society of women. Berowne knows that this is a futile defiance of human nature, but even he is not prepared for the totality of the subjugation which loves causes.

> And I forsooth in love! I that have been love's whip,
> A very beadle to a humorous sigh,
> A critic, nay a nightwatch constable,
> A domineering pedant o'er the boy,
> Than whom no mortal so magnificent.
> This wimpled, whining, purblind, wayward boy,
> This senior-junior, giant-dwarf, Dan Cupid,
> Regent of love rhymes, lord of folded arms,
> Th' anointed sovereign of sighs and groans,

> Liege of all loiterers and malcontents,
> Dread prince of plackets, king of codpieces,
> Sole imperator and great general
> Of trotting paritors—O my little heart!
> And I to be a corporal of his field,
> And wear his colours like a tumbler's hoop?
> What? I love, I sue, I seek a wife?
>
>   Go to! It is a plague
> That Cupid will impose for my neglect
> Of his almighty dreadful little might.
>
>   (III. i. 174–89, 201–3)

Lucentio in *The Shrew* arrives in Padua in order to institute a programme of study of the philosophy 'that treats of happiness / By virtue specially to be achieved'. But the first sight of Bianca changes all that. It is nearly always love at first sight. Lucentio, like Rosalind with her wrestler, has good luck in this spontaneous appetence, but Olivia is appalled by the effect which the handsome youth Cesario has on her, a dignified lady, mistress of a household, in mourning for her brother.

> Well, come again tomorrow. Fare thee well.—
> A fiend like thee might bear my soul to hell!
>
>   (III. iv. 216–17)

She feels herself possessed, and has no power to restrain what she really has no wish to restrain.

> There's something in me that reproves my fault,
> But such a headstrong potent fault it is
> That it but mocks reproof.
>
>   (III. iv. 203–5)

This is one of the countless versions of Medea's cry in Ovid's *Metamorphoses*: 'Video meliora proboque; deteriora sequor'—I see and approve of the better things; I follow the worse. Fortunately Olivia is in a comedy, and, by mistaking the manly Sebastian for his disguised twin sister, her rash dedication of herself to Cesario turns out all right.

At the end of *Love's Labour's Lost*, the penitent Berowne ingeniously manages to blame the women for the extravagance of the men's behaviour.

> Your beauty, ladies,
> Hath much deformed us . . .

> Therefore, ladies,
> Our love being yours, the error that love makes
> Is likewise yours.

(v. ii. 756–7, 770–2)

The 'deformities' of love are partly of course the exaggerated behaviour of lovers which all the comedies constantly make fun of. Silvius in *As You Like It* actually *boasts* of his ridiculous behaviour as being a measure of his love, and Touchstone nostalgically remembers his follies when he wooed Jane Smile. 'We that are true lovers run into strange capers; but as all is mortal in nature, so is all nature in love mortal in folly' (ii. iv. 54–6). But deformity goes deeper. 'Love is merely a madness,' says Rosalind in the safety of her role as Ganymede. In Sir Philip Sidney's *Arcadia*, published in 1590, which Shakespeare had read carefully, Musidorus said:

O heaven and earth! . . . to what a pass are our minds brought, that from the right line of virtue are wryed to these crooked shifts! But, O love, it is thou that dost it; thou changest name upon name, thou disguisest our bodies and disfigurest our minds. But indeed thou hast reason, for though the ways be foul, the journey's end is most fair and honourable.

(I. 18)

It seems to be the most light-hearted comedy, *A Midsummer Night's Dream*, which has the most ominous things to say about love. The gloomy catalogue of Lysander and Hermia in the first scene, to demonstrate that 'the course of true love never did run smooth', is of course their response to the gloomy situation in which they find themselves, but 'So quick bright things come to confusion' is a line which seems to have come across from the tragic love story of *Romeo and Juliet* written at the same period. And how dejected Hermia is when she tells Helena that she and Lysander are running away!

> Before the time I did Lysander see
> Seemed Athens as a paradise to me.
> O then, what graces in my love do dwell,
> That he hath turned a heaven into a hell.

(I. i. 204–7)

Left alone, Helena gives voice to the most bitter speech in the comedies.

> Things base and vile, holding no quantity,
> Love can transpose to form and dignity.
> Love looks not with the eyes, but with the mind,
> And therefore is wing'd Cupid painted blind.
>
> (I. i. 232–5)

She blames Demetrius for transferring his affections to Hermia, and herself for loving Demetrius. By 'the mind' she is specific that she does not mean the judgement. It would have been easy to say that the trouble with love is that it goes by the *eyes*—that is, by superficial outward appearance—when it should be governed by the *mind*—that is, by the considering judgement. What Helena means by the mind is what is imagined and not real, the fancy whose obsessions cloud, distort, and deny the truth that is seen by the eye. This is the world of the dark-woman sonnets:

> O me! what eyes hath love put in my head
> Which have no correspondence with true sight!
>
> (148)

This is the lover whom later in the play Theseus compares with the madman and the poet whose 'shaping fantasies' apprehend 'more than cool reason ever comprehends'.

> The lover, all as frantic,
> Sees Helen's beauty in a brow of Egypt.
>
> (v. i. 10–11)

In the opening lines of *Twelfth Night* Orsino speaks enigmatic words about the transforming power of love. 'O spirit of love, how quick and fresh art thou!' he exclaims, ending,

> So full of shapes is fancy
> That it alone is high fantastical.

To tease out the meaning of this mysterious remark, we need to note that 'shape' means either a bodily presence or an outward semblance; that 'fancy' means love and devotion (Orsino at the end calls Viola 'his fancy's queen'), but it also means imagination; that 'fantastical' means either imaginary, or whimsical, wayward, affected. Putting all that together, we understand Orsino to be implying that the lover, sudden and capricious in the guises he

adopts as in the fitfulness of his devotions, demonstrates that love
is in the mind, is the great fabricator, coining its own world,
leading its devotees (or its victims) into the wilderness of irrationality. 'Thou art as wise as thou art beautiful,' says Titania,
embracing the donkey head of Bottom.

It is just as well that Shakespeare wrote *As You Like It*, or we
should begin to suspect that the comedies, which are all about
love, are all surreptitious attacks on love. Rosalind and Touchstone are realists about love; they know the world and they know
the human heart. If the relationships they form with the other sex
are very different, that is because of a difference in temperament,
not intelligence. As Ganymede in her teasing sessions with
Orlando, Rosalind shows no mercy in cutting through the lover's
false sentiments, protestations, and hopes. At the end of one of
the liveliest and most amusing scenes in Shakespearian (or any
other) comedy (IV. i), in which she lays waste to every cherished
belief of a lover in the holiness or permanence of his or her
emotions, Rosalind turns to Celia as Orlando leaves: 'O coz,,coz,
coz. My pretty little coz, that thou didst know how many fathom
deep I am in love!' (IV. i. 205). So liberated, so clear-sighted, and
so deeply in love; no question here of 'Venus toute entière à sa
proie attachée'. The good humour and balance of Rosalind is
shared by the whole play. In the closing ceremony Rosalind gives
herself to her father and to Orlando, and Hymen sings:

> Wedding is great Juno's crown,
>   O blessed bond of board and bed.
> 'Tis Hymen peoples every town,
>   High wedlock then be honourèd.
> Honour, high honour and renown
> To Hymen, god of every town.

(v. iv. 141–6)

The union of Touchstone and Audrey won't last long, and
Jaques is a determined non-joiner, but the audience's pleasure in
the union of Rosalind and Orlando is unalloyed. It is the perfect
completion of the pattern of delight, from severance and misfortune through confusion to union and happiness.

Endings

There is no other comedy so free of uncertainty. The ending of the

Dream is enchanting, with Oberon's blessing on the issue of the
marriages to come and Puck's epilogue appealing to us not to
take the play too seriously—so we all hope that Theseus, whose
earlier seductions, betrayals, and infidelities have been pointedly
referred to by Oberon (II. i. 77–80), will not be tempted to leave
Hippolyta, and that the juice which has caused Demetrius to
transfer his affection back to Helena will not lose its effect. Most
comedies end with marriage in prospect, but *The Shrew*, in going
beyond the wedding, has its own comment to make on lovers'
expectations by showing in Bianca an indifference to her husband
that seems quite out of keeping with the heroine of a Shakespearian comedy. But the bigger problem about the ending of that play
is of course the nature of Petruchio's victory over Katherina. As
she makes her eloquent speech defining the proper submission of
wives to husbands, there are those who think of her as intimidated into repeating a lesson taught by cruelty. There are those
who think that her spirit is unbroken and that she doesn't mean a
word of what she says; what Petruchio has taught her is prudence
and dissimulation; she will exercise her power through other
means than tantrums. There are those who think that these two
high-spirited people have achieved an affectionate and mutually
respectful equilibrium which will continue beneath their observ-
ance of the conventional social disequilibrium. Certainly, a
working *modus vivendi* has come about since the encounter with
Vincentio on the road back to Padua. But no one can lay down
the law about the ending. It is really for the actors in each new
production, and especially the actress playing Kate, to work out
what final relationship the play intimates.

Love's Labour's Lost deliberately moves away from the usual
happy ending. The ladies doubt what at the end of other comedies
the audience doubts: the permanence of an affection which has
grown up so quickly. They send their lovers away for twelve
months' meditation and hard work. Berowne protests:

Our wooing doth not end like an old play.
Jack hath not Jill. These ladies' courtesy
Might well have made our sport a comedy.
KING. Come sir, it wants a twelvemonth and a day,
And then 'twill end.
BEROWNE.   That's too long for a play.

(v. ii. 874–8)

The sudden change of focus by which Shakespeare makes us subject the love relationships to a deeper scrutiny than is usually found in comedy is our justification for looking quizzically at other endings. It might be thought that Viola deserves a better match than Orsino and Portia a better match than Bassanio. Hero in *Much Ado* and Julia in *The Two Gentlemen* will have to continue to be very forgiving of their husbands' earlier insufferable behaviour. The ending of *The Two Gentlemen* is a very special problem that we have already looked at (see above, pp. 35–6. At the beginning Proteus feels himself transformed or, to use his own word, 'metamorphised' by love. Love then captures Valentine too (see above, p. 90). It was under no compulsion from his source that Shakespeare ended the play by making Valentine place friendship above sexual love. Sexual desire has dislocated their relationship and led Proteus into betrayal and violence. In accepting Proteus' penitence, Valentine tries to reconstruct the relationship by refusing to let a woman stand between them:

> And that my love may appear plain and free,
> All that was mine in Silvia I give thee.
>
> (v. iv. 82–3)

Valentine thus works himself into a very awkward either/or situation from which Shakespeare extricates him by producing Julia, Proteus' cast-off love who is standing by disguised as a page.

> It is the lesser blot, modesty finds,
> Women to change their shapes than men their minds.
>
> (108–9)

Proteus is as ashamed of his treatment of Julia as he is of his treatment of Silvia. The idea of the conclusion of the play is that friendship and love are not mutually exclusive; the friendship of Valentine and Proteus is strengthened in its renewal and each moves forward to marriage—the weddings to be celebrated on the same day:

> One feast, one house, one mutual happiness.
>
> (173)

The ending of *The Two Gentlemen of Verona* is not botched or silly as is so often said. It is an interesting and suggestive 'open' ending, like the ending of *The Shrew* and *Love's Labour's Lost*. *The Two Gentlemen* degrades women only if the ethics of Valentine are supposed to be the author's, and they cannot be, any more than Petruchio's are. *The Shrew* portrays male domination; *Love's Labour's Lost* portrays female domination. One viewpoint balances another. If either sex is treated unfavourably in *The Two Gentlemen*, it is the men, in their wavering and uncertainty as well as in their casual indifference to women as persons. The women remain single-minded, constant, and true. Throughout the comedies it is not women who are unconstant but men; all the bad behaviour, the fickleness, and the betrayals, come from them. Julia, Hero, Helena, Viola remain true, while the objects of their affection do not reciprocate, drift away, build up slanders. With typical male vanity Orsino (whose mind Feste tells him to his face is 'a very opal') claims that love in women is 'appetite' and that their hearts 'lack retention'. The comedies disprove him.

Controlling forces

It is often said that women dominate the comedies. It is a perilous generalization. The matter can only be debated within a much wider context of who or what it is that is shown to govern and control the course of life in the comedies. It is no easier to answer this for the comedies than for the tragedies. The world of comedy is a topsy-turvy world; its spirit has often been compared with that of the licensed anarchy of medieval and renaissance revels and the 'lord of misrule'. If happiness comes to those who deserve it, it can hardly be said that they have achieved it by thought and effort in a rational and just world; it has come their way.

The engineering of tricksters and manipulators is much less present in Shakespearian comedy than in that of other dramatists—Ben Jonson notably—though it commands two plays, *A Midsummer Night's Dream* and *Much Ado About Nothing*. The *Dream* has a whole supernatural machinery to 'explain' what controls human lives. The dispute of the fairy king and queen is described as having terrible effects on earth; harvests lost, rivers flooding, seasons out of order. The schemes of Oberon, erratically administered by Puck, are responsible for all the wild happenings of the central part of the play. Puck is identified in Act ii, Scene i as Robin Goodfellow; the readiness of the common people to attribute all mishaps to the activities of this creature had been scornfully attacked by Reginald Scot in his *Discovery of Witchcraft* (1584). The identification helps us to see the supernatural machinery of the *Dream* for the joke it is (like that of the sylphs in *The Rape of the Lock*). The play pretends to explain the irrationality at the heart of sexual desire, as people believe they can explain unforeseeable mishaps by the activity of Robin Goodfellow. It succeeds of course in emphasizing the sheer inexplicable fact of irrationality at the heart of things. Lysander interestingly calls this irrationality reason, when under the influence of Puck's potion he sets off in pursuit of Helena:

> The will of man is by his reason swayed,
> And reason says you are the worthier maid.
>
> (II. ii. 115–16)

In *Much Ado* the tricksters are very human, one good one (Don Pedro) and one bad one, his half-brother (Don John). Neither can refrain from scheming. Don Pedro wishes to take over from Cupid the honour of generating love; Don John wishes to destroy it. Don Pedro strives to bring Benedick and Beatrice together; Don John to separate Claudio and Hero. Both succeed, but Don John only temporarily. The attachment of Benedick and Beatrice is of some importance in deciding what the comedies show as the governing force in life! Is it caused by the manipulation of others? Or is Don Pedro's scheming another joke 'explanation' of the 'changeable taffeta' that is the stuff of our lives? Or is it the emergence of a concealed love that needs no ulterior explanation? Many people feel that the bickering between Benedick and Beatrice is a kind of sexual play and that the double deception by which each is led to believe the other is in love only accelerates their recognition of a deep attachment. The actor and the actress have only a brief moment in the final scene of the play to indicate to the audience how *they* see their strangely-wrought relationship when they learn about the deception. They both say that they actually love the other 'no more than reason', but, in a burst of laughter, agree to accept the situation. Every audience delights in the union as they have delighted in the bickering. Whether the couple are sensible people making the best of things, or whether they have been helped to realize their true selves, is one of the open questions with which Shakespeare continuously leaves us, as a sign of the amplitude and generosity of his art. Whatever way we take it, the play as a whole goes to a lot of trouble to show what little say our wills and determination have in governing our lives. Don Pedro is as completely taken in by Don John's contrivance of Hero's 'adultery' as Benedick and Beatrice are taken in by *his* contrivance. Shakespeare makes a tantalizing web of the solving of the play's problems. It appears that the stupid and bumbling Dogberry is to be the unexpected means of revealing Don John's plot, and that the Friar's scheme for pretending that Hero is dead will bring Claudio back to his sense. But these are spoofs. The Friar's scheme has no effect on Claudio; and the truth comes trickling out in spite of, not because of, Dogberry, who hasn't the faintest perception of what's going on. This elaborate plotting by Shakespeare in a play full of characters plotting produces the strangest effect; it certainly does absolutely nothing to reduce the sense of how mysterious in the end, despite all contrivance and effort, is the outcome of things.

No woman directs events in these two plays, and no man either. The direction of only one comedy is in the will of a man, *The Taming of the Shrew*, and only one comedy, *The Merchant of Venice*, is directed by the will of a woman. In *As You Like It* Rosalind is certainly in command for much of the time, but the play is extraordinarily plotless, more meetings than happenings, and she takes command more in the disposings of the final scene than as a director of events. Portia's role in *The Merchant of Venice*, is perhaps rather curious. It is Shylock's loan, sending Bassanio off to Belmont, and Portia's father's incredible scheme for marrying his daughter to a man who chooses a leaden casket, that initiate the action. Portia is fortunately won by the man she wants, and she offers herself to him with a rather surprising humility and submissiveness as 'an unlessoned girl, unschooled, unpractised'. From then on she takes charge and everyone yields to her. Her knowledge of the law is like Helena's knowledge of medicine in *All's Well*: it makes her almost a priestess in possession of arcane knowledge able to solve problems too difficult for ordinary mortals. And as she returns to the more womanly role of Bassanio's wife, she is certainly no 'unlessoned girl' but one who with her control of the rings is all-powerful.

The Merchant of Venice

Shakespeare's earlier comedies are so richly different from each other that they don't compete and it's impossible to have a favourite play. There is a particular brilliance about *A Midsummer Night's Dream* and *As You Like It*. But there is also a very special achievement in *The Merchant of Venice*, in incorporating Shylock, one of the greatest figures in the whole range of Shakespeare's plays.

We have seen that Shakespeare has a habit of tilting the plane of his comedies so that these light-hearted fantasies of love's fulfilment are momentarily seen in the light of a graver valuation. In *The Merchant* the plane is being tilted one way and the other almost scene by scene, exchanging valuations scene by scene, so that at the end when Portia judges Shylock, Shylock judges Portia. The play begins in the familiar way of identifying strands. First Antonio and Bassanio, then Portia at Belmont, then Shylock. Bassanio's courtship of Portia is aureate indeed.

> Her sunny locks
> Hang on her temples like a golden fleece,
> Which makes her seat of Belmont Colchis' strand,
> And many Jasons come in quest of her.
>
> (I. i. 169–72)

But this figurative gold involves matters of real gold, 3,000 ducats. Bassanio says frankly that winning the rich Portia will be the means of getting clear of his heavy debts. To set himself up as a suitor is going to cost money which he hasn't got, and hence his application to Antonio for funds, and hence Antonio's application to Shylock. Down to the waist *The Merchant of Venice* is romance; beneath is all realism, or, to change the image, the flower of romance is rooted in a heavy clay of sordid pecuniary needs and their consequence.

In the crucial scene in which Bassanio, arrayed as splendidly as Shylock's ducats will allow, has to choose the right casket of three, gold, silver, and lead, he makes a famous speech in which he inveighs against the world's concern with ornament and outward show, rejects the 'gaudy gold' casket and the casket made of silver—'thou pale and common drudge / 'Tween man and man'—and chooses lead. The inscription on the lead casket is,

'Who chooseth me must give and hazard all he hath.' What Bassanio is hazarding is Antonio's life-blood. Considered so coldly, Bassanio's conduct and his attitudinizing over 'ornament' are contemptible. He is indeed, as famously described by Quiller-Couch, a 'fortune-hunter', and a hypocrite to boot. But he is none of these things when the plane of comedy is tilted to catch the light of romance. If anyone is guilty of inconsistency or deception, it is Shakespeare, with his *trompe-l'œil* skill by which he engages our concentration of the values of this beautiful casket scene as it is acted out before us. Questions come afterwards, when Rialto and Belmont come together in the courtroom.

Shylock is one of Shakespeare's two great studies in hate, the other being Iago. But whereas Iago, possessed by paranoia, hardly knows why he hates, feeling himself (Satan-like) impaired by others whose mere existence seems to taunt him with ugliness, Shylock knows whom he hates and why he hates. His entry in the third scene of *The Merchant of Venice* is a great moment in the history of world drama. Marlowe had already given the stage in *The Jew of Malta* the extremely imaginative figure of a powerful wealthy Jew, whose crimes were accompanied with a scathing contempt for the ethics of the 'superior' Christian race. Barabas helped Shylock into existence, but Shylock is far and away the more complex, interesting, and provocative figure. He maintains his impressiveness—you cannot exactly call it dignity—even while he spits out his hatred. Shakespeare avoids the Scylla and Charybdis of making Shylock on the one hand a mere stage-Jew villain or on the other the pathetic victim of centuries of persecution. Nor is he concerned to elicit specific quantities of approval and disapproval. Shylock is not greatly in need of audience sympathy. There is a magnificence in Shakespeare's Jew that, even in the perpetration of evil, dwarfs his Christian opponents and dwarfs the comedy he is in. There is no better illustration of the magnitude of the conception than the great prose speech of Act III, Scene i, 'Hath not a Jew eyes?' Here the appeal to recognize the Jew as a human being, the pride in his 'sacred nation', the deep sense of unending persecution, the recognition of Christian hypocrisy, blend into a great climax of overpowering hatred and vindictiveness. The assurance and the cool contempt of the Shylock of the opening scenes have disappeared, as hate begins to overmaster him. This whole scene is one

of Shakespeare's masterpieces. As Shylock's emotions veer wildly
in rejoicing at Antonio's losses and curses at his daughter's flight,
Shakespeare never lets him become ridiculous. The comic effect
of the division of his rage between the loss of his daughter and his
ducats is suddenly modified by his words about the ring that
Jessica has taken and exchanged for a monkey: 'It was my
turquoise, I had it of Leah when I was a bachelor. I would not
have given it for a wilderness of monkeys' (III. i. 121–3). The scene
is both comic and terrible. 'No ill luck stirring but what lights o'
my shoulders, no sighs but o' my breathing, no tears but o' my
shedding.'

Shylock is cunning, cruel, implacable. If *he* has urged the
claims of humanity, so must we, against him, as his sharpened
knife threatens the bared breast of Antonio in the courtroom.
Portia's plea for mercy is absolutely rejected. But he is outwitted
and defeated; and he is destroyed. His life is spared, but most of
his wealth is taken away from him, and what remains is allowed
to him only on condition of his becoming a Christian. All his
wealth is to go after his death to his Christianized daughter and
her husband. Even in full recognition of the murderousness of
Shylock's intentions, it is very difficult to share the delight of the
characters in the crushing of Shylock. We feel that Baudelaire was
right; there is something satanic in the laughter at his utter
discomfiture. But in the uncertainty about our response to the
ending of the play, how far are we importing into the play our
post-holocaust views of Jew and Gentile? Of course we are
importing our own responses; we could not do otherwise. But
when we try to ballast our response with what we surmise to be an
Elizabethan response, we are amazed to recognize how Shakespeare, with his uncanny proleptic historical imagination, has been
expecting us. The values of Shakespeare's day were indeed not
ours. The Jewish problem of later centuries simply did not exist in
his England. (The Jews had been banished in Edward I's time.)
Peoples of different creeds and race were not considered equal.
And yet! Shakespeare was not of his own day either. He breathed
such life into a stereotype villain-Jew that it is not just in our
modern eyes that he is a challenge to the assurance of Portia and
Bassanio.

It is interesting that Shakespeare should illustrate his counter-
pointing method by leaving us with another figure in this play

whose isolation makes us knit our brows a little at the conclusion, and that is Antonio. The deep affection that Antonio has for Bassanio—which is the cause of his willingness to borrow money for his friend and accept Shylock's bond for it—is movingly expressed in the court scene.

> Commend me to your honourable wife,
> Tell her the process of Antonio's end;
> Say how I loved you, speak me fair in death.
> And when the tale is told, bid her be judge
> Whether Bassanio had not once a love.
>
> (IV. i. 273–7)

His resignation to his fate ('I am a tainted wether of the flock, / Meetest for death') has something to do with the loss of Bassanio as well as the loss of his argosies. Whatever we may have thought of Bassanio's shallowness at various points in the play, he is at this tense moment in the action very much in earnest when he responds to Antonio's testament of friendship.

> Antonio, I am married to a wife
> Which is as dear to me as life itself,
> But life itself, my wife, and all the world,
> Are not with me esteemed above thy life.
> I would lose all, ay, sacrifice them all
> Here to this devil, to deliver you.
>
> (282–7)

This dangerous moment of truth is beautifully put aside by the laugh that greets the intervention of Portia, disguised as the young lawyer Balthazar: 'Your wife would give you little thanks for *that*!'

It is not Shakespeare's way to sabotage his comedies. His early comedies are fantasies about the gaining of happiness in the achievement of sexual love. But in introducing into the plays such features as this deep friendship of Antonio or Shylock's sense of racial injustice, and other sometimes disconcerting problems which we have discussed in this chapter, he has put a perspective into these fantasies which deepens their thoughtfulness and in the end enriches our delight.

5

History

Writing in 1592, the same year in which the baleful Robert Greene attacked Shakespeare as an 'upstart crow', Thomas Nashe paid a remarkable tribute to Shakespeare's Henry VI plays:

How would it have joyed brave Talbot, the terror of the French, to think that after he had lien two hundred years in his tomb he should triumph again on the stage, and have his bones new-embalmed with the tears of ten thousand spectators at least, at several times, who, in the tragedian that represents his person, imagine they behold him fresh bleeding!

(Pierce Pennilesse)

The death of Talbot is a crucial moment in the first part of *Henry VI.* He and his son, the soul of English honesty and valour, are overcome by the French only because they are let down and betrayed by the petty rivalries and squabbles of noblemen competing for power in an England rapidly sinking into anarchy. The death illustrates two of the many components of Shakespeare's great cycle of historical plays. The plays originate in England's pride in itself as a nation, curious about its past and hopeful about its future. Taken as a whole, they are the national epic of an emerging and ambitious world-power. Their patriotism, being written for a people who had just overcome the might of Spain in the English Channel, is often sturdy enough to be embarrassing, but that part of them which is devoted to trumpeting the superiority of the Englishman is really quite small. Pride in one's nation can show itself in strong self-criticism and admonishment. The death of Talbot is both a celebration of English courage and a warning against those political tendencies which time and again had brought England into chaos and misery. As a youthful aspiring dramatist Shakespeare set about his ambitious task of a series of plays on the Wars of the Roses, accepting the views of Englishmen of his time that the strong rule of the Tudors had rescued England from an abyss of self-lacerating civil war and tyranny. The sense of development towards the promise of his own day is inescapable. National pride, the mainspring of the histories, shows itself therefore in warnings as well as fanfares, and in a noticeably Tudor view of the shape of history.

To say so much is to take us only to the threshold of the histories. Whatever the young Shakespeare's plans and intentions, grappling with the persons and events he found in the chronicles of Holinshed and Hall and creating plays out of them was a process which generated something very much deeper and richer than a narrowly national or nationalistic programme. Each play became an exploration and a discovery of the dramatic potential of history, of the meaning of politics, of the nature of kingship, and of the shape of life itself. Moreover, as the series grew, new units came into being, asking us to attend to the significance of the plays in ones and twos and threes as well as in 'tetralogies', until we consider in the end the significance of the whole cycle of plays, all nine of them, going from 1389 to 1485, from Richard II to Henry VII, with the earlier detached reign of King John.*

It hardly needs saying that Shakespeare took enormous liberties with historical fact in the histories—even such fact as the chronicles presented him with. The reasons for distortion are many. History, then as now, was required to subserve many ulterior purposes, political and moral, and the opportunities and restrictions of drama played havoc with historical fidelity. Queen Margaret could not have spoken all those long speeches in *Richard III*, because she was dead. The Bastard could not have played his brilliant and decisive role in *King John*, because he was never alive. Richard II's Queen Isobel, his second wife in a dynastic marriage, was a mere child. Edward IV's reign, occupying a few scenes in two plays, actually lasted twenty-two years. Richard III's wooing of Anne is fictitious. Shakespeare took from Daniel the Procrustean arrangement whereby Prince Hal and Hotspur are the same age; actually Hotspur was old enough to be Prince Hal's father. Falstaff is Shakespeare's invention. The peaceful last years of Henry IV's reign are entirely ignored. The bay-trees that withered in *Richard II* withered in England, but Shakespeare thought it more poetic for them to wither in Wales.

*This is to exclude *Henry VIII*, discussed in Chapter 1, p. 24.

Henry VI

The first part of *Henry VI* opens with a brilliant symbolic pageant of England's nobility falling into dissension even around the coffin of the dead hero-king Henry V. This quality is not maintained. There are many fine things in the first two plays, but in general the progress is that of a lumbering wagon looking for a good road. The first play deals with the loss of France. The most exciting character is not Talbot but Pucelle, Joan of Arc, a Marlovian character of lowly birth utterly confident of her high destiny. She is quite a challenge to the play's patriotic values, with her pungent contempt for pomposity and the fanaticism of her belief in the French cause. But Shakespeare betrays her in an infamous last scene of lying and wriggling. Two triumphs in the play are the scenes which look to the past and to the future. Act II, Scene iv is the Temple Garden scene, in which the division which is to grow into the great dynastic clash of Yorkists and Lancastrians has its symbolic start in the plucking of the white rose and the red. This is immediately followed by a descent into the past. The future Duke of York visits his kinsman, the aged Mortimer, who is dying as a prisoner in the Tower, and who initiates the young man into the dark happenings of the deposition of Richard II and the struggle against Bolingbroke; he passes on to him the good old cause as his inheritance. The scene is Greek in its sense of the ineluctable weight of the past. The brooding pitiable figure of Mortimer must have been in Shakespeare's mind years later when he turned to dramatize the events here recounted, and created the ineffective young rebel with the Welsh wife who spoke no English.

During the first part of *Henry VI* we see poison spreading steadily through a country which lacks a strong ruler until, in the second play, self-devouring violence erupts, first in the grim scenes of Jack Cade's rebellion and then in York's armed bid for power culminating in the battle of St Alban's. Henry VI develops into a saintly figure, uncertain of his rights, longing only for peace, brushed aside by people of greater confidence and resolution, including his wife as well as York. These last two, Queen Margaret and Richard Duke of York, face each other for the last time in the third part of the trilogy, in the finest of the rituals in a play which is largely organized in terms of stylized scenes of ritual violence. Margaret circles her captive enemy, accuses him, and taunts him, shows him a napkin drenched in his son's blood, and places a paper crown on his head. He replies with a magnificent speech, beginning 'She-wolf of France!', which clearly left a deep impression on the audience's memory.

> O tiger's heart, wrapped in a woman's hide.
> How couldst thou drain the life-blood of the child,
> To bid the father wipe his eyes withal,
> And yet be seen to wear a woman's face?
> Women are soft, mild, pitiful and flexible;
> Thou stern, obdurate, flinty, rough, remorseless.
> Bidst thou me rage? Why now thou hast thy wish.
> Bidst thou me weep? Why now thou hast thy will.
>
> (*3 Henry VI*, I. iv. 137–44)

Margaret and Clifford stab him in turn. They order his head to be cut off and placed on the walls of York.

There are three kings in the third part of *Henry VI*. The pathetic figure of Henry himself moves through the play clutching his prayer book, dispossessed and despised. He laments the unenviable lot of a king after the battle of Towton (II. v) and watches while a son drags in the body of the father he has killed, and a father drags in the body of the son he has killed. Then there is Edward IV of York, his successor, a jolly, amorous fellow seen chatting up Lady Grey. But he is only a shadow king. The real monarch to arise from the marsh of anarchy is Richard of Gloucester, grotesque and deformed, who is awaiting his opportunity. In Act III, Scene ii, he has a speech of seventy-one lines, pulsating with the force of an ambition that cannot yet see its way forward.

> I'll make my heaven to dream upon the crown,
> And whiles I live, t' account this world but hell,
> Until my mis-shaped trunk that bears this head
> Be round impalèd with a glorious crown.
>
> (III. ii. 168–71)

He takes an enthusiastic share in the ritual killing of Henry's son in the sight of his mother, and then goes into the Tower and murders the patient, saintly Henry, who is expecting him. He is then ready to begin his own play, *Richard III*, one of

Shakespeare's two studies in the hero-villain. Whereas Macbeth moves to possess the future in a trance of horror, to Richard of Gloucester it is all a great joke.

Richard III

History and drama now concentrate on a single personality (with much help from Sir Thomas More's life of Richard). The brilliant Marlowe-style prologue, light-hearted and dreadful, is the keynote. History is malleable material lying there for Richard to shape. Misshapen himself, he can shape the future. This is to be done by replacing fact with fiction. Misrepresentation is a way of life.

> Plots have I laid, inductions dangerous,
> By drunken prophecies, libels and dreams,
> To set my brother Clarence and the king
> In deadly hate, the one against the other.
>
> (I. i. 32–5)

The winning of Anne, whom he had orphaned and widowed, is his first exhibition of his misrepresentation of himself. He despises her for being taken in by his protestations while being proud of his prowess.

> Was ever woman in this humour wooed?
> Was ever woman in this humour won?
>
> (I. ii. 227–8)

What is so extraordinary at the height of Richard's malpractices in Act III, with the liquidation of Hastings before a trembling council, is the combination of horror with the ridiculous. In the audience, with our guilty enjoyment of the perpetration of this infamy, we feel we are taking part in some monstrous satanic comedy. Richard and Buckingham are quick-change artists of unending resourcefulness, playing for a reward no smaller than the Crown of England. Their double-act is full of outrageous lies, sanctimonious sorrow, saintly patriotism, and so on. Oddly enough, brilliant though the performance is, the common people are completely unconvinced, even when Catesby lends a hand at the ludicrous presentation of Richard on the balcony 'between two bishops'. It is curious that, when Buckingham raises the enthusiastic cry, 'Long live King Richard, England's worthy king!', in the Quarto text of 1597 only the compliant Mayor says 'Amen'. This is in keeping with the sullen silence of the intimidated populace as reported earlier in the scene (III. vii) and as described by More. But the Folio and modern editions give the Amen to 'All'; this is surely wrong.

Richard's enjoyment of his own villainy and his zest for improvisation cease abruptly when he actually gets the crown. The game is over and very soon the game is up. The brilliance of Shakespeare's conception of Richard's rise is hardly matched by the routine pattern of his fall. This is in the manner of the age's understanding of tragedy, namely, the fall of great tyrants as the wheel of fortune spun. We have to remind ourselves that he's no longer hamming some role when he says:

> Murder her brothers and then marry her?
> Uncertain way of gain! But I am in
> So far in blood that sin will pluck on sin.
> Tear-falling pity dwells not in this eye.
>
> (IV. ii. 63–6)

The night before Bosworth, the ghosts of his many victims assemble and pass before his tent and that of his conqueror Henry Richmond, cursing him and blessing Richmond. He wakens in terror, afflicted by 'coward conscience'. He who had once proudly boasted 'I am myself alone', now cries:

> I shall despair. There is no creature loves me,
> And if I die no soul shall pity me.
>
> (v. iii. 200–1)

The ending of *Richard III* is an ending of the tetralogy. 'The day is ours; the bloody dog is dead!' says the future Henry VII, and his final speech puts a formal end to the Wars of the Roses.

> And then, as we have tane the sacrament,
> We will unite the White Rose and the Red.
>
> England hath long been mad and scarred herself,
> The brother blindly shed the brother's blood,
> The father rashly slaughtered his own son,
> The son compelled been butcher to the sire.

O now let Richmond and Elizabeth,
The true succeeders of each royal house,
By God's fair ordinance conjoin together.
And let their heirs, God if thy will be so,
Enrich the time to come with smooth-faced peace,
With smiling plenty and fair prosperous days.

(v. v. 18–19, 23–6, 29–34)

We have had a prolonged exhibition stretching over four plays of cruelty, grasping ambition, and belligerence, of a vacuum of power filled by a monstrous tyranny, and now it is all ended by a saviour who bears remarkably little resemblance to that Machiavellian Welshman Henry VII. Tudor historiography enabled Shakespeare to compose a sort of gigantic historical tragicomedy, in which the happy ending belongs more to the-world-as-we-would-wish-it-to-be than to the world as it is.

King John

Although the date of *King John* is uncertain, it seems likely that it was when he had finished *Richard III* that Shakespeare wrote this most interesting and sometimes underestimated work, almost a political morality play, reflecting what the writing of the Henry VI–Richard III sequence had taught him and preparing the themes that he was to explore in the Richard II–Henry V sequence.

It is perhaps difficult in these days to enter into a sympathetic comprehension of Shakespeare's concept of kingship in the histories. Having broken away from Rome, the Tudor monarchy clothed itself with mystical ideas about kingship. Its authority, lacking the divine sanction of the Catholic church, was given its own sacerdotal protection. The theory of the divine right of kings blossomed and the Crown became the centre of the nation's emotional and spiritual life, as well as of its political life. While Elizabeth never claimed the role of high priestess of England, this very practical and hard-headed monarch became a cult-figure; not merely a popular monarch, but an object of devotion. A business-like government laid claim to its own sacredness. Elizabeth's successors, James and Charles, responded with more enthusiasm than caution to the concept of the divinity of their states, with disastrous consequences.

Shakespeare was another who fell under the spell of the carefully nurtured mystique about kingship. It is for this reason that we find deeply woven into the barbaric dynastic rivalries of the histories ideas about the sacredness of kingship which seem more appropriate to *The Golden Bough* than to late feudal England. The lesson of the first tetralogy might seem to be that England needs a strong king. It would be better to put it that England needs its true king. (Henry VI is haunted by doubts about his right to the throne.) The more deeply Shakespeare gets into the continuous contention for the Crown that is the basic story of his histories, the more troubling the implications of the Elizabethan theory of the divinity of kingship become. No merely mortal man can fill *this* job-description. Many may claim to be the looked-for divine protector of a people, but the real king is a messiah who never comes. In Shakespeare's histories we are always waiting for Godot. Was he there in that coffin at the beginning of the first part of *Henry VI*? Is he there in Richmond at the end of *Richard III*?

The real King John had a perfectly good title to the throne of England, but Shakespeare took it away. He made him a *de facto* monarch who had usurped the rights of his elder brother's young son, Arthur. 'Our strong possession and our right, for us!' says John defiantly. 'Your strong possession much more than your right,' whispers his mother to him (I. i. 39–40). The claims of young Arthur are being advanced by the arch-enemy of England, France. Here is a nice pickle of loyalties, which Shakespeare makes worse by mischievously introducing from his source (*The Troublesome Reign of King John*) a totally anachronistic Reformation conflict between Rome and England over sovereignty. Shakespeare then adds his brilliant invention, the Bastard Faulconbridge, the reckless, witty, intelligent, romantic scapegrace who is in fact the illegitimate son of Richard Coeur-de-lion and would be king of England if his father and mother had been married. John can for a time fill the bill by standing up to the Pope and licking the French, but Shakespeare shows his hollowness by an almost melodramatic collapse, beginning with his guilty instructions for putting Arthur to death. The scene of the royal child brought in to be blinded is of great importance, in that cruelty is compounded by the sense of sacrilege in the defilement offered to this helpless embodiment of England's kingship. As

John crumbles, the sight of the child's corpse creates a new Bastard, who recognizes 'all England' in 'this morsel of dead royalty'.

> And England now is left
> To tug and scamble and to part by th' teeth
> The unowed interest of proud-swelling state.
> Now for the bare-picked bone of majesty
> Doth dogged war bristle his angry crest
> And snarleth in the gentle eyes of peace.
>   (IV. iii. 145–50)

Majesty—the true kingship of England—a bone fought over by snarling dogs! The nobles have deserted John and are fighting with France's invading army. The Bastard assumes the accoutrements of kingship without any of the ambition for personal power that, given his birth, he would have had some right to seek. He stuffs the emptiness of John with his own resourcefulness, courage, and rhetoric, and acts in his name to reassert the overarching claim of the integrity of England.

> Now hear our English king,
> For thus his royalty doth speak in me ...
>   (v. ii. 128–9)

The young Prince Henry appears at the end as a convenient rallying point to give some feeling of hope for the future as the Bastard enunciates the play's famous closing lines:

> This England never did, nor never shall,
> Lie at the proud foot of a conqueror,
> But when it first did help to wound itself.
> Now these her princes are come home again,
> Come the three corners of the world in arms
> And we shall shock them. Nought shall make us rue
> If England to itself do rest but true.

'Nought shall make us rue.' This is hope, not history. 'If England to itself do rest but true ...' This is the condition which is never fulfilled in the long search of the histories.

> Hope springs eternal in the human breast,
> Man never *is* but always *to be* blest.

Richard II

The histories show England continuously unable to find the self
to which it must be true because unable to find the king who is the
true king. *King John*, with potential royalty looming up and
disappearing again in the separate figures of John, Arthur, and
the Bastard, is a fine preparation for Shakespeare's great tragic
story of the 'original' loss of true kingship in *Richard II*. Richard
II was the last of the Plantagenet kings to rule with undisputed
title to the throne. His deposition by Bolingbroke was generally
seen as the *fons et origo* of nearly a hundred years of internecine
strife, relieved only by the foreign conquests of Henry V. Shakespeare makes the dethronement almost another fall of man,
showing his audience a tragic inevitability that permanently lost
for the English people the possibility of a happiness which in fact
they'd never enjoyed.

Although *Richard II* is very much of a companion piece to
Marlowe's *Edward II*, the actor taking the part of Shakespeare's
king should avoid at all costs representing him as the epicene
hedonist of Marlowe's play. *Richard II* embodies Shakespeare's
vision of feudal England at its best and worst, and the worst
comes first. Richard is the undoubted king, and he is maltreating
his own people. He is autocratic, impulsive, imperious, irresponsible. There is the dark stain of his implication, never properly
explained, in the murder of his uncle Woodstock. But he is above
all majestic in the solemnity of the early 'medievalizing' scenes of
ceremonious accusation and counter-accusation, tournament and
banishment; the actor who goes for a 'weak' king is going to have
heavy work on his hands for the rest of the play. John of Gaunt
knows that the correction of a divine king is not in human hands.
Speaking of Woodstock's death, he says,

> God's is the quarrel, for God's substitute,
> His deputy anointed in his sight,
> Hath caused his death, the which if wrongfully,
> Let heaven revenge, for I may never lift
> An angry arm against his minister.

(I. ii. 37–41)

But it is in a way Gaunt who prepares the way for his son's
violation of that great credo. The vehement attack on Richard
which Gaunt makes immediately before his death (in the

'sceptred isle' speech) puts Richard's rule over 'this land of such dear souls, this dear, dear land', as having gone past the stage of reclamation, past the stage of men's endurance. 'This royal throne of kings . . . hath made a shameful conquest of itself.' He dies before he has to face the decision facing his brother York, torn between the wrongs done both to his kinsman Bolingbroke and to the people of England, and his manifest obligation to be loyal to the anointed king. But it doesn't really matter what he decides, as Bolingbroke's march through England, like Octavius' advance on Mark Antony, is the march of history.

From Act III, Scene ii, when he returns from Ireland to meet Bolingbroke's army, until the end of the play, the portrayal of Richard in decline, defeat, and death is a sustained masterpiece. There is almost no action; Richard's cause is lost from the start. It is one long 'passion', Richard Agonistes, as adversity pushes the king further and further into recognition of who he really is and what it is he has done. Those who talk of Richard as an actor, playing with the situation, have simply turned the play upside-down. It is the divestment of role-playing that Richard undergoes. True, until solitary confinement forces it upon him, he has no use for soliloquy; he argues out his assessment of his situation in public, conscious of his audience and with a bitter enjoyment of the only power he has left—that of embarrassing his listeners. It is an act, but he is not acting. He very soon detects the hollowness of his own proud assertion of his inviolability as anointed king. The mere name of king has no potency on a battlefield.

> All souls that will be safe, fly from my side,
> For time hath set a blot upon my pride.
>
> > (III. ii. 80–1)

It is Time—which is his last scene he recognizes he has abused and wasted—that has put an end to the exalted and invulnerable position he believed he had. Understandably, with his recognition of just how vulnerable he really is, he sees himself as Lear was later to do, deceived by all those voices who proclaimed he was a being above all others, immune from adversity.

> Cover your heads, and mock not flesh and blood
> With solemn reverence; throw away respect,
> Tradition, form, and ceremonious duty,

For you have but mistook me all this while.
I live with bread like you, feel want,
Taste grief, need friends. Subjected thus,
How can you say to me, I am a king?

(III. ii. 171–7)

But this awareness of his humanity is only a stage, though an essential stage, in his progress to his too-late understanding of what he is as king. This understanding emerges in the most important speech in the play, his defiant challenge to Bolingbroke from the walls of Flint Castle (III. iii. 68–100). Here his sense of kingship is of a divine stewardship.

Show us the hand of God
That hath dismissed us from our stewardship,
For well we know no hand of blood and bone
Can grip the sacred handle of our sceptre
Unless he do profane, steal, or usurp.

Richard knows himself as a sacramental being. He is a mortal being invested with sacredness; he knows the mortal side is destructible, but that to destroy it is profanity. Even by consenting to his own compelled abdication, Richard believes he is conniving at an act of sacrilege.

I find myself a traitor with the rest,
For I have given here my soul's consent
T' undeck the pompous body of a king.

(IV. i. 248–50)

He invents a rite of dethronement in which he is both priest and victim while Bolingbroke stands by impatiently. In renouncing kingship, Richard sees himself as demolishing his own being and creating a nothingness. Kingship is not a presidency but a mystical office whose holiness fuses with the being of the person who holds it; to cast it off is self-destruction, as, again, Lear is to find. Richard is the true king, but he corrupted the royalty invested in him. Everyone knows what he might have done to be a better ruler; but he has something that Bolingbroke cannot take from him as he seizes power.

Bolingbroke's reward is a care-worn reign spent subduing the violence he has introduced into the land. He and his son are kings of a new kind, who have read *Il Principe* and know how to tailor their public image and when to engage in foreign wars. The 'intertissued robe' of kingship is something you take on or put off at will. It and the other accoutrements of majesty form the 'thrice-gorgeous ceremony' whose purpose, Henry V says, is 'creating awe and fear in other men'. The Tudor monarchs have indeed taken over from their obsolete and inefficient feudal predecessors.

Shakespeare's portrayal of history as both loss and gain is clearly shown in the progress from the autocracy of Richard II to that of Henry V. In saying this, we recognize the two levels, or two of the levels, on which the histories take place. Shakespeare was surely nostalgic for some qualities in a feudal past which he saw being replaced by materialist, selfish, opportunistic values; but he also recognized not only the inevitability of change but the advances made under the Tudors towards internal peace and international standing. Here is an historical understanding of both loss and gain. But there is also a poetic valuation, by which the histories speak in parable of an intractable present troubled by dreams of what man has been and may again be. In this valuation Richard is Adam, who has wrecked the people's heritage on the rock of his irresponsibility and denied to them their link with the divine. But *there will come a time* when deliverance is at hand and the blessed peace so lost will be restored. Mankind is between paradise lost and paradise regained, perpetually.

Henry IV and *Henry V*

The change in artistic tone between the sacred tragedy of *Richard II* and the strikingly original format—modified from the comedies—of the first part of *Henry IV* is very noticeable. But the overall design of the sequence of three plays on the reigns of Henry IV and Henry V needs looking at first. That Shakespeare's plan was flexible is clear from the epilogue to *2 Henry IV*.

If you be not too much cloyed with fat meat, our humble author will continue the story, with Sir John in it, and make you merry with fair Katharine of France; where, for anything I know, Falstaff shall die of a sweat, unless already a be killed with your hard opinions.

That the popularity of Falstaff engendered new plays is clear from the existence of *The Merry Wives of Windsor*—even if it wasn't Good Queen Bess who commissioned it. In this epilogue we can see that *Henry V* has been planned but is not written. Sir John is most notably not 'in' the play we have, except for the moving account of his death. The epilogue shows us Shakespeare keeping his options open. He may already have made major modifications to an earlier plan. It has been argued (by Malone) that the second part of *Henry IV* was written only because the first part was such a resounding success. It has also been argued (by Capell) that both parts were written in fulfilment of an original plan. More recently Harold Jenkins (following Dr Johnson) has argued that the two parts are a single artistic unit which could not be accommodated in a single play. The trouble with all these theories is that they do not take into account what Shakespeare may originally have intended to do with *Henry V*.

The reason for the debate about the shape of *Henry IV* is the repetitiveness of the second play. Part One shows Hal emerging from his father's disfavour to declare himself in his victory over Hotspur and the glory of the battle of Shrewsbury. But Part Two shows the paternal disfavour continuing, with Hal under the necessity of proving himself yet again. The play ends with the death of Henry IV, the crowning of Hal, and the rejection of Falstaff. Besides being repetitious, *2 Henry IV* is a very leisurely play. The opening, with Rumour and the long Northumberland scene, is not only leisurely but boring. There is in fact very little action in the play. There is a great deal of character-creation: Pistol, Mrs Quickly, Doll Tearsheet, Shallow, Silence; and a great many reflective arias on themes many times presented: the strain of kingship, the uncertainty of Henry's title, fears about Hal's behaviour, the iniquity of rebellion, and so on. The writing in the comic scenes is brilliant; that of the verse scenes calm, masterful, unexcited. Shakespeare is exceedingly unhurried. The thought that he was stretching out his material to fill a bigger space than was originally intended is irresistible. What might the original plan have been? The coronation of Hal and the rejection of Falstaff must always have been an integral part of the overall plan; the rejection is prepared for in the first soliloquy of *1 Henry IV*. It seems most likely that Shakespeare originally thought of *two* plays, one on Henry IV showing the emergence of Hal in triumph at Shrewsbury, and one on Henry V starting with the coronation and the rejection of Falstaff and ending as now with the conquest of France. Then the tremendous success of Falstaff in the first play led Shakespeare to extend his scheme and make three plays for the sequence instead of two. Material for the new intermediary play had to come from the original second play, which now became the third. At the end of the new intermediary play, *2 Henry IV*, he was still prepared to bring Falstaff on for a third time, but wisely enough decided against it. If *Henry V* had some of its original material taken from it to form *2 Henry IV*, it would explain the great tediousness of the Archbishop of Canterbury's exposition of the Salic Law and the muddle of the lame ending of the Prologue to Act II, 'Now all the youth of England are on fire', when the audience are told to expect the king at Southampton and then are told to wait:

> But till the King come forth, and not till then
> Unto Southampton do we shift our scene.

Then, ludicrously, enter Nym and Bardolph!

If this suggestion is correct—that, after the great success of Falstaff, an original scheme for one play on Henry IV's reign and one on Henry V's reign was expanded by the insertion of an extra play—we can see how one of the major problems of the Henry IV plays, the division of sympathy in the rejection of Falstaff, may have become accentuated. Being displaced from being a mere prelude to Henry's victories in France to become the climax of a whole play, the rejection has taken on a centrality and a finality that was never originally intended. We can only discuss what we have and not what we might have had, but it looks highly possible that, in winning a new play from his creator, Falstaff won a new life indeed.

In *1 Henry IV*, Prince Hal faces three people who radiate tremendous influence, Hotspur, Falstaff, and his father. Hotspur and Hal do not meet until the last battle, and it is a pity we do not see the two together. Hotspur is all spontaneity and incautious impulse; it is hard not to be attracted by his impetuous and passionate volubility. His romantic devotion to honour is not matched by judgement or forethought. His commitment to the rebel cause has such a frankness about it that we sometimes forget that he is proposing to carve Britain up and rule over one of the pieces. He is at least utterly open; he can no more conceal his contempt for Bolingbroke's crafty self-interest or Glendower's self-satisfied pomposity than Coriolanus can conceal his feelings about the plebeians.

Falstaff is unrestrained, too, but his ardour is not for Hotspur's ascetic goals. He is for sack and self-indulgence, for life unbuckled, unbuttoned, unbraced. Honesty is not *his* strong point, but no one takes offence at his preposterous fabrications. Obese and slovenly alcoholics in real life rarely have the wit and charm of Falstaff. Shakespeare has made his fat reprobate the tempter not only of Hal but of all who are troubled by the super-ego, the protestant work ethic and the competition for success. At the same time, a career like Falstaff's is not devoid of effort; he has to live by his wits. Nor is his self-indulgence without its rationale. His catechism on honour, which Shakespeare includes in its reasoned prose to counterbalance the ardent imagery of Hotspur's honour speech (I. iii. 201–8), makes a compelling case. Honour will not repair a smashed limb and will neither live with the living nor be felt by the dead. 'Therefore I'll none of it— honour is a mere scutcheon' (v. i. 129–41).

As for King Henry, this cheerless man believes that the end justifies the means, and that the end is the acquisition and maintenance of power.

Each 'way of life' in the *Henry IV* plays challenges the other. Falstaff's instinct for self-preservation challenges the romanticism of Hotspur's honour; his laughter challenges the humourlessness of the king. Hotspur's energy challenges Falstaff's laziness; his impulsive emotionalism challenges the king's cautious self-control. King Henry's sense of responsibility challenges the social and political heedlessness of both Falstaff and Hotspur.

Hal does not have to choose his way from among those opposed figures; he has already chosen, as his first soliloquy makes clear ('I know you all . . .'). What we are watching, as has many times been said, is the education of the ablest king in Shakespeare's repertoire. It is basically by suppression that his mastery is achieved, stopping off those qualities in a man that lead to rebellion, to imagination, and even to love. The austere self-discipline of the ruler in Shakespeare is not attractive but Shakespeare insists on its necessity (see Chapter 2, pp. 45–8). That he who would govern others must first govern himself was an aphorism going back to antiquity. Self-government in *Henry IV* is a kind of self-mutilation. No one doubts that Falstaff has got to be rejected, and Hal's withdrawal from him begins in his first soliloquy (I. ii. 195–217). But there has been a long tolerance of Falstaff's 'unyoked humours', and the pharisaical severity of the rejection is a shock to every playgoer.

Just before the rejection, Hal has received the frankest of testaments from a dying father on whom the guilt of deposing Richard II still lies heavy.

> Yet though thou stand'st more sure than I could do,
> Thou art not firm enough, since griefs are green,
> And all my* friends, which thou must make thy friends,
> Have but their stings and teeth newly tane out,
> By whose fell working I was first advanced,
> And by whose power I well might lodge a fear
> To be again displaced; which to avoid,
> I cut them off, and had a purpose now
> To lead out many to the Holy Land,
> Lest rest and lying still might make them look
> Too near unto my state. Therefore my Harry,
> Be it thy course to busy giddy minds
> With foreign quarrels, that action hence borne out
> May waste the memory of the former days.
>
> (*2 Henry IV*, IV. v. 202–15)

Friendship, foreign policy and religious commitment are all to be fashioned as the interests of retaining power dictate. When in *Henry V* the battle of Agincourt is at its most critical point, with the wasted band of the English struggling against the might of the French, who have just rallied their forces for a new attack, Henry orders his soldiers to kill their prisoners, a ruthlessness justified by the extremity of the peril his troops are in. He reinforces his instruction on learning that the French, against the rules of war, have attacked the English camp and killed the boys and 'the luggage'. Somehow or other Fluellen and Gower manage at this juncture to have a discussion about Henry's likeness to Alexander the Great. Fluellen says that Alexander,

in his rages, and his furies, and his wraths, and his cholers, and his moods, and his displeasures, and his indignations, and also being a little intoxicates in his prains, did in his ales and his angers, look you, kill his best friend Cleitus.

*The original texts have 'thy'.

GOWER. Our king is not like him in that; he never killed any of his friends.
FLUELLEN . . . As Alexander killed his friend Cleitus, being in his ales and his cups; so also Harry Monmouth, being in his right wits, and his good judgements, turned away the fat knight with the great belly doublet; he was full of jests, and gipes, and knaveries, and mocks; I have forgot his name.
GOWER. Sir John Falstaff.

(IV. vii. 34–51)

'The king hath killed his heart', says the Hostess of Falstaff just before his death. It is clear that Shakespare wants us to remember Falstaff even at the most desperate moment of Agincourt; he wants us to understand Henry not as a romantic chivalric figure but as a man of iron will and determination, who will be absolutely merciless, to his prisoners or his friend, when he judges it necessary. And it *is* necessary, for his own survival and the survival of those who depend on him, for him to be merciless on each occasion. It was 'in his right wits, and his good judgements' emphasizes Fluellen, that Henry turned away the fat knight, not in a fit of drunken rage.

'I know thee not, old man.' We mustn't be sentimental about Falstaff, any more than about Shylock or Caliban. Be sorry for them by all means, but recognize in all three a challenge to the maintenance of established authority. One or the other has to go under; as Shakespeare presents each case, no comfortable accommodation of the one to the other is possible. Eat or be eaten. It is the greatness of Shakespeare to make the devouring of the challenge such a very awkward meal. As every reader and playgoer notices, Henry V's long denunciation of the treachery of Cambridge, Scroop, and Gray, condemned to death for treason, is followed immediately by the very moving scene reporting the death of Falstaff. Betrayal comes in different shapes and sizes.

The question of survival is basic to the play *Henry V*. The fabric of this great imaginative pageant which the language of Shakespeare created for his new theatre is more subtly woven than is sometimes realized. We are not to think that Henry's greatness is nibbled at and eroded by challenges and oppositions that Shakespeare mischievously included in an otherwise simple hero-play. Henry's greatness is the greatness of the devourer. His greatness is defined in the presence of the oppositions and in his conquest of them. How attractive that greatness is is quite another matter.

At Henry's heels in France are Pistol, Bardolph, and Nym. Theatrically and militarily they threaten Henry; they puncture his rhetoric and endanger the campaign. Henry says:

> Cheerly to sea! The signs of war advance!
> No king of England, if not king of France!
>
> (II. ii. 192–3)

In the next scene Pistol chimes in with his own version of this *andiamo*.

> Yoke-fellows in arms,
> Let us to France, like horse-leeches, my boys,
> To suck, to suck, the very blood to suck!
>
> (II. iii. 54–6)

After the tremendous roar with which Henry concludes the speech urging his men on to the attack at Harfleur—'Once more unto the breach dear friends, once more'—there enters behind everyone else the sweating quartet led by Bardolph, the big-nosed companion of Falstaff, panting, 'On, on, on, on, on, to the breach, to the breach.' Nym calls them to a halt: 'Pray thee corporal, stay. The knocks are too hot.' These parodic anti-heroic voices have got to be stifled. Henry gives no sign of acquaintance when Fluellen tells him that Bardolph has been caught robbing churches. Bardolph and Nym are hanged and Pistol is disgraced.

The most famous challenge to Henry is very direct, being put to him as he walks about his camp in disguise on the night before Agincourt. In a moving speech Michael Williams urges the responsibility of the king.

I am afeard there are few die well that die in a battle; for how can they charitably dispose of anything, when blood is their argument? Now, if these men do not die well, it will be a black matter for the king, that led them to it; who to disobey were against all proportion of subjection.

(IV. i. 141–6)

The disguised king gives a perfectly satisfactory answer: the state of his soldiers' souls is not *his* responsibility. If they are sinners who have not repented, he cannot be held guilty for their judgement if they die in battle. 'There is no king, be his cause never so spotless . . . can try it out with all unspotted soldiers.' But it is only in this sentence that Henry recognizes the conditional clause with which Williams began his challenge: 'If the cause be not good, the king himself hath a heavy reckoning to make . . .' Williams's charge was complex: concerning the king's responsibility for creating the occasion of the sudden death of an unprepared man by leading his subjects (who are bound to obedience) in an unjust war. So much heavy weather has been made at the beginning of the play about the justice of the French war that it is curious that Henry does not at this point assert the justice of the campaign more fully and thus more fully absolve himself from Williams's charge.

Shakespeare insists on putting these troubling matters just before the climactic battle; and he also includes a reference to the usurpation of Richard II:

> Not today, O lord,
> O not today, think not upon the fault
> My father made in compassing the crown.
>
> (IV. i. 292–4)

The incredible victory of Agincourt is won. The victory is over the French and all others who in their various ways have challenged Henry. One's personal assessment of the quality of that which he has defeated is naturally a vital part of one's assessment of the greatness of Henry. For all the enthusiasm Henry generates in an English audience in times of war, there is no doubting that mastery of his kind, however necessary for the survival of societies, is achieved only at the price of a limitation of humanity. What fortunately Henry has not sacrificed is his sense of humour, as we see in the rich scene of the wooing of Katharine of France, where he is so much at his ease, so much in control of himself, enjoying his role as blunt soldier-wooer.

KATHARINE. Is it possible dat I sould love de enemy of France?
HENRY. No, it is not possible you should love the enemy of France, Kate; but in loving me you should love the friend of France, for I love France so well that I will not part with a village of it; I will have it all mine . . .

Take me by the hand and say, Harry of England, I am thine. Which word thou shalt no sooner bless mine ear withal, but I will tell thee

aloud England is thine, Ireland is thine, France is thine, and Henry
Plantagenet is thine ... Wilt thou have me?

KATHARINE. Dat is as it sall please de roi mon père.

HENRY. Nay, it will please him well, Kate. It shall please him, Kate.

(v. ii. 169–75, 236–49)

This banter, mixing courtship and conquest, is touching on very
serious matters. France is absolutely defeated, and the Duke of
Burgundy movingly describes her desolation (v. ii. 38–67). France
accepts England's terms for peace, which include Henry's marriage with the French princess. For the French king and queen
this marriage symbolizes the new relation of the two countries;
not subjugation but a wedding of partners. This relationship is a
very interesting anticipation of the ending of *Cymbeline*, in which
Britain, victorious yet again, this time over a Roman army,
forgoes an assertion of independence and enters into a kind of
marriage with imperial Rome, having renegotiated her position
more as partner than as serf by the prowess of her army. In both
Henry V and *Cymbeline* there is an idea of empire in which,
though one country is dominant, the image of the alliance is
marriage and not serfdom. The queen of defeated France speaks
thus to Henry and Katharine:

> God, the best maker of all marriages,
> Combine your hearts in one, your realms in one.
> As man and wife, being two, are one in love,
> So be there 'twixt your kingdoms such a spousal
> That never may ill office or fell jealousy,
> Which troubles oft the bed of blessed marriage,
> Thrust in between the paction of these kingdoms,
> To make divorce of their incorporate league;
> That English may as French, French Englishmen,
> Receive each other. God speak this amen.

(v. ii. 359–68)

Henry V was for Shakespeare a very modern play. Its mention
of Essex, identifying him with King Henry, shows this, as does the
completely anachronistic presence in the army of the four cap-
tains, the English Gower, the Scottish Jamy, the Welsh Fluellen,
the Irish Macmorris. Here we see Shakespeare making the past
give an account of a post-Elizabethan future, in which the equal
members of a Great Britain co-operate freely to extend by

conquest the partnerships of a new British empire. This is certainly to look at past, present, and future with rose-coloured spectacles. But the *idea* of such a breakthrough, by which the assertive and savage rivalries of contending peoples are calmed into an imperial *pax Romana*, is not contemptible. It may seem strange that a play which is at times so stridently patriotic and nationalistic as *Henry V* is should end with a vision of the surrender of nationalism and the blessings of union. It is the ending Shakespeare chooses not for *Henry V* alone but for his whole series of histories. We have to say again that this ending reflects hopes or dreams more than reality. If Shakespeare really expected Essex's campaign in Ireland to end with 'marriage', he was very, very quickly to be disillusioned. But I don't think he did. The idleness of the hopes of the king and queen of France and of King Henry himself is shown by the flat words of the Chorus speaking the epilogue, reminding us that the child of the marriage was Henry VI,

> Whose state so many had the managing
> That they lost France, and made his England bleed;
> Which oft our stage hath shown . . .

Which oft our stage hath shown! So we are back again with Talbot and his son dying in France, deserted by the irresponsible nobility, back again in an England unable to locate its true king, back in a cycle of hope destroyed by cruel fact. In so far as *Henry V* is a Tudor play, celebrating the inauguration of a British empire, with peace arising from conquest, this rather callous redirection of our thoughts to the failure of the hopes for union and peace at the end of the play must make us pause, and make us wonder as we do at the end of *Richard III* whether ultimately Shakespeare could have had a deep faith in the permanence of Tudor peace. Civil war broke out in England twenty-six years after his death.

6

Tragedy

Tragedy can be defined in many different ways, but however it is defined it needs a theatre. A novel may be tragic but it can't be a tragedy. A tragedy is a theatrical event, the performance of a text, which provides a special kind of experience for the audience. This was the foundation of Aristotle's view of tragedy, as something which, arousing pity and terror, accomplished a *catharsis* of those emotions—for the general good of the city. This was also the foundation of Nietzsche's view of tragedy as a tension of the Apollonian and the Dionysiac, balancing the drive towards order against the impulse to break through.

Tragedies are rare and most of them are Greek. It is not the writers who have been lacking—they try hard in every generation in every country, it is the setting and the occasion that are so rarely right. The ancient Greeks had the inestimable advantage of theatres so designed they could hardly fail to generate audience-emotion and a tradition that made the presentation of tragedies an occasion of deep importance in the life of the community. Everything else in tragedy seems a kind of aftermath to the great ritual doom-laden plays of Aeschylus, Sophocles, Euripides. But England had its moment, and it belongs almost entirely to Shakespeare. To look at the ancestry of Shakespearian tragedy in the drama of medieval church and city, following the story up to his predecessors Kyd and Marlowe, is fascinating and illuminating. And there are great plays in the tragic vein in the work of his later contemporaries and successors, Chapman, Webster, Tourneur, Middleton, Beaumont and Fletcher, Massinger, Ford. But before and after Shakespeare there's a fire-trench that's hardly crossable. His tragedy is of its own kind, and stands alone. All the same, the theatre and the audience which were essential conditions for his tragedy were provided for him not created by him. And he could not have taken advantage of *these* if the conflicting pressures of a unique moment in history hadn't demanded voice and utterance.

The outer edge

Although Shakespearian tragedy is anything but homogeneous, I shall argue that there is real kinship among the plays. There are, however, some special cases. *Cymbeline* was included in the 'tragedies' by Heminges and Condell in the 1623 First Folio, but though it has tragic elements it is a tragicomedy and I discuss it in the next chapter. Other plays belong to Shakespeare's tragic world but do not provide what I regard as the Shakespearian tragic experience.

Titus Andronicus

Titus Andronicus, one of Shakespeare's earliest plays, suffers from its demand for notice. Everything is strain and effort. Its incidents are of the wildest savagery, with a peculiar insistence on dismemberment, and, as all this horror is couched in a poeticism of elaborate richness, the play has a distinctive phosphorescent sheen. What is of interest for the later tragedies is the figure of Titus himself, a patriarch steeped in tradition, by his obstinancy opening the floodgates to evil and then becoming a crazed figure trying to reorganize the world. He is a remarkable foreshadowing of King Lear. Again, considered as a revenge-play, *Titus* looks forward to *Hamlet* in the hero's search for justice in a society which he considers 'a wilderness of tigers'. Thirdly, there is Aaron the Moor, outsider and wrecker, whose cool amusement at his own monstrous schemes both attracts and repels the audience. With Aaron, Shakespeare begins to make his way towards Iago.

Troilus and Cressida

Troilus and Cressida is often and quite wrongly discussed as a 'problem play' along with *Measure for Measure* and *All's Well That Ends Well*. It belongs among the tragedies though it seems deliberately to avoid tragedy or indeed sets itself as a foil to tragedy, with its lack of a hero, lack of pattern, lack of a concluding death, lack of evil, lack of dignity. The play is unnervingly anti-heroic. Though it may seem strange that Shakespeare, who gave a sombre magnificence to Roman and British themes, should treat the great Greek theme in so grimly reductive and deflationary a way, he was not exactly the first major writer to be moved to cynicism by the Trojan War. Ideals of love, ideals of war, ideals of the human community, as expressed by Troilus, Ulysses, and others sound splendid, but are quite hollow when measured against what people actually do and what actually happens; these ideals do not seem to understand Helen and Cressida and Achilles.

All Shakespeare's plays, perhaps all drama, deal with the failure of expectations, but *Troilus* makes a special feast of it. Somewhere, not in the expressed ideals of men and women and not in the visible behaviour of men and women, truth lodges; but it is inaccessible. Troilus fondly believes he is 'as true as truth's simplicity'. Hector does his very best to speak 'in way of truth'; in his famous speech to the Trojan council—when after all these years they are *still* debating the justice of their cause—he firmly enunciates a principle of conduct based on a concept of absolute value when he urges that they should return Helen to the Greeks:

> 'Tis mad idolatory
> To make the service greater than the god.
>
> (II. ii. 56–7)

What is the use of being able to recognize principles like this? Hector astoundingly concludes his speech with a 'ne'ertheless', propending (or inclining) to his brothers' opinion, 'in resolution to keep Helen still',

> For 'tis a cause that hath no mean dependence
> Upon our joint and several dignities.
>
> (II. ii. 192–3)

Hector's story is a micro-tragedy set within an anti-tragedy. Like most of us, he cannot in the end exclude himself from the good will and esteem of those closest to him. (In this he is utterly unlike Hamlet, who severs himself from everyone in the cause of what he believes to be truth.) At the beginning of the play he is shown to us uncomfortably dislodged from his own ideals of conduct, in petty anger from having been humiliated by Ajax. He is fighting in a war he does not believe in, and in that predicament cannot derive much solace from his effort to hold fast to ideals of chivalry and honour. The remoteness of his code of military ethics—which includes the long-drawn-out business of the courtly challenge to the Greeks—from the actual course of war is brutally shown at the end of the play when he courteously spares

Achilles only to have Achilles treacherously set on him with his Myrmidons and slay him when he is unarmed and resting.

Ulysses sets up an ideal of human society governed by absolute value in his 'degree' speech in Act I, Scene iii (see Chapter 2, pp. 45–6), but what he really believes in is policy, in craftily manœuvring society the way you want it to go. For most of the play he is scheming to get Achilles back into action. Elaborate stratagems to work on Achilles' vanity include an important debate on reputation and merit in man: whether there *is* such a thing as absolute merit, or whether, as Ulysses seems to believe, everything depends on what people think of you. But in the end Achilles returns to the battle for very personal reasons, quite unaffected by Ulysses' ideals or his schemes.

Troilus' view of value is an emotional Keatsian one. You commit yourself to what your imagination fixes itself on, in love and in war. His self-intoxication is exhibited in his rhetoric, as we saw in Chapter 3 (p. 73). He never really sees Cressida but has a cloudy vision of a blessed damozel. He has little right, when he discovers Cressida and Diomedes together, to exclaim so vehemently that the 'bonds of heaven' have been 'unloosed'. His disillusionment is the puncturing of a self-inflated world. There is something truer in Cressida than he recognized though alas it did not express itself in constancy. Her worldly prudence in not showing her affection for Troilus too quickly (I. ii. 282–95) is a wisdom she has acquired from many sources in Shakespeare and elsewhere: 'Men prize the thing ungained more than it is.' She is wishing to postpone what was commonly supposed to be the decline of male affection once desire was satisfied. She may have been right, even about Troilus, who protests too much. Her level words in the scene before the consummation contrast strongly with the windy extravagance of Troilus. But she can't keep faith. The scene between her and Diomedes is at a level of psychological realism that Shakespeare rarely attempted in wooing scenes. It is a mystery to her why her conduct doesn't follow her intentions.

The scurrilous and vituperative commentator Thersites is one who, like nearly everyone else in the play, is disappointed by the gap between expectations and reality. There would be no force in his scathing contempt for what men and women actually do if he were not like Swift filled with *saeva indignatio*. 'Still wars and lechery! Nothing else holds fashion. A burning devil take them!'

He may not be at the centre of the play's valuation of the human scene but he's not far off. *Troilus and Cressida* is disenchantment most powerfully expressed: an account of society as a meaningless mix of stupidity, pomposity, sensuality, brutality, self-regard, self-indulgence, obstinacy, and vanity. It is like the tragedies in asking what is truth, but unlike the tragedies it does not tantalize us with the possibility that there is an answer.

Timon of Athens

In *Timon of Athens*, too, the last of these plays on the outer edge of Shakespearian tragedy, the vision of humanity is full of darkness and disgust. Whereas *Troilus* rejects tragic form as a means of accommodating its perceptions, *Timon* seeks tragic form and fails to find it. Shakespeare perhaps gave it up and never finished it; if so, whoever managed to produce the manuscript for the First Folio saved a minor treasure, intense, powerful, and different, whatever its defects. It toys with many things more fully developed in other tragedies, *Coriolanus* and *Lear* especially, but it develops more fully than any other tragedy two particularly interesting formal experiments: one the blending of tragedy with satirical citizen comedy and the other the blending of tragedy and pastoral. *Timon* is the tragedy most concerned with economic man, and its attack on money as corroding every relationship and corrupting every principle is blistering. It is also the tragedy which most powerfully uses city, city-walls, cave, and sea-shore as symbols of human states. A life cynically based on hard cash is located in symbolic geography.

Part of its weakness as a tragedy is the simplicity of the hero's course and the facile allocation of responsibility for his catastrophe. Timon is deeply affected by the rot that infects all Athens. Money dominates his life as it dominates the lives of his crafty creditors and clients. He rejoices in what money can buy, or seems to buy—the affection of people. He is quite blind to the shallowness of the friendships he wins and of the gratitude he is shown. While others are greedily covetous and acquisitive, he is munificent, generous, heedless—but his life like theirs is based on considering material possessions as the highest good. When the crash comes and no one will assist him, the violence of his indignation, like that of Troilus, is quite excessive. Only unthinking men could be so shocked. Prodigal generosity rewarded with ingratitude leads to misanthropy. Timon tries to hasten the destruction of mankind by increasing the circulation of gold and syphilis. But it looks as though warfare will do it first, as Alcibiades, like a more justified Coriolanus, brings an avenging army against the city that has banished him. Timon's death, with the tide washing gently over the grave he has made 'upon the beachèd verge of the salt flood', together with a sudden relenting in Alcibiades, changes the mood of the play in its final moments from wrath to forgiveness. *Timon* is very strong both in the power of the invective with which Timon denounces Athenian society and in the satirical wit with which the complacency and hypocrisy of the time-serving poet and painter, creditor and senator, are drawn. It has wit, power, and occasional beauty, but its components do not coalesce into tragedy.

Tragic commitment

Shakespeare's main tragedies divide into tragedies of violence and tragedies of love. The tragedies of violence are *Julius Caesar*, *Hamlet*, *Macbeth*, and *Coriolanus*. The tragedies of love are *Romeo and Juliet*, *Othello*, *Antony and Cleopatra*, and *King Lear*. In both kinds we recognize an apartness in the hero (man or woman), a dissatisfaction with society and what it has to offer, a commitment to an objective that sets him or her even farther outside society, a failure that must provoke an audience's recognition of both the folly and the greatness of the aspiration; and a death. The initial stage of the hero's indeterminacy and dissatis-fied aspiration seems very important. It is there in Romeo, despondent, irresolute, questioning his own identity ('I have lost myself'), not taking part in the fray, in love but not loved. It is there in Brutus, in Macbeth, in Richard III, in Troilus. Most notably it is in Hamlet, bereaved, disinherited, disillusioned, meditating suicide.

> How weary, stale, flat, and unprofitable
> Seem to me all the uses of this world.

> (I. ii. 133–4)

To every one of the heroes comes what is seen as the opportunity for deliverance, deliverance through love or violence to an entirely new life of purpose and fulfilment.

Deliverance through violence

Julius Caesar

In the tragedies of violence the fulfilment is social and political as
well as personal. In *Julius Caesar* Cassius seeks out a Brutus who
is 'with himself at war', 'vexed ... with passions of some difference'. What Cassius offers him is in a sense a recovery or a
restoration: an obliteration of bad new ways and a return to an
older society in which honour and equality had prevailed.

> Brutus had rather be a villager
> Than to repute himself a son of Rome
> Under these hard conditions as this time
> Is like to lay upon us.
>
> (I. ii. 172–5)

Infinite damage has been done to *Julius Caesar* by the supposition
that the fiery republican Cassius is an unprincipled schemer
manœuvring Brutus into a shady conspiracy which is to serve his
own unworthy purposes. Everything depends upon a pronoun:

> If I were Brutus now and he were Cassius,
> He should not humour me.
>
> (I. ii. 314–15)

So often taken to mean that Cassius would not allow himself to
be inveigled as he has inveigled Brutus, that *he* would know on
which side his bread was buttered, the play as a whole *insists* that
this means that if Cassius were Brutus he would not allow *Caesar*
to humour him; that is to say, be nice to him and make much of
him—and thus weaken and sap his political principles. Brutus is
as it were responding to this fear of Cassius when he says in the
night-time soliloquy (II. i), 'It must be by his death!'; arguing
against his own affection and respect for Caesar, trying to let
nothing stand in the way of 'redress'. They are to be 'purgers, not
murderers'. Brutus proposes to square his personal feelings for
Caesar and his desire for political change by renaming death. But
violence, however named, is indispensable. The bloody act of
assassination is performed centre-stage. The concept of violence
as liberation is summed up in Brutus asking the conspirators to
stoop and wash their hands in Caesar's blood:

> And waving our red weapons o'er our heads
> Let's all cry peace, freedom, and liberty!

(III. i. 109–10)

Within most of Shakespeare's tragedies there is a subordinate tragedy playing against the movement of the main tragedy. In *Julius Caesar* the micro-tragedy is that of Cassius, who makes what turns out to be the fatal mistake of engaging Brutus in a political enterprise and sees everything come to ruin through the temperamental unfitness of his partner for his role. With supreme confidence in his own ability, Brutus makes one error of judgement after another, and Cassius is the prisoner of the man he has himself recruited. The painful quarrel scene shows Cassius in the better light. But, says Antony in his hour of victory over the conspirators, Brutus was 'the noblest Roman of them all'. It is the enterprise to which he commits himself that makes all his excellent qualities appear meretricious, and turns this selfless man of honour into a self-righteous self-deceiver. *Julius Caesar* is a simpler tragedy than most. Recreating the political structure of the past is clearly an impossibility in the Rome of Caesar; the means used to achieve it are presented as odious and repulsive; the hero is darkened and defaced by his commitment; the political result is civil war and the personal end is suicide. Failure is too clear in *Julius Caesar* for us to regard it as one of the greatest tragedies; it is too easy for us to stand back and say that Brutus was misguided rather than feel our own involvement with him. Yet the balance of opposites which is the very stuff of tragedy still obtains in this play. There is little satisfaction to be found in Caesar and his regime, or in Antony's opportunism. In *Antony and Cleopatra* Brutus and Cassius are referred to as 'courtiers of beauteous freedom' (II. vi. 17). There can't be any pleasure in the obliteration of their vision and the perpetuation of Caesarian society.

Hamlet

In many ways *Julius Caesar*, as a story of the failure of the intellectual in the world of violent political action, is a prelude to *Hamlet*, although the two plays could not be more different in form, style, and tone. The only thing we know for certain about the earlier play of *Hamlet* which Shakespeare rewrote is that it

contained a ghost crying out to Hamlet to take revenge. It may
have been this crudity that sparked Shakespeare's imagination,
for it is the extra dimension of the supernatural that completely
transforms the hero's commitment and mission as found in *Julius
Caesar*. The solid earth of Denmark is surrounded by the invisible
world of salvation and damnation. The Ghost is Hamlet's link—a
link of uncertain validity—with a world which would provide him
with the meaning and purpose so utterly lacking in his life. The
Ghost tells him of adultery and murder; commands him to wreak
vengeance on Claudius but to leave Gertrude to her conscience
and to heaven. Hamlet accepts the mission with a fervent
dedication of himself—and then shrinks from what is his own
interpretation of how far that mission extends.

> The time is out of joint. O cursèd spite,
> That ever I was born to set it right!
>
> (I. v. 188–9)

Already in his suit of mourning a man set apart from the rest of
the Court, Hamlet symbolizes his alienation yet further by his
pretended madness. But what, apart from such gestures, is he
actually to do? His eagerness to carry out the Ghost's command
seems to evaporate. Was the spirit in fact a devil trying to procure
the damnation of his soul? The native hue of resolution is sicklied
o'er with the pale cast of thought. It is 'conscience' he says that
restrains him both from committing suicide and from other
'enterprises of great pitch and moment'. Claudius's reaction to
'The Murder of Gonzago' convinces him that the Ghost was
telling the truth, but then follows the central irony of the play: he
spares the king when he finds him praying and then strikes home
when he finds him as he thinks eavesdropping behind the arras,
only to discover that he has killed Polonius. It is extraordinary
how little this accidental killing seems to worry Hamlet. It is
evident that what he has committed himself to at this stage is
precisely what the Ghost had forbidden, the castigation of his
mother, whom he continues to upbraid and reprehend with the
dead man at his feet. The shaming of his mother seems to exhaust
his passion for revenge, and he allows the king's plan to send him
to England to take effect. He is brought back to Denmark by a
strange series of events which he believes manifests the hand of
heaven. The conviction is now strongly upon him that he has been

appointed by a higher power to perform a cleansing of society in the punishment of Claudius, and that it is not for him to organize and direct events as he has been trying to do but to be aware of and respect heaven's direction. Duty is now given a deeply religious context.

> Is't not perfect conscience
> To quit him with this arm? And is't not to be damned
> To let this canker of our nature come in further evil?
>
> (v. ii. 67–9)

But Laertes, quicker in his revenge for *his* dead father, gives Hamlet his death-wound before Hamlet finally kills Claudius. A foreigner, Fortinbras, inherits the kingdom which Hamlet had tried to purge of a usurper. The forfeiture of the kingdom, together with the madness and death of Ophelia, seem the strongest indictment of Hamlet's activity and inactivity.

Hamlet is the most enigmatic play in the canon and after nearly four hundred years and whole libraries of comment and interpretation we seem to be no nearer the heart of its mystery. The traditional question, 'Why did Hamlet delay?', still demands an answer, but to that question there has been added during this century the question whether Hamlet should have committed himself to revenge at all. The two questions are interconnected, and they prompt a third, 'What *is* revenge?' The coarse convention of Elizabethan revenge-tragedy had a way of posing profound and difficult questions about justice, human and divine—whether there is any such thing, and if there is who initiates it. In the hands of a master like Shakespeare, with a hero like Hamlet, such questions do not become less searching. Hamlet's commitment to revenge is beset by doubt and uncertainty, and that is why he delays; and when he acts, he blunders terribly. Could it be otherwise with a matter of such magnitude? 'Revenge' in *Hamlet* is about justice, about rightful inheritance, about moral discrimination, about the punishment of evil, about the relation of society to the divine will. To say that Hamlet should have acted quickly and resolutely is to make light of these problems; to say that he should not have acted at all is to acquiesce in what the play unequivocally states to be evil. The question that Hamlet asks the Ghost, 'What should we do?', is not one that we are allowed to evade. Hamlet, we may well say, made a terrible mess of things.

But at least he was trying to keep alive the distinction between right and wrong, trying not to compromise with evil, trying to establish a justice which he believed had an authority higher than the merely human. We may be dreadfully mistaken if we say *he* was dreadfully mistaken. There is no play in which the conflict of emotions and ideas in those who witness it is so finely balanced as in *Hamlet*, as we respond to and try to adjudicate his failure and his triumph. It is often held that tragedy consists in the resolution of oppositions; I am not sure that this is so. The balance of the oppositions in *Hamlet* is anything but the resolution of them.

Macbeth

The deed that is to liberate the hero in *Julius Caesar* and recreate his society is all too quickly decided on and carried out. Yet it is often noted that Brutus' words about the gap between commitment and action could apply very forcefully to *Hamlet*, in which the deed of liberation does not take place until the play's last moments.

> Between the acting of a dreadful thing
> And the first motion, all the interim is
> Like a phantasma or a hideous dream.
> The Genius and the mortal instruments
> Are then in council; and the state of man,
> Like to a little kingdom, suffers then
> The nature of an insurrection.
>
> (II. i. 63–9)

But how much more forcefully, even, do these words apply to Macbeth, as he moves in horror to encompass the deed which is to bring about a longed-for future? He moves forward in a trance to convert a fantasy into reality.

> Is this a dagger which I see before me?

> Art thou but
> A dagger of the mind, a false creation
> Proceeding from the heat-oppressèd brain?

> Thou marshal'st me the way that I was going.
>
> (II. i. 33, 37–9, 42)

'Thou marshal'st me the way that I was going.' Macbeth could have said to the Witches what he says to the dagger in the air. He and Lady Macbeth, in an extraordinary *folie à deux*, must have shared a vision of glory, of themselves as king and queen ministering bounty to their reverent subjects, and must have got as far as speaking of the only act that could bring this about (see I. vii. 41–9). The prophecy of the Witches, drawing aside the curtains and displaying this very fantasy, leaves Macbeth stunned, a prey to 'horrible imaginings'.

> My thought, whose murder yet is but fantastical,
> Shakes so my single state of man, that function
> Is smothered in surmise, and nothing is
> But what is not.
>
> (I. iii. 139–42)

It was a wonderful stroke of Shakespeare's to choose to award a brave, efficient, ruthless general the richest imaginative life of all his heroes. Macbeth lives two lives, as a soldier and as a dreamer. The dreams seem a kind of possession, not instigated by him. They force themselves upon him as reality does, without any seeking; and they can terrify him more than reality does, as with the airborne dagger and later Banquo's ghost.

In the sixteenth century England was full of debate and controversy about the extent to which the eternal world physically offered its presence to men, women, and children. There was no single belief about ghosts, spirits, angels, demons, witches. At one end was the noble scepticism of Reginald Scot and at the other the tortuous reasoning of scholars who thought that to deny demonic possession in women was to question the existence of God. In two plays Shakespeare uses the uncertainty of his age about manifestations of the spirit world to convey a sense of uncertainty about supernatural communications. Both the Ghost in *Hamlet* and the Witches in *Macbeth* are perplexing and mysterious; the extent of their knowledge and their authority puzzles us in both plays, and is meant to puzzle us. These supernatural messengers powerfully suggest that mankind is not alone in the universe, free to do what it will. But *who* is out there, and in what ways and for what purposes mankind is being influenced and directed is more than Hamlet or Macbeth or the audience can say. The voices are distorted, the messages cryptic. *King Lear* explicitly presents in the questions and assertions of the

different characters the wide range of views on the relation of
human affairs to the divine and infernal, and it is with this
spectrum of possibilities in mind that we must approach the
supernatural in *Macbeth* and *Hamlet*.

Although Macbeth longs to fulfil his 'black and deep desires', it
is the infernal encouragement of the Witches, added to the very
human taunting of his wife, that pushes him to the murder of
Duncan, the horror-filled act of violence by which the fantasy of
'the swelling act of the imperial theme' will become fact. Macbeth's strong sense of right and wrong is never confused or
overcome in this extraordinary passage of evil. 'To know my
deed, 'twere best not know myself.' From the very moment of the
murder, with voices in his head crying 'Sleep no more!', the inner
life of the mind becomes devastatingly more real, as the reality of
kingship, the supposed 'ornament of life', becomes illusory.
'Better be with the dead,' says Macbeth,

> Than on the torture of the mind to lie
> In restless ecstasy.
>
> (III. ii. 21–2)

'These terrible dreams that shake us nightly' cannot be got rid of
by further murders or further recourse to the Witches. It is Lady
Macbeth, for all her tough scorn for Macbeth's cowardice and his
fear of the coinings of his mind, who gives way first to the jarring
confusion of the real and the unreal as she walks in her sleep,
trying to wash away imaginary blood. 'Who would have thought
the old man to have had so much blood in him?' The conclusion
for Macbeth, who has sleep-walked his way into murder and then
lived out his own nightmares, is more extraordinary. As he hears
'the cry of women' he is aware of a new numbness in his life. The
fear that has been a constant attendant on this bold soldier—not
in the field but in the privacy of his imaginings—has disappeared
(v. v. 9–15). At this moment of realizing that something has
deadened in his life, there comes the news that the cry signalled
the death of his wife. In the great 'Tomorrow, and tomorrow, and
tomorrow' speech we understand that for Macbeth, just as the
torturing inner reality of the mental life has died, so has the life of
reality itself. Neither the intangible nor the tangible has meaning
any more.

Life's but a walking shadow, a poor player
That struts and frets his hour upon the stage,
And then is heard no more. It is a tale
Told by an idiot, full of sound and fury
Signifying nothing.

(v. v. 24–8)

The hero who was so much an inhabitant of two worlds that 'nothing is but what is not', finds now mere 'nothing' in both worlds. He fights his opponents with all his soldierly courage in the last battle, but is defeated, and his severed head is brought on. So perish all traitors! But the audience must demur at Malcolm's reference to 'this dead butcher'. *Macbeth* contains some of Shakespeare's greatest poetry; and this poetry draws the audience into the closest communion with Macbeth and the torture of his mind. Macbeth's acts are villainous and evil, but that horror-filled imagination is not easily dismissed. The tragic balance in *Macbeth* is not as in *Julius Caesar* and *Hamlet* a sort of fundamental ambiguity in the quality of the enterprise; Macbeth's selfish enterprise is totally wrong. The balance comes through our being admitted by the force of poetry into the heart of darkness which as in Conrad's story we have to recognize as ours. The source of Macbeth's monstrous crime is hard to identify. It comes both from within and without, with the strongest evidence of satanic interference and temptation. Whatever he's in the grip of, the quality of the poetry doesn't allow us to disown him or what he does. Aristotle held that pity and terror were essential in the tragic experience: pity for one like ourselves and terror at what he does. Another way of putting this is 'There but for the grace of God go I.' *Macbeth* is supreme in engendering that complex and powerful emotion in which empathy blends with fear and repulsion.

Coriolanus

Coriolanus is a tragedy of violence in which the liberating act of violence never happens. By the destruction of his own city the hero was to initiate a new self and a new society, forging himself a name in 'the fire of burning Rome' (v. i. 14–15). Volumnia averts the disaster and Coriolanus goes instead to his death at the hands of his new allies the Volsces.

Destruction is Coriolanus's answer to every problem. He is the great revolutionary among Shakespeare's heroes. It is true he is a man of the past, who hates the direction society is taking. He has been shaped by his mother to become the very incarnation of the values of a society whose continuance depended on a military class protecting it against the physical assaults of its enemies. But there is no sentiment in the man for the happier days of old, as there is in Hamlet longing for the beauteous majesty of his father's Denmark, or in Brutus longing for the ways of republican Rome. Coriolanus is a root-and-branch innovator, as Sicinius recognizes (III. i. 174), believing in a new order based on principles of genetic difference between himself and ordinary mankind. He is a man apart. His mother's moulding of him was only the beginning: he has grown into something dreadful, a scourge, separated from his fellow-patricians as well as the plebeians. The 'sovereignty of nature' (IV. vii. 35) which his enemies as well as his friends speak of is not something to argue about. He is, by himself, the city's protector, a man of incredible valour. He believes in absolutes and scorns compromise. The ideal city for which he strives is based on a political philosophy which is clearly thought out and eloquently if over-vehemently expressed (III. i. 91–161). If we say that no one could live in such a city, it being founded on the idea that the common people, the 'musty superfluity', being genetically inferior have no representation or voice whatsoever in the government of their affairs, we have to remember that some twentieth-century communities have survived longer than Nazi Germany did on the principle of the *Herrenvolk*.

The enemies of Coriolanus, the tribunes, will have to destroy him if they themselves are to survive. Their words are as full of hate as his—yet there are shrewd truths told on either side.

BRUTUS. You speak o' th' people
    As if you were a god to punish, not
    A man of their infirmity.

(III. i. 80–2)

SICINIUS. Where is this viper,
    That would depopulate the city, and
    Be every man himself?

(III. i. 262–4)

Coriolanus's attempt to accommodate himself to the civilian customs of the new society is bound to fail, given the fatal chemistry of his irascible pride and the skilful manœuvring of the tribunes, who carefully engineer the final breach. With the sentence of banishment Coriolanus' real separateness becomes apparent.

> You common cry of curs, whose breath I hate
> As reek o' th' rotten fens, whose loves I prize
> As the dead carcasses of unburied men
> That do corrupt my air, I banish you!

> Thus I turn my back;
> There is a world elsewhere!
>
> (III. iii. 120–3, 134–5)

The real 'pride' of Coriolanus is now seen in a kind of exultation in his image of himself, magnificent and terrible in his isolation.

> Though I go alone,
> Like to a lonely dragon, that his fen
> Makes feared and talked of more than seen, your son
> Will or exceed the common or be caught
> With cautelous baits and practice.
>
> (IV. i. 29–33)

The concern of this final phrase, that in its attempt at a free soaring flight the heroic spirit is particularly vulnerable, in its noble innocence as it were, to the crafty tricks of lesser men, is something we find expressed time and again in Shakespeare's tragedies. Coriolanus cannot work with the tribunes: they are lesser spirits but they are too artful and tricky for him, as Octavius is for Antony, and Iago is for Othello.

The 'world elsewhere' is to be built on the smoking ruins of Rome. Coriolanus sides with his arch-enemy Aufidius to wreak this destruction. He refuses all negotiation and all mercy. When his mother, wife, and child arrive to plead with him, he has to steel himself to

> stand
> As if a man were author of himself
> And knew no other kin.
>
> (V. iii. 35–7)

But the lonely dragon cannot face it out. Volumnia his mother created this monster, as her proud boasts earlier in the play sufficiently indicate (I. iii. 1–47), and she uncreates him. Honourably and with dignity he yields to her view of his intended actions and abandons his enterprise of destruction. It is a great moment in the theatre as 'he holds her by the hand, silent'. But how extraordinary that this dread alienated figure, a brand to sear and cauterize the infected world, should be subdued by his mother! The submission reduces and belittles the enterprise itself. It is as a 'boy of tears' that Aufidius taunts him and provokes him to the childish rage of his final defiance.

> Boy? False hound!
> If you have writ your annals true, 'tis there
> That like an eagle in a dovecot I
> Fluttered your Volscians in Corioles.
> Alone I did it. Boy?

(v. vi. 112–16)

Coriolanus is a tremendous play, brilliantly written, passionate and intense throughout, utterly absorbing to later times as no doubt it was in its own for its political and psychological subtlety and insight. Shakespeare's almost-unbearable tolerance and fair-mindedness make the case for and against the people and for and against Coriolanus endlessly disputable; but from the point of view of our four tragedies of violence the special interest is in the *reduction* in this play of the motivation for the violent liberating act. No messengers from heaven or hell, no search for justice, no punishment of wickedness or vice, but the passionate anger of a thwarted man. The avenging extra-terrestrial hero is shown in the end to be still tied to the umbilical cord that gave him being and nourishment. There is no doubt that in this diminution of the hero *Coriolanus*, fine play though it is, is less tragic in its final mood than *Hamlet* or *Macbeth*.

Deliverance through love

Romeo and Juliet

Romeo and Juliet, the earliest of the Shakespearian love-tragedies, presents their main features in a clear and simple form. The love of the tragic pair rises out of hate like a sudden rainbow over

Verona. It is a fulfilment for themselves that has to be kept secret from feuding families to whom the relationship would be a scandal. Friar Lawrence sees this youthful love as a possible means of ending the hostility of the families; in fact things go the other way: the hostility destroys the lovers. By the juxtaposition of scenes Shakespeare sharply demonstrates the incompatibilities that form tragedy. Love cannot thrive in Verona, as is shown by the masterly ironies of the scene leading to the deaths of Mercutio and Tybalt and the banishment of Romeo (III. i.). It starts from Romeo trying to be friendly to Juliet's family. In this context of hatred, love ignites the fuse.

All along, Juliet's vision of happiness comprehends its ending:

> Too like the lightning, which doth cease to be
> Ere one can say, it lightens.
>
> (II. ii. 119–20)

When the 14-year-old bride hears of the Tybalt affray, she says:

> I'll to my wedding bed,
> And death, not Romeo, take my maidenhead.
>
> (III. ii. 136–7)

They are able to consummate their love but are immediately separated. The Friar's desperate scheme to avert the marriage to Paris and to reunite the lovers goes wrong and the reunion in the tomb is a reunion of the dead. Death is seen as safety.

> O here
> Will I set up my everlasting rest,
> And shake the yoke of inauspicious stars
> From this world-wearied flesh.
>
> (v. iii. 109–12)

No one will say that Romeo is unworthy of Juliet, but when we see or read the play we feel that Juliet's love is its true centre. Her naïve directness in the balcony scene and in the betrothal scene in Friar Lawrence's cell makes Romeo seem a little wordy, and there is a tinge of extravagance in nearly all his conduct and protestations after the fatal brawl. We don't really need to contrast the two in the quality of their love or behaviour—but there is nothing in Romeo's part like Juliet's grim determination to kill herself rather than marry Paris (IV. i. 50–67), or her isolation just before she takes Friar Lawrence's potion (IV. iii). At this latter moment she is utterly alone, estranged from her family, her new husband banished, her nurse turned traitor. She cannot even be sure that the Friar is not playing false with the potion. Juliet is more *important* in the tragedy than Romeo.

Romeo and Juliet is not concerned with tragic flaw and tragic error. The impetuousness of the lovers and the compliance of the Friar are not being entered up in a balance sheet of culpability. In the world's eyes such things might be scandalous, but the play shows the affection of Romeo and Juliet as something that momentarily transfigures the world, alters its values, and might redeem it if the world were not so determined to eclipse and destroy it. In the later love-tragedies, the protagonists are more closely implicated in their own destruction; but *Romeo and Juliet* is most effective in presenting the idea of the opposition of love and society on which the later plays are built.

Othello

As Juliet's love is the centre of *Romeo and Juliet*, Desdemona's love is the centre of *Othello*, and Cleopatra's of *Antony and Cleopatra*. In the two late plays, however, the hero fails the heroine, being unable to comprehend or reciprocate the quality of the other's affection.

Of the Duchess of Malfi's commitment to her steward Antonio, Cariola said:

> Whether the spirit of greatness or of woman
> Reign most in her I know not, but it shows
> A fearful madness.

                                                    (I. i. 576–8)

That alternative is not open in Desdemona's commitment to Othello. In *Cymbeline*, Imogen has like Desdemona chosen a husband outside her own social group and married him in absolute defiance of her family. When later she finds herself betrayed and calumniated by her husband, she says he will learn that her choice of him was

> no act of common passage, but
> A strain of rareness.

                                                    (III. iv. 91–2)

The spirit of greatness and the spirit of woman are together in Desdemona marrying Othello, but 'a strain of rareness' is the aptest description of her choice of this foreigner, whose way of life was so utterly different from that of the 'wealthy curlèd darlings' whom she might have had in order to settle into the conventional life of an aristocratic Venetian wife. She calls her act one of 'downright violence' in her great speech at the Duke's palace.

> My heart's subdued
> Even to the very quality* of my lord.
> I saw Othello's visage in his mind,
> And to his honours and his valiant parts
> Did I my soul and fortunes consecrate.

(I. iii. 250–4)

Her choice is inexplicable to her father: he believes Othello must have used witchcraft to enchant her. Iago has a different explanation: Othello won her by 'bragging' and telling tall stories; it was 'a violent commencement' but 'when she is sated with his body she will find the error of her choice' (I. iii. 350–1). To the often-made charge that Desdemona was naïve to love Othello, that she did not really know him, the only answer is that she did know him: she knew truly what was noble and distinctive in Othello from his presence and from his account of his life. What she could not know was what Iago could do to the man she knew. Yet there is indeed more to it than that. Shakespeare has given touches to the initial presentation of Othello which—while we must still be in awe of Desdemona's independence and courage in such a reckless adventure—make us fear that faith of that sort in any human being is misplaced.

Othello, like Coriolanus, is conscious and proud of his apartness and his own qualities.

> I fetch my life and being
> From men of royal siege; and my demerits
> May speak unbonneted to as proud a fortune
> As this that I have reached. For know, Iago,
> But that I love the gentle Desdemona,
> I would not my unhousèd free condition
> Put into circumscription and confine
> For the sea's worth.

(I. ii. 21–8)

*The Quarto reads 'utmost pleasure' instead of the Folio's 'very quality'.

He doesn't need to feel small by the side of the Venetian aristocrats—he is more than their equal in terms of birth. The office he has achieved in their service is nothing to him: his deserts ('demerits') warrant a position at least as high as that. Then the very surprising confession that he sees himself as tying himself down, putting himself into 'circumscription and confine', amongst a people he regards as inferior. The syntax of the sentence, 'But that I love ... I would not ...', puts the emphasis just away from where we feel it should be. Somehow the disadvantages of compromising 'my unhousèd free condition' are not quite outweighed by the new element of love. To the Senate in the next scene, describing his courtship, he concludes:

> She loved me for the dangers I had passed,
> And I loved her that she did pity them.
>
> (I. iii. 167–8)

This is said with a smile of course, as he closes with 'This only is the witchcraft I have used.' But we are a little disconcerted at the difference between this and Desdemona's free and complete gift of herself. 'I loved her that she did pity them': he recognizes the achievements of his own life and what he says he responds to is *her* recognition of them. Desdemona's love is the dedication of herself to unpathed waters, to new possibilities of existence; his, however sincere and full, is in his own regard a limiting rather than an expansion. To understand this is to understand better his later terrible cry, 'Othello's occupation's gone!'

As with Romeo and Juliet, the happiness of Othello and Desdemona is intense and brief. Whatever trace of foreboding we have found in Othello's words, the moment of their coming together after their short separation on the stormy seas gives us a glimpse of what it is that the heroes and heroines of the love-tragedies hazard everything for (II. i. 182–99). It is not 'society' that breaks their love and happiness, but hell. There is a super-natural dimension in *Othello* as in *Hamlet* and *Macbeth* and the same difficulty in being clear about the source and shape of supernatural intervention. Iago constantly speaks of himself as a collaborator with hell, working by its methods with its assistance. At the very end, a disabused Othello sees him as a demi-devil who has sought to ensnare his soul for Satan's kingdom. Perhaps this is no more than to say that if hell has its agency on earth it is in a villain like Iago, and that if damnation is true it exists in doing what Othello is led to do.

Iago is not only a witty and joky man in public, as in the sea-shore scene with Desdemona and Emilia (II. i. 100–66), but like Aaron the Moor and Richard III can take a mischievous delight in the monstrousness of his schemes, and like the traditional Vice of the medieval drama share his relish with the audience. But in the recesses of his soul there is no laughter whatever, rather the absolute darkness of smouldering hate. The very quality of other people's lives is an attack on him, slighting and humiliating him. 'He hath a daily beauty in his life that makes me ugly.' The famous 'motive-hunting', which Coleridge ascribed to 'motiveless malignity', during which he piles up wholly improbable accusations against Othello and Cassio for having had relations with his wife, is really the irrational bubbling of his fermenting paranoia; everyone is more successful than he and persistently takes advantage of him.

That Iago has been passed over by Othello in favour of Cassio is only the superficial cause of Iago's swelling programme of destruction. The greatest offences are the calm success of Othello, the married happiness of Othello and Desdemona, and, above all, the virtue and innocence of Desdemona. Several times Shakespeare dwelt on the urge to deface, pollute, and destroy which purity in women provoked in some men—that urge of which Yeats gave a crystalline description when talking of the whiteness of swans:

> So arrogantly pure, a child might think
> It can be murdered with a spot of ink.
>
> ('Coole Park and Ballylee, 1931')

Shakespeare makes Desdemona's virtue 'out of this world', as her naïve last conversation with Emilia demonstrates. It is very important to Iago to keep her scale of values out of this world: she has to be destroyed. The 'divinity of hell' recognizes that her virtue can itself be the agent of her destruction. He could not destroy Othello through her, because her trust is impregnable; but he can destroy her and Othello through Othello's comparatively frail armour.

> So will I turn her virtue into pitch,
> And out of her own goodness make the net
> That shall enmesh them all.
>
> (II. iii. 360–2)

The most terrible thing about the chemical change which Iago brilliantly and speedily works in Othello's nature is that he gets him to accept the values of Venetian society—of which Iago is always the extreme exponent. He becomes in his own eyes elderly, black, ignorant, excluded, and inferior, and he accepts the white man's view that it was *unnatural* for Desdemona to love him: 'And yet,' he reflects, 'how nature erring from itself . . .' In the greatest failure of trust in Shakespeare's plays, Othello accepts not only society's image of himself but its image of Desdemona as an 'ordinary' woman, *varium et mutabile* as her irrepressible sexual desires waft her from one man to the next. For Othello, the disintegration of his love engineered by Iago's remorseless lies and insinuations is the destruction of the whole man.

> There, where I have garnered up my heart,
> Where either I must live or bear no life . . .
>
> (IV. ii. 57–8)

It is for this reason that the moment he has lost his faith in Desdemona he speaks the extraordinary elegy for the 'pride, pomp, and circumstance of glorious war'. His being as a man apart, a strange adventurer in foreign fields, was forged anew as soldier-lover, and the fusion of the new being was recognized and accepted by Desdemona in her determination to accompany him as his bride to the place of battle. The new fused being cannot be taken apart again into its separate components; when love ceases the whole being shatters.

Romeo and Juliet die in each other's arms, their love for each other confirmed and held in death. In 'the tragic loading of this bed' at the end of *Othello* there is intense separateness. 'No way but this,' says Othello, 'Killing myself, to die upon a kiss.' But his suicide is his judgement on himself as one who because of his own insane act of 'justice' is 'damned beneath all depth in hell'.

Thus the world takes its revenge on those who glimpse visions of fulfilment which reveal all too clearly society's inadequacies and deficiencies. Othello and Desdemona are no Faustian rebels

any more than Romeo and Juliet are. Othello is a faithful servant
of the Venetian State. But their love, transcending the values of
society, is an offence society won't endure. Iago, the honest
soldier trusted by Othello beyond his trust in his own wife, is the
very extraordinary incarnation Shakespeare chose for hellish
forces in the world determined to prevent escape from the world's
values.

Antony and Cleopatra

The offensiveness to the world of the love between Antony and
Cleopatra is strongly and thematically stated in Philo's words at
the very opening of the play. His disgust at seeing

> The triple pillar of the world transformed
> Into a strumpet's fool

is easy to understand as we listen to Antony's inflated avowal of a
love that denies the importance of anything except Cleopatra and
her wishes.

> The nobleness of life
> Is to do thus!

(I. i. 36–7)

How can we help being embarrassed by this display of the higher
hedonism, or feeling that the only word to use in connection with
his extravagant protestation about 'new heaven, new earth' is
'besotted'? 'Excellent falsehood!', says Cleopatra, and she is right.
The language of transcendence, which is indeed the proper
vocabulary for the potential relation between Antony and Cleopatra, is being misused here by Antony; he does not really mean
it. When 'a Roman thought' strikes him, her spell over him is seen
as a spell: 'I must from this enchanting queen break off;' 'These
strong Egyptian fetters I must break.' This conception that
Cleopatra is an enchantress who ensnares her victims by unnatural powers never leaves him; after the disgrace of the last battle
(IV. xii), he says she has 'beguiled' him 'to the very heart of loss'.
'The witch shall die!' It is in response to Antony's violence after
the earlier defeat at Actium that Cleopatra says, 'Not know me
yet?' Her question runs through the entire play.

Critics often suggest that *Antony and Cleopatra* is a kind of
problem play in that Shakespare has painted Cleopatra and the

love between her and Antony in a double perspective, so that
sometimes and from some angles she seems noble and sometimes
a mere strumpet, and the love seems sometimes majestic and
sometimes sordid and meretricious. Or else that Cleopatra is a
wayward, sensual, designing, high-class whore who eventually
attains the dignity and nobility of wife and queen. Both these
views of alternative and opposed valuations of Cleopatra seem
wrong. She is one person throughout, a person too complex and
profound for anyone in the play to perceive or understand, with
the partial exception of Enobarbus. As the heroine of a love-
tragedy, her sensuality and promiscuity put her at the opposite
pole from Desdemona. But Desdemona would not try to vie with
her majesty. Cleopatra lives at all times on all levels that are
perceived in her. Her wilfulness, waywardness, sensuality, selfish-
ness, and vanity are inextricably part of her mysterious grace, and
they contribute to a quality of love as splendid as anything in
Shakespeare. If Antony did not recognize this he would not love
her as he does, but he never recognizes it wholly, and he
constantly doubts the quality of her affection. He glimpses the
uniqueness of Cleopatra in the first scene, the 'wrangling queen, /
Whom everything becomes'. That which is 'bad' becomes transformed in Cleopatra, and moral judgements fall away before this
inexplicable alchemy. Enobarbus in the second scene, contradict-
ing Antony about her 'cunning', says, 'No, her passions are made
of nothing but the finest part of pure love.' This is the burden of
Enobarbus' remarks about her in the all-important speech in Act
II, Scene ii. She makes 'defect perfection'.

> Vilest things
> Become themselves in her, that the holy priests
> Bless her when she is riggish.
>
> (II. ii. 237–9)

A 'rig' is a sexy woman. The priests bless her when she is in an
amorous mood, summoning men to her arms and her bed.
Enobarbus gives (by courtesy of Plutarch) his famous description
of the luxurious magnificence of her stately progress on the barge
on the river Cydnus, and immediately follows it with:

> I saw her once
> Hop forty paces through the public street,
> And having lost her breath, she spoke, and panted ...
>
> (II. ii. 228–30)

Material magnificence, voluptuousness, a simple physicality, are all parts of a strange spirituality. Cleopatra says she was persuaded to believe that 'eternity was in our lips and brows'. The depth of her love for Antony is aroused by her recognition of something transcendent in him. 'Did I, Charmian, / Ever love Caesar so?' Her question perfectly illustrates what Shakespeare is doing. At once we have the strumpet-queen proud of her seductive talent, and also, 'wrinkled deep in time', some scarcely namable being who requires the rare experience of an encounter with an Antony to create herself in fulness, and spiritualize an experience which begins in sex and generally remains in sex.

Antony can neither commit himself to her nor reject her. But he is not a free agent. *Antony and Cleopatra* is not a love-and-honour tragedy, weighing Egyptian luxury against austere Roman virtues, though Antony sees it that way. There is no either/or in it. Antony cannot return to his former life any more than Othello could. His occupation's gone. Even if there weren't the irresistible magnetism of Cleopatra, there is no place for him in a Roman setting in which he has hastened his own supersession. After the inevitable break-up of Antony's patched-up relationship with Rome, the young Caesar comes on with unbelievable pace. In alliance with Cleopatra, Antony's soldiership crumbles and disappears. Enobarbus kills himself because he cannot reconcile himself to staying with Antony or to leaving him.

The final crisis is pitiful. After the last defeat, to avoid Antony's fury, Cleopatra sends the lie that she is dead; and, finding all hope in life gone with this news on top of his military defeat, Antony gives himself his death-wound. He postpones his happiness with Cleopatra to a curious vision of an afterlife 'where souls do couch on flowers'. This is perhaps generous in him; in the world they are forced to live in she has failed him time and again. When he is hoisted up, dying, to the monument, he says nothing whatsoever of reproach or forgiveness to Cleopatra. He tells her to seek her safety, and not to lament him but remember his former greatness. Not their love, but his former greatness. He wants to be remembered as the great soldier and not the fated lover.

Cleopatra's transformation at Antony's death is, I have suggested, not so much a transformation as a realization. The ecstatic imagery in which she conveys the greatness, the *difference* of Antony, and her recognition and adoration of that greatness, is the perfect expression of the vision which impels; but it is a tragic vision because fulfilment, which can now be so perfectly expressed, is now unattainable. 'Husband, I come.' She is still what she always has been; in her great speech welcoming death her nobility and majesty include her indefeasible coquetry.

> Give me my robe, put on my crown, I have
> Immortal longings in me. Now no more
> The juice of Egypt's grape shall moist this lip.
>
> (v. ii. 280–2)

But the image of death itself is of a sexual embrace.

> The stroke of death is as a lover's pinch,
> Which hurts, and is desired.
>
> (295–6)

The fatal asp is 'the baby at my breast', and she wishes to die quickly in case Charmian reaches Antony first and he 'make demand of her'.

It is given to the brisk and efficient Caesar to sum up the play in a rare imaginative moment. Looking at the dead queen, he says:

> She looks like sleep,
> As she would catch another Antony
> In her strong toil of grace.
>
> (v. ii. 346–8)

'Toil' is a word from hunting, and perhaps all Octavius means is that even in death she's beautiful enough to enmesh someone else with her charms. But 'grace' is such a strong word. What she ensnares people with is not her charms but a net of grace. She bestows this grace in a relationship which the protesting Antony referred to as 'Egyptian fetters'. The lover is caught by what liberates him. Interestingly, Cleopatra uses the trap imagery in the reverse direction. She welcomes Antony after a victory which is a false hope between two defeats.

> O infinite virtue! com'st thou smiling from
> The world's great snare uncaught?
>
> (IV. viii. 17–18)

The world can trap the free spirit, and the free spirit can escape by being trapped. In service is perfect freedom. Antony fails to realize fully the contrast between the two snares. 'The nobleness of life is to do thus'—'Here is my space'—'New heaven, new earth.' These are the phrases he should have been using at the end of the play; at the beginning they were unearned and unmeant; at the end they were forgotten, and they pass to Cleopatra, who means them.

King Lear

The paradox of the two traps has been used by Shakespeare before, at a supreme moment in *King Lear*, which though it was written a year or two before *Antony and Cleopatra* I have left until the last. It is when Lear says to Cordelia, 'Have I caught thee?', when they are being led away to prison after their defeat.

King Lear is obviously quite unlike all the tragedies we have been discussing in which the hero stakes all on love or violence to initiate a new mode of being in opposition to more obvious rewards lying nearer at hand. To speak of it as a love-tragedy may seem perverse, yet its driving force is the love between father and daughter, the relationship that dominates Shakespeare's last years of writing for the stage. Lear's decision to divide his kingdom between his daughters and to make his home with the youngest of them is a matter of the greatest magnitude both politically and in terms of ordinary family concerns, but it does not resemble those reckless commitments we have been talking about. No, Lear's commitment is in fact the disastrous one of a negation of love, a severance and a banishment.

> I loved her most, and thought to set my rest
> On her kind nursery.

> Thou hast her, France, let her be thine, for we
> Have no such daughter, nor shall ever see
> That face of hers again.
>
> (I. i. 123–4, 262–4)

There is no hope in this act of wounded pride. Nothing will come of nothing. Lear punishes himself, opens the gates to evil, and secures his own humiliation and degradation. *King Lear* differs from the other tragedies in being an extended 'passion', all stemming from an act in the first scene. After that first scene, Lear's acts are mostly speeches and journeys until he kills the 'slave' who hanged Cordelia. Action belongs to others, the people of ill will making the most of opportunities given them to achieve power, and the people of good will trying to rescue Lear and restore his position and relationships.

The plays which deal most with tragic suffering are *Richard II*, *Timon of Athens*, *King Lear*, and *Antony and Cleopatra*. These are the plays of dispossession, where men of power and authority are being superseded in a world that no longer has use for them. Each of the heroes has a kind of grandeur in his desolation that he did not possess in his prosperity. Each learns truths about the world and himself when it is too late to make use of the knowledge. It is in *King Lear* that the suffering is most prolonged, the dispossesion most fierce, and the discoveries about the world most deep and painful.

There is constant questioning in *King Lear* about who has the responsibility for the course of events, and each questioner has his or her own opinion, which the play as a whole refuses to endorse or reject. Edmund believes confidently in his own freedom to carve out his own future; his father Gloucester comes to believe in the casual hostility of unknown deities; Albany believes that a caring God will eventually protect his own. It is Edgar, the man who has such remarkable influence over the ruined Lear and Gloucester, who has the most daunting and complex answer. Like Cordelia the victim of a father's rashness, he disguises himself as the least of mankind, an utterly destitute mad beggar, 'Poor Tom'. His scenario is that he has been brought to this state by the devil who is now a constant inescapable presence in all sorts of shapes and forms. He was formerly 'a servingman proud in heart and mind', a lustful, lying, vain, well-to-do villain. His present destitution is his punishment for the crime and vanities of his previous life; here he is, in the hovel on the heath in the storm, convinced he is pursued and hunted by the foul fiend, and handing out the gratuitous advice of a born-again Christian. 'Keep thy foot out of brothels, thy hand out of plackets.' The fascinated Lear seizes on this philosopher and asks him the cause of thunder. Then, getting no answer, 'What is your study?' he says. 'How to prevent the fiend, and to kill vermin,' is the reply. Tom volunteers that 'the Prince of Darkness is a gentleman'. He is indeed, like Claudius in *Hamlet* or Cornwall in this play, or (to take Poor Tom's example) like Nero, who was 'an angler in the lake of darkness' and killed his mother. 'Child Rowland to the dark tower came'—the dark tower of this world where the prince of darkness keeps his court. Edgar already sees himself in his role as the knight in armour who in the final scene challenges and defeats that prince of darkness and illegitimate gentleman, his half-brother Edmund. When the mad Lear arraigns his daughters, with Poor Tom as his 'most learned justicer', Lear can see the 'she-foxes' where the Fool can see only a joint-stool. But Poor Tom knows who is standing there: it's the Prince of Darkness, the foul fiend: 'Look where he stands and glares!' So to Lear's great question, 'Let them anatomize Regan . . . Is there any cause in nature that makes these hard hearts?', the unspoken answer must be, no, it is the foul fiend. In the very next scene (III. vii) is the culmination of the reign of evil, the blinding of Gloucester by Cornwall, set on and assisted by Regan.

Edgar's laborious missionary efforts have extraordinary success. His blinded father he saves from suicide and despair—convinced that it was a fiend who had led him to the cliff from which he proposed to leap. Both Lear and Edmund accept some of his philosophy (see p. 40). Poor Tom provides a wild view of the world as a place of demonic possession, in which disappropriated man turns at last to fight the prince of darkness for his own soul. Shakespeare culled the names of the spirits that terrify Poor Tom—Smulkin, Frateretto, Hoppedance—from the derisory account which Bishop Harsnett gave of exorcisms in his *Declaration of Egregious Popish Impostures* (1603). But in *King Lear* they are not there for us to deride. They provide a 'local habitation and a name' for the inexplicable evil which courses through the tragedies. The mad scenes in *King Lear* are alive with cryptic intimations and messages suggesting more wisdom than ever came the way of the sane. The idea that the evil in man is too strong to be self-created is given us in Macbeth's witches, in Iago, and in Poor Tom's fiends. Like the emissaries from heaven on Shakespeare's stage, the messengers from hell appear in unexpected ways and sometimes in rather crude shapes. Their presence is always shadowy and their influence indefinable.

The progress of King Lear from imperious confidence and blind anger in the first scene, through the complex emotions of guilt, self-pity, shock, and fury in the succeeding scenes, to the raging madness of the storm and the crafty lunacy of the aftermath, is one of the great wonders of artistic creation. The story is conceived entirely in terms of theatrical presentation, especially the eerie symphony of the alienated intelligences and personalities on the heath. But the capacities and resources of the theatre have always been and always will be unequal to the task of bringing those storm scenes to their full life. By contrast, the waking of Lear into reunion with Cordelia is something of which only the stage can show us the full meaning and effect, and the stage very rarely lets us down.

As he comes 'out o' th' grave', scarcely awake, Lear has a vision, as Othello did of Desdemona and himself, of Cordelia as a 'soul in bliss' and himself as a damned soul upon a 'wheel of fire', forced eternally to know his own deed. *Othello* ended there. Lear lives, to recognize that Cordelia too is alive.

> Do not laugh at me,
> For as I am a man, I think this lady
> To be my child Cordelia.
> CORDELIA. And so I am, I am.
>
> (IV. vii. 67–9)

He is humble and contrite: 'Pray you now, forget and forgive; I am old and foolish.' After the reunion there is the battle, in which the old man and his daughter are defeated, and they are led away as prisoners. In a strangely ecstatic state for a defeated king, Lear wants to hasten to confinement.

> CORDELIA. Shall we not see these daughters, and these sisters?
> LEAR. No, no, no, no. Come let's away to prison.
> We two alone will sing like birds i' th' cage.
> When thou dost ask me blessing, I'll kneel down
> And ask of thee forgiveness. So we'll live,
> And pray, and sing, and tell old tales, and laugh
> At gilded butterflies; and hear poor rogues
> Talk of court news and we'll talk with them too,
> Who loses and who wins, who's in, who's out;
> And take upon's the mystery of things
> As if we were God's spies. And we'll wear out,
> In a walled prison, packs and sects of great ones,
> That ebb and flow by th' moon.
> EDMUND.   Take them away.
> LEAR. Upon such sacrifices my Cordelia,
> The gods themselves throw incense. Have I caught thee?
> He that parts us shall bring a brand from heaven,
> And fire us hence like foxes.
>
> (v. iii. 7–23)

Everything spoken here in this major moment in Shakespearian tragedy is of the greatest importance. It is the ultimate expression of the vision which so many have glimpsed, of a human relationship bathed in a light that never was on sea or land, the consecration and the poet's dream. Based on the mutual forgiveness celebrated in the later sonnets to the young man, it comes to existence in adversity, in the active disfavour and hostility of society, and it rises supremely above both the adversity and those who are responsible for it. This relationship within the walls of a prison, founded on the need of each person for the other, is an avenue to a transcendent knowledge. The 'mystery' of things means their secret significance. Cordelia and Lear (to Lear's mind) will be in the service of heaven, aliens and strangers among mankind, knowing the vanity and absurdity of what men and women spend their lives trying to achieve. This offering of themselves to each other in the spiritual liberation of a place of deprivation and confinement is a 'sacrifice' pleasing to the gods.

Like Hamlet's revelation on shipboard that he was receiving divine guidance, Lear's revelation is personal to him and not something that the play 'confirms'. The frailty of the vision lies in 'He that parts us shall bring a brand from heaven'. It is the villainy of Edmund that parts them. Lear's belief that by being together they could endure suffering is not put to the test, for Cordelia is brutally seized and hanged. The rejection of Lear's faith that only heaven would part them is followed by the rejection of Albany's prayer, 'The gods defend her!', just before Lear's final entry with Cordelia dead in his arms. The ending of *Lear* like the ending of *Hamlet* is utterly impassive as regards what lies beyond the grave.

> What do we know but that we face
> One another in this place?*

Lear knows she will come no more—'never, never, never, never, never'. He dies knowing that, calling the others to witness in the final bitterness of his cry, 'Look there!' As in all the love-tragedies, there has been the achievement of a relationship which like a sudden flame momentarily illuminates undreamt-of regions of experience even as it is extinguished.

*Yeats, 'The Man and the Echo'.

Conclusion: the tragedies in their time

On the whole, Shakespearian tragedy is not concerned with the
slow unfolding of the secrets of past misdeeds and their ineluctable burden as are *Oedipus Rex*, *Ghosts*, and many other
tragedies. *Hamlet* is a major exception, as Claudius' closely
concealed crime is made known. The burden of the past is heavy
in *Troilus and Cressida*. But in general Shakespearian tragedy is
about meeting the future, not the past. It looks back to a happier
and richer past and is in mourning for it, representing it as
something colourful, with power to inspire loyalty and affection
even if it was full of faults. The past no longer works, but what
replaces it arouses no enthusiasm whatever. Antony and Lear are
men of the past; Coriolanus and Hamlet are young men attached
to the values of the past. 'Modern' men are often villains, like
Claudius or Edmund, or at best men without colour like Octavius
Caesar. In the passing of the individual's life we are given the
strong undertone of the movement of history, unavoidable and
always regrettable. In Shakespeare's century, momentous change
was everywhere, in religion, in social organization, in politics,
international relations, economic structure, in man's knowledge
about the world and in his views about the world. Shakespearian
tragedy is the creature of a rapidly changing world and the doubt
and questioning which rapid change breeds. Perhaps the changes
in religion embrace the other changes. The Reformation is not
only a fundamental shift in doctrine; it involves a shift in
allegiances, in one's recognition of one's identity, one's place in
the universe, and indeed in the meaning of one's entire activities.
In speaking of Shakespeare's tragedies I have stressed their
extraterrestrial concern, their location of the cruelty and of the
aspirations of man in a dimension wider than that of mortal life, a
dimension of salvation and of damnation, of the divine and the
satanic. Yet most certainly, though inevitably steeped in Christian thought and feeling, the tragedies are not Christian, doctri-
nally speaking. They are plays written when the weakening of
traditional Christianity has generated an intense and fearful
inquisitiveness. Lear in the storm is newly aware of the 'dreadful
summoners' in the skies showing him truths he had never guessed
at in the somnolence of his security. The tragedies are full of
religious anxiety and have little religious confidence. The big

questions are always those on which depend all hope and despair: what we are put on earth *for*, why there is cruelty and suffering, and what if anything is directing the course of events. Shakespearian tragedy encourages hope as it denies it, encourages despair as it denies it. It fights to maintain a transcendent context for the squabblings and striving of man, yet it cannot clearly name or locate that context. Since tragedy is tragedy, failure is more pronounced than success, and yet failure always has a double hue, with failure in the world sometimes having the lustre of success by the half-understood values of a less identifiable world.

The tragedies are not lessons in conduct. Rather than teach us what to do and what to avoid, they show us how in extreme situations the utmost rectitude or probity can be led astray, nobility weakened, determination dissolved, dignity lost. In tragedy no one is unassailable. It's not only that unsuspected weaknesses suddenly come to the fore, but that the very merits and strengths of the heroes contribute to undermining them. It is common in an anti-heroic period of history like ours to dwell on the imperfections of Shakespeare's tragic heroes—and this book doesn't seek to sentimentalize them—but it is as well not to feel superior to them, as in our more smug moments we may feel inclined to. A tragedy with an audience of pharisees is a contradiction in terms. The whole energy of Shakespearian tragedy is directed towards an experience in which our confidence in ourselves, our opinions and beliefs is (at least) shaken. Positiveness is not encouraged. The confidence of scepticism is undermined equally with the confidence of faith as these plays about disaster awaken in us

> a dim and undetermined sense
> Of unknown modes being . . .
>
> . . . an obscure sense
> Of possible sublimity.*

.

*Wordsworth, *The Prelude* (1805), I. 419–20; II. 336–7.

Tragicomedy

Thou dost make possible things not so held,
Communicat'st with dreams—how can this be?
With what's unreal thou coactive art,
And fellow'st nothing.

(*Winter's Tale*, I. ii. 139–42)

Leontes' words, part of his cryptic and disordered apostrophe to 'affection', make an appropriate epigraph for Shakespearian tragicomedy, especially as they come from a play in which the element of wonder is so strongly stressed in the conclusion. The Second Gentleman says, 'Such a deal of wonder is broken out within this hour that ballad-makers cannot be able to express it.'

Shakespeare's early comedies, as we saw, had little use for verisimilitude, but the improbabilities in the tragicomedies seem much more striking because they occur in plays which contain serious and extended treatment of grave moral problems. As 'tragicomedy' is not a familiar category in the taxonomy of Shakespeare's works, we had better name the plays: *All's Well That Ends Well, Measure for Measure, Pericles Prince of Tyre, Cymbeline, The Winter's Tale, The Tempest, The Two Noble Kinsmen*. The term 'problem comedies' has had too long an innings with reference to *All's Well* and *Measure for Measure*. It is time they were put in better company, and the true affinity of these middle comedies is with their successors, Shakespeare's last plays, the romances. That the romances (*Pericles, Cymbeline, Winter's Tale, The Tempest*) form a special group is true enough. Coming as they do after years in which Shakespeare had been writing some of the profoundest tragedies the world has seen, these plays with their fanciful plots and relaxed structure have a great deal in common and seem to constitute a particular endeavour. But to treat them as a self-contained and exclusive group is to make light of the dissimilarities between them, and their links with earlier plays. Romance is a form of narrative not easy to define; in the Renaissance we think of it as the conscious literary heir of Hellenistic and medieval romance, as we see it in

Ariosto's *Orlando Furioso*, Sidney's *Arcadia*, Spenser's *Faerie Queene*, an episodic adventure story of great complexity, involving quests, love, misfortunes, fights, marvels, villains, shepherds, kings, knights, gods, twins, shipwrecks, and what have you. *Pericles Prince of Tyre* seems to be a definite attempt by Shakespeare to accommodate a romance-style narrative to the seemingly antithetical requirements of drama. But romance features have been an indispensable element of Shakespearian comedy from the very beginning. *The Comedy of Errors* actually uses the same Hellenistic romance as *Pericles*, the story of Apollonius of Tyre. *Cymbeline* is a romance only in that it contains the element of a king's stolen sons growing up among the mountains. *The Winter's Tale* has strong links with *As You Like It* in its pastoral escape from the evils of Court and a triumphant return. *The Tempest* is different from every other play—though it seems to gather up threads from them all. If it is a romance in that it contains marvels and the supernatural, then *A Midsummer Night's Dream* is also a romance; and as for its shipwreck, they are common in Shakespeare. Romance is a useful term in Shakespeare criticism, but it is not confined to the last comedies and it does not explain them. It is better to take the late 'romances' as a sub-group of particular importance within the wider category of tragicomedy.

Giambattista Guarini, author of the influential *Il Pastor Fido* (published 1590), wrote that 'he who makes a tragicomedy does not intend to compose separately a tragedy or a comedy, but from the two composes a third thing that will be perfect of its kind'. From tragedy, he said, tragicomedy takes 'the danger but not the death'. In Shakespearian tragicomedy, a tragic crisis develops but it is dissolved, and the consequences evaded, by extraordinary interventions which often seem to belong to another level or kind of drama. *The Winter's Tale* and *Measure for Measure* provide the ideal forms of this tragicomedy. The first three acts of *The Winter's Tale* give us the onset and growth of Leontes' paranoid jealousy until in its hideous course it has destroyed his queen and two children. Then in the third scene of the third act we move into true romance geography on the seacoast of Bohemia, with a shipwreck, a bear, and an abandoned babe found by shepherds. The enigmatic but reassuring figure of Time appears to take us over an interval of years to the rustic happiness of Perdita's love for Florizel and the eventual 'miracle' of the restoration of Hermione. *Measure for Measure* develops over just the same portion of the play the unique conflict of Angelo and Isabella concerning the life of Claudio, culminating in Angelo's offer to save the brother's life if the sister will submit to him sexually. The sister refuses—but then the disguised Duke steps in to initiate the remarkable chain of stratagems which lead to the reasonably happy ending. In *All's Well*, Helena's determined love wins its prize only to encounter hatred and repudiation. It is she and no outsider who moves into a priestly role and organizes the (again) moderately happy ending. In *Cymbeline*, we have once more a chaste wife calumniated and vilified by an irrationally jealous husband. His plan to kill her miscarries, and the play moves into an extreme intricacy of plot in the wildness of Wales to emerge in the unprecedented denouement of the last act. Not all these mini-tragedies have the stamp of the tragic commitment discussed in the last chapter, though both *Measure for Measure* and *All's Well* do. In other tragicomedies the tragic crisis takes different forms. The whole of *The Tempest* is devoted to miraculous solution, the crisis being related in the first act.

The earlier tragicomedies

All's Well That Ends Well

The tragicomedies provide some brilliant portraits of women, Hermione, Imogen, Perdita among them, and perhaps the two most interesting ones are the heroines of the two earlier plays, Helena and Isabella. The love of Helena, the humble doctor's daughter, for the aristocratic Bertram is of a kind and intensity that is new in the plays and perhaps unique. She burns with longing, though she knows that

> 'Twere all one
> That I should love a bright particular star
> And think to wed it, he is so above me.
>
> (I. i. 85–7)

She broods on his physical appearance with a kind of desperation: 'His arched brows, his hawking eye, his curls.' What she describes as 'the ambition in my love', 'my idolatrous fancy', will not be curbed. In her speech at the end of the first scene, she asserts almost like Edmund in *Lear* that man is master of his fate. Our imaginations are not given us in order to tantalize and frustrate us, but to impel us forward to realize what they conceive.

> Our remedies oft in ourselves do lie
> Which we ascribe to heaven. The fated sky
> Gives us free scope; only doth backward pull
> Our slow designs when we ourselves are dull.
> What power is it which mounts my love so high,
> That makes me see, and cannot feed mine eye?
>
> (I. i. 216–21)

So she commits herself to follow Bertram to the court of the ailing king, with the mission of curing the king of his mysterious disease. The interview in which she forces the king to try the efficacy of her healing powers is extraordinary. In her incantatory rhymed couplets she *now* presents herself as the humble agent of heavenly providence. Her womanly passion for Bertram and her priestly belief in her curative skill are in curious partnership. She is in a strange exalted state and she will *not* be sent away. In curing the king lies the only possibility of gaining Bertram—a prize for a cure. If she succeeds, 'what do you promise me?' Whatever she demands, the king says.

> Then shalt thou give me with thy kingly hand
> What husband in thy power I will command.
>
> (II. i. 193–4)

How Macbeth-like is this staking of everything on a single act which is magically to usher in a dreamed-of future! To heal a king not murder a king—but the deed is just as futile. Helen is appalled when, having wonderfully cured the king, she fails with Bertram. She has a husband in name only and has won the emptiest of rewards, having neither his love nor his company. What sympathy we have for Bertram, trapped by this extraordinary pact between Helena and the king, is much lessened by his arrogance and contempt for her. But this behaviour increases our amazement at Helena. So much effort for this shallowest of men?

'Let the rest go!' she beseeches the king, meaning the marriage bargain. But there's no release for her either. In wretchedness she leaves France so that her husband will be free to return, for he has said 'Till I have no wife, I have nothing in France', and vowed not to acknowledge her till she gets the ring from his finger and bears his child. So she undertakes a pilgrimage, to get out of his way and to expiate her 'ambitious love'. Thus ends the tragic movement, as usual in the middle of Act III. It is important that we accept Helen's pilgrimage as a truth. For many people accept the the implication of Rowe's tendentious stage-direction in Act III, Scene v: 'Enter Helen disguised like a pilgrim.' They see Helena pursuing Bertram and the pilgrimage as a pretext. It is true that, each trying to get out of the other's way, they both turn up in Florence, and that it is curious for Helena to go to St James of Compostella by way of Florence—but all the other pilgrims are taking that route (III. v. 94–6). Having come across Bertram disgracefully attempting to seduce Diana, she does indeed pursue him, as she pursued the king, relentlessly saving him. She defrauds him of Diana and makes him her husband in full by means of the 'bed-trick', which is central to this play as it is to *Measure for Measure*. Bertram returns to France thinking Helena is dead, quite unaware that she has slept with him and conceived his child. He tries to lie his way out of the final confrontation but is thoroughly exposed, and has to ask pardon and accept Helena.

Shakespeare cannot have been entirely satisfied with the way *All's Well* turned out. The idea is brilliant, but the play is padded out with some dreary material. It is the ending, however, that is the real trouble. Helena at the beginning of the play is an extraordinarily interesting person; at the end she has become a kind of smothering Amazon with the feeble male cowering at her feet. Bertram is a consistently good portrayal of an unlikeable young man. But as such he's not worth her trouble, and likeable or not she should not have trapped him, twice. By contrast, the ending of *Measure for Measure* (a very great play) is exuberant in its openness as *All's Well* is simply depressing.

Measure for Measure

However profound and far-reaching the major tragedies may be in their philosophical implications, there is no play of Shakespeare's which so fully and explicitly argues about problems of belief and conduct as *Measure for Measure* does. The issues range widely; but the two main heads are sexuality and justice. The debates are carried on not by formal argument but in conflicts which are often struggles for survival. Even Pompey's irrepressible condoning of human frailty is in the context of saving his own skin. Claudio's Hamlet-like broodings, first over the sexual drive and later over the nature of the afterlife, are forced from him by the extreme peril he is in. The Duke's experiment in law-enforcement has started it all off; the debate which he has had with himself on the relative merits of firmness and severity on the one hand and tolerance and leniency on the other (as regards sexual permissiveness) is continued as a matter of life or death for his subjects. Angelo's belief in the absoluteness of law, unaffected by the moral condition of those who administer it, is strengthened by his confidence in his own virtue; and it crumbles in his confrontation with Isabella, not because of her wonderful invocation of Christ's teaching and sacrifice, but because of a sudden access of lust for her, which gives her words a dreadful meaning:

> Go to your bosom,
> Knock there, and ask your heart what it doth know
> That's like my brother's fault.
>
> (II. ii. 136–8)

Angelo's shock at the collapse of his prized impregnability swiftly transforms itself into the cunning of his bargain. She who has dedicated herself to the asceticism of a nun's life sees herself in the position of either denying God or putting an end to her brother's life. This 'debate' on the value of her chastity is at the very centre of the play; but it is suspended when, at the moment of Isabella's almost hysterical refusal of Claudio's plea to let him live, the duke-friar steps forward to take charge of the play. No doubt it is callous to feel cheated by the intervention which saves Isabella from the consequences of her decision, yet many people are so caught up by the intensity of the crisis as it has developed that they don't welcome the change in theatrical atmosphere as the duke produces from nowhere Mariana, whose engagement with Angelo, we now learn, he had improperly broken off. Adding this meanness to Angelo considerably lessens his standing. Isabella is also lessened by being made to agree without question to the bed-trick by which Mariana performs the same act that Isabella had disapproved of in Juliet. The duke is lessened by his sweating labours and by his rationalization of his deceiving of Isabella (IV.

iii. 107–10). Only Barnadine the condemned prisoner keeps his dignity. This is the price we pay for tragicomedy. The ending itself is superb, but the means to the end ask too much of our loyalty. Angelo broken and contrite; Mariana's fierce protectiveness towards him; Isabella pleading he should be forgiven—none of this needs apology. The duke tests Isabella as he tested Angelo and finds in *her* no chasm between words and deeds. He is able to produce Claudio still alive and pardon all except Lucio. He also offers Isabella marriage. As there is no sign in the text to indicate whether Isabella accepts or not, it seems important that the actress playing Isabella should herself decide how to play the final moment of the play. She should feel that the final gesture truly emanates from the person she has been portraying. Clearly the duke has too much evidence of the perils of asceticism to wish Isabella or himself to continue celibate. It is, however, asking a lot of Isabella and an actress that she should suddenly and silently abandon that dedication of herself which has brought about the play's crisis. Better if she at least thought about it; but that perhaps is the hardest task for the actress—to indicate neither assent nor refusal.

Whatever happens in the duke's personal life, the state of Vienna is no better for all that has happened, except for the total disqualification of Angelo and all he stood for. It is not just that Angelo's fall discredits the idea of repression and impersonal law. Isabella's magnificent invective against the presumption of men in the exercise of power (see pp. 47–8) undermines every principle of government. The negativeness of repression is replaced in the play with the enlarging power of forgiveness. No one can run a city on forgiveness. Vincentio's problems with his unruly citizens have defied one attempted solution and remain with him, made worse indeed by Isabella's denunciation of 'man, proud man' which would only have confirmed what we would feel to be an indwelling scepticism of his own about the exercise of authority.

The bed-trick

The task of bringing deep moral crises to a fortunate conclusion does not always go smoothly in the two tragicomedies of Shakespeare's middle years. What was he trying to achieve? The bed-trick is the most awkward device, yet Shakespeare used it twice as the centre-point of his play, the means by which a man's wickedness is neutralized and an evil intention circumvented. An illicit sexual act is at the heart of each play; its transformation by the substitution of another partner is the beginning of what is intended to be a process of rescue and salvation. Surely the very unlikelihood of the bed-trick is a key to its importance in these plays? For all the seriousness of their moral crises, these two plays draw heavily on folk-tale elements, which boast unlikelihood as their stock-in-trade. Shakespeare positively calls attention to the unreality of his solutions. The route towards the fortunate outcome in both these plays is over a bridge of unconcealed make-believe, namely the bed-trick, by which 'wicked meaning' becomes 'lawful deed' (*All's Well*, III. vii. 45). There is a strong religious atmosphere in both *All's Well* and *Measure for Measure*. The latter is more steeped in Christian sentiment than any other play of Shakespeare's, and many attempts have been made to see its rescue-story as an allegory of divine protection and providence. There is no doubt about the religious aura attending both Helena and the duke and the sense of blessedness about the fortunate outcome. So here is a perplexing blend of fanciful make-believe and supernatural mystery. As the same blend is to be found in the final plays, we should turn to them for further enlightenment.

The last plays

Pericles Prince of Tyre

Pericles Prince of Tyre was not included in the 1623 Folio and the text published in 1608, which is the only one we have, hardly contains a single line that can be confidently greeted as pure Shakespeare. It is an unauthorized text, a 'bad quarto' which was never superseded. The last three acts are much more suggestive of a Shakespearian original than the painfully wooden first two acts. It is likely, however, that it is the different abilities of two people putting the unauthorized text together which is responsible for the marked difference between the two halves of the play, and that *Pericles*, like *The Two Noble Kinsmen*, was the work of Shakespeare and a collaborator alternating irregularly throughout the play. We lose a great deal because of the absence of the proper text of *Pericles*, because it seems to have the key to much that is going on in the final plays.

Like *Henry V*, *Pericles* uses a presenter. He is the medieval poet John Gower (whose poem is one of the play's sources). Gower insists from the start that what we are going to see is an old tale. He strikes a note of Keatsian medievalism in talking of the pleasure it has brought to 'lords and ladies' 'on ember-eves and holy-ales'. He is a powerful presence, conducting us with his quaint couplets and gnomic sentences through the strange series of adventures which constitute the play. All this exasperated Ben Jonson, who called *Pericles* 'a mouldy tale'—therein at least recognizing what it fundamentally is, a tale. The story is Gower's; it is essentially narrative. He as chorus relates some parts and chooses those parts which are to be vivified on stage:

> And what ensues in this fell storm
> Shall for itself itself perform.
> I nill relate; action may
> Conveniently the rest convey.
>
> (Chorus to Act III)

'Action' means acting. So the power of performance on stage makes real selected parts of what is explicitly offered as a romantic old tale.

Pericles journeys from one Mediterranean port to another, fleeing a tyrant, enduring shipwreck, winning a tournament, finding a bride. In the very Shakespearian scene of the storm at sea, Thaisa dies giving birth to a daughter and is buried at sea—

> And humming water must o'erwhelm thy corse,
> Lying with simple shells.
>
> (III. i. 63–4)

But a scene of mysterious solemnity follows when the priestly Cerimon finding the body washed ashore discovers Thaisa is not dead and restores her to life. The gap in time which now follows, allowing us next to see the daughter Marina grown to young womanhood, is of course repeated in *The Winter's Tale*, and it is interesting that this was a marked feature in the pre-Shakespearian romantic drama, as we know from Sidney's irritation with it in the *Apology for Poetry*: 'Two young princes fall in love. After many traverses, she is got with child, delivered of a fair boy; he is lost, groweth a man, falls in love, and is ready to get another child, and all this in two hours' space. . . .'

From the perils of the brothel (whose murky humour is Shakespearian indeed) Marina escapes by force of shining innocence, and is brought to a ship where lies a grief-stricken prince, her own father. In spite of the halting verse, the recognition scene vies with that in *Lear*.

> O come hither,
> Thou that beget'st him that did thee beget,
> Thou that wast born at sea, buried at Tarsus,
> And found at sea again.
>
> (v. i. 194–7)

These extraordinary lines, using for the *redintegratio* of father and daughter the words of the Christian paradox whereby Mary is greeted as the mother of the son who as God the Father created her, and emphasizing the symbolism of the sea, resound throughout both *The Winter's Tale* and *The Tempest*. The goddess Diana appears in a vision directing Pericles to Ephesus where Thaisa is discovered still living.

In spite of the tattered dress of its inferior language, *Pericles* holds the secret of Shakespearian tragicomedy. It always amused Shakespeare in the earlier comedies to call attention to the fictionality of his scenes. This constant illusion-breaking was on the one level good-humoured banter, a conspiratorial wink at the audience, agreeing with them that it's all only a joke. But as we have seen, in *A Midsummer Night's Dream* something much more serious is hinted at. 'The best in this kind are but shadows,' says Theseus. The best that drama has to offer differs from *Pyramus and Thisbe* only in degree. Bringing moonlight into a chamber is always an artistic contrivance. Yet, as Theseus draws all art within the definition of shadow-play and airy nothing, so the 'concentric circles' of the play begin to assert the shadowiness of human life itself: the play of Pyramus and Thisbe is watched by the confident Theseus and his courtiers, who are unaware that *they* are being watched by Oberon and Titania, who control their lives. Oberon is the creature of Shakespeare and is being watched by the audience in the theatre—and WHO is watching them? Our sense of reality may be an illusion.

> Life's but a walking shadow, a poor player
> That struts and frets his hour upon the stage,
> And then is heard no more ...

In the tragicomedies of his last years of writing for the stage Shakespeare returned to his earlier insistence that all he was offering was simply make-believe, but he is referring now to a more obviously serious drama. He exploits his whole mastery of language and the dramatist's art to obtain credence for scenes of terror and of beauty; and he persistently withdraws that credence from them. In *Pericles* we can only half-perceive the effect, because of the ruined language. But it is crystal-clear in *The Winter's Tale*.

The Winter's Tale

There is no presenter to introduce *The Winter's Tale* and explain the insidious growth of Leontes' jealousy. The jealousy is suddenly there, acted out before us in all its force, a demented, contorted vision of things that ceases as suddenly as it began. At the beginning of Act IV, however, it is made clear to us that *The Winter's Tale*—an ambiguous title meaning both a tale of darkness and an old wives' tale—is the offering of a crafty presenter not unlike Gower, dressed up as Father Time. Perhaps he is a forgiving recreation of Robert Greene, whose romance *Pandosto. The Triumph of Time* Shakespeare used for the play as he had used Gower's poem for *Pericles*. This figure now takes upon him 'in the name of Time' to use his wings and do what Time can never do—jump over sixteen years, to show us Perdita alive and in love with the son of Polixenes. All the narrative-links in *The Winter's Tale* emphasize the insubstantiality and indeed the absurdity of the story. The Clown makes a comic business of his gruesome tale of the preposterous coincidence of the bear and the shipwreck, by which all witnesses to the abandonment of Perdita are destroyed at a stroke. This whole contrivance is Shakespeare's addition to Greene's story. The passage from the terror of the Leontes/Hermione story to the beauty of the Perdita/Florizel story is via a signposted bridge of make-believe.

The scene of the sheep-shearing feast contains the renowned argument between Perdita and Polixenes on art and nature, in which she says she won't grow 'gillyvors' because they need artificial assistance. Polixenes patiently explains that all art derives from and depends on nature, and improves it; but Perdita will have none of it. Shakespeare has put this child of 'great creating nature' in a contradictory position. She is embarrassed at wearing clothes not her own, 'most goddess-like pranked up' as Flora, goddess of spring. The season of this feast is with 'the year growing ancient, / Not yet on summer's death, nor on the birth / Of trembling winter'. Yet Perdita, if she refuses to create gillyvors by grafting, has the power (when wearing a costume which she fears 'does change my disposition') to bring into being an entire springtime of flowers:

> daffodils
> That come before the swallow dares, and take
> The winds of March with beauty; violets, dim,
> But sweeter than the lids of Juno's eyes
> Or Cytherea's breath . . .
>
> (IV. iv. 118–22)

In spite of herself Perdita demonstrates the power of art to create life.

> Each your doing,
> So singular in each particular,
> Crowns what you are doing in the present deeds,
> That all your acts are queens.
>
> (IV. iv. 143–6)

Even if the acts are 'acts' in the theatrical sense.

In describing in the final act the reunion of Perdita with her contrite and penitent father Leontes, much play is made of the idea that *narrative* cannot grapple or cope with such extraordinary events: 'such a deal of wonder is broken out within this hour, that ballad-makers cannot be able to express it'; 'so like an old tale that the verity of it is in strong suspicion'; 'I never heard of such another encounter, which lames report to follow it, and undoes description to do it'; 'like an old tale, still, which will have matter to rehearse though credit be asleep and not an ear open'. Shakespeare had already given to an incredible reunion of father and daughter the truth and reality of enactment, in *Pericles*; in *The Winter's Tale* the reunion is passed by, too marvellous for mere words, in order to concentrate on the reunion of Leontes and Hermione. The statue-scene is no miracle, though it seems so to Leontes, and must have seemed so to the original audience who if they knew Greene's story would assume that the queen had indeed died—an assumption that Shakespeare drops no hint to discredit, keeping a major turn of the plot a secret from his audience for the first time in his career. Paulina has kept Hermione in concealment for sixteen years. But it is as a statue that Leontes and the audience see her, a statue that turns into a wife long thought to be dead. Paulina says:

> That she is living,
> Were it but told you, should be hooted at
> Like an old tale, but it appears she lives.

> (v. iii. 115–17)

Here the contrast between the incident *narrated* and the incident *enacted* is strikingly presented. 'It *appears* she lives.' Seeing is believing. The characters, overcome with emotion, are hurried off-stage. Hermione begins to explain, but Paulina is quick to quieten her: 'There's time enough for that!' Leontes promises they will all explain what has been happening. 'Hastily lead away!' Even during Shakespeare's great triumph in this statue-scene, he insists on hinting at explanations and narrations which would surely destroy everything if they were permitted—the absurdity, or the immorality, of Hermione's sixteen-year deception of her husband.

As Leontes gazes at the 'statue', he thinks he sees life in the eye—but, he reflects, that is the way 'we are mocked with art'. 'Mocked' does not here mean laughed at derisively, but simply deceived. We mistake the copy for the real thing. It turns out he is deceived not by art but by Paulina's contrivance: the eye is truly alive. But we in the audience accepting that this is really Hermione are being mocked with art because of course Hermione is a boy-actor pretending to be Hermione acting as a statue. In the play, Shakespeare is constantly telling us what we already know perfectly well, that we are in a theatre and that the play is only a play. His desire to mock us with art is not in the least derisive. He knows we know we are in a theatre. But he knows the power of the theatre—at least his own power in the theatre. In *The Winter's Tale* he realizes for us a sequence of extremely vivid and powerful scenes—Leontes' jealousy, the sheep-shearing feast, the statue-scene—but so introduces and links them that, even as he makes them substantial, he highlights their fragility and artificiality. We can assent to the 'truth to life' of these scenes with all the eagerness felt by generations of audiences, but, if in a moment of scepticism we say it's all made up or life is not like that, Shakespeare will be the first to agree. They are dramatic images which he has made, and they are put forward as nothing more than that. Shakespeare has two analogues for the dramatist in the last plays: the great magician Prospero and the ingenious trickster Autolycus.

The Tempest

The Tempest, proudly placed first by Heminges and Condell in their collection of their dead colleague's works, bears every sign of being considered a rather special play and, although *Henry VIII* and *The Two Noble Kinsmen* come later, Shakespeare may well have meant it to be his farewell to the theatre. The sprawling construction of *Pericles, The Winter's Tale, Cymbeline* gives way to a strict obedience to the unities of time and place. The entire play is devoted to the solution of the tragic crisis, the expulsion of Prospero from his dukedom by his brother Antonio, which is tucked away into Prospero's bitter account of it to Miranda.

The engineering of the fortunate outcome is not by means of bed-tricks or bears or concealed wives but by magic: an improbability openly proclaimed. Prospero hauls his enemies back into his power by raising a storm and wrecking, or seeming to wreck, their ship. Absorption in study lost him his dukedom in the first place; now it is the sedulous use of those books (that Gonzalo mercifully placed in the boat) which has given him command over the spirits, who now do his bidding and place Antonio and the King of Naples as his prisoners on the island. Opinions differ on what revenge if any Prospero had it first in mind to exact. There are those who think that it is only Ariel's pity for the victims that turns him from retaliation to forgiveness—'The rarer action is / In virtue than in vengeance' (v. i. 27–8). But all along Prospero's main concern is not with the past but with the future of Milan and Naples, for he brings his daughter and Alonso's son together with one thing in mind: the hope that they may fall in love, marry, and so unite the two territories. There is a great deal in the play about the past, present, and future of Milan and Naples. Questions of territory, of possession, of sovereignty, abound in this very political play. In usurping his brother in Milan, Antonio brought the independence of the dukedom to an end in exchange for Alonso's aid; this dukedom 'yet unbowed' was reduced to 'most ignoble stooping' and became a tributary of Naples (I. ii. 111–16). Prospero wants his dukedom back; but he wants to end this new servitude to Naples not by annexing Naples nor by reverting to the status quo; he looks for the union of the territories in the freely chosen marriage of the two heirs. It is for this reason that he is such an anxious onlooker at the meeting of Ferdinand and Miranda:

> It goes on I see
> As my soul prompts it. Spirit, fine spirit, I'll free thee
> Within two days for this.
>
> (I. ii. 420–2)

> Fair encounter
> Of two most rare affections. Heavens rain grace
> On that which breeds between 'em!
>
> (III. i. 74–6)

This play not only resolves a preceding tragic crisis, it re-enacts it, twice. This little island seems to provide a controlled experiment in the operations of human nature; greed and violence emerge as surely as love between the sexes. Antonio incites Sebastian to repeat his own act of usurpation by murdering Alonso; Caliban persuades Stephano and Trinculo to murder Prospero and take over the island. Caliban was of course in sole possession of the island before Prospero came, though his rights in it are recent enough with his mother coming there from Algiers. Now with his drunken singing of 'Freedom, high-day, high-day, freedom!' he puts himself into a new servitude to Stephano.

The deformed and misbegotten Caliban is (after Macbeth and Shylock) Shakespeare's most sympathetic exploration of the heart of evil. As with them, though, to understand everything is not to pardon everything. The story of initial mutual trust and affection, of Prospero teaching Caliban, followed by a flare-up, mutual recrimination, harshness, and slavery, has a sickening resemblance to the pattern of the worsening relations between the

English colonizers and the Virginian Indians in Shakespeare's own time. But Caliban is not in the play to 'stand for' colonized Indians. In so far as he is a 'savage', although it is clear he is not Montaigne's noble savage, there is more poetry in him and less unmotivated violence than in the civilized Sebastian and Antonio, and his readiness to rape is not half so dastardly as the preparation of the queen's son Cloten to rape Imogen in *Cymbeline*. He is natural man, instinctively poetic and instinctively brutal, longing for freedom and seeking it in the wrong quarter.

Prospero is a theatre-person. He puts on shows. The first of these, in Act III, Scene iii, is a performance by Ariel and his fellow-spirits to threaten and terrify the visitors. Ariel enters like a harpy and thunders out a magnificent denunciation.

> You are three men of sin, whom Destiny
> That hath to instrument this lower world
> And what is in it, the never-surfeited sea
> Hath caused to belch up you, and on this island . . .
>
> You fools, I and my fellows
> Are minister of fate . . .
>
> You three
> From Milan did supplant good Prospero,
> Exposed unto the sea, which hath requit it,
> Him and his innocent child, for which foul deed
> The powers delaying not forgetting have
> Incensed the seas and shores, yea, all the creatures,
> Against your peace.
>
> (III. iii. 53–6, 60–1, 69–75)

All this is the script which Prospero has written for Ariel. He is delighted with its effectiveness.

> Bravely the figure of this harpy hast thou
> Performed, my Ariel; a grace it had, devouring.
> Of my instruction hast thou nothing bated
> In what thou hadst to say.
>
> (III. iii. 83–6)

Powerful though Prospero's art is, he is a human being. This confrontation of his enemies with the 'ministers of fate', arresting them and charging them in the name of the sempiternal powers, is a human view of what Providence ought to be doing. It is he and not God who 'incensed the seas and shores'. This fabricated 'theophany', or manifestation of the deity, needs to be compared with other theophanies in the last plays, particularly that in *Cymbeline*. It has been common in criticism to stress the religious quality of the late romances. But the careful way in which the theophany in *The Tempest* is presented as a human contrivance should make us aware that religion in the last plays is presented through a filter. The theophany in *Cymbeline* is deliberately put in the form of a court-masque. Posthumus in prison, deeply penitent for the supposed death of his wife on his orders, falls into a sleep. Then with 'solemn music' there enter 'as in an apparition' the dead parents and brothers of Posthumus, chanting in turn their appeal to Jupiter to help the afflicted couple Imogen and Posthumus.

JUPITER *descends in thunder and lightning, sitting upon an eagle: he throws a thunderbolt. The* GHOSTS *fall on their knees.*

Magisterially, Jupiter assures them that all has been forethought.

> Be not with mortal accidents oppressed,
> No care of yours it is; you know 'tis ours.
> Whom best I love I cross, to make my gift,
> The more delayed, delighted. Be content.
>
> Mount, eagle, to my palace crystalline.
>   *Ascends*
>   (v. iv. 99–102, 113)

The naïvety of all this, and the rather crude verse, led critics to repudiate it as non-Shakespearian. Wilson Knight went to the other extreme of seeing it as a supreme moment of mystical experience. The whole manner of it is carefully fashioned to establish that what we are witnessing is a masque; NOT the voice of God but the sort of thing that we in our court entertainments confidently present as the voice of divine beings blessing the endeavours of our monarch and the nobility. As in *The Tempest*, we hear a divine voice speaking of the concern of the gods for mortal welfare and justice, promising to rescue and redress. But the divine voice is exhibited as a human voice; the voice of human hope not of human certainty. To present a theophany in terms of theatre is consonant with the general endeavour in the last plays that we have been describing: to *advertise* fabrication and make-believe. The dramatist wishes to be seen forging the promises of God.

So we move to the masque in *The Tempest*. No question here that the divine blessing on the betrothal of Ferdinand and Miranda is not the work of the Duke of Milan. 'Some vanity of mine art,' he calls it modestly. As Juno and Ceres sing their very beautiful invocations of fertility, Prospero says in reply to Ferdinand's question about this 'most majestic vision' that it is an enactment by spirits of 'my present fancies'. He suddenly stops the masque on recollecting the approach of Caliban's conspiracy against his life. 'Our revels now are ended.'

> And like the baseless fabric of this vision,
> The cloud-capped towers, the gorgeous palaces,
> The solemn temples, the great globe itself,
> Yea, all which it inherit, shall dissolve,
> And like this insubstantial pageant faded
> Leave not a rack behind. We are such stuff
> As dreams are made on, and our little life
> Is rounded with a sleep.
>
> (IV. i. 151–8)

A dramatist cancels his shadow-play on remembering the reality of personal danger, and reflects that the very transience of the stage images he has created and dismissed is yet another way in which they imitate the real—which is just as fleeting and illusory. 'We are such stuff / As dreams are made on' is rightly one of the most famous sayings in Shakespeare. All that we create in art is make-believe and dream, our 'present fancies'; but is that to disparage it, when everything that is non-art, all the lived-through reality of everyday, is a kind of dream too? Whether we call this scepticism or faith, we have to be wary in giving it a finality as Shakespeare's scepticism or faith, as against Prospero's. All the same, the attitude to art and life accords with so much that goes on in the final plays, and the identification of author and hero seems much closer in *The Tempest* than in say *Macbeth* or *Hamlet*. It is always a moving experience to imagine that in the Epilogue Shakespeare speaks in the person of Prospero:

> Now I want
> Spirits to enforce, art to enchant,
> And my ending is despair,
> Unless I be relieved by prayer.
>
> (13–16)

If there are to be no more plays, if there is to be an end of that
cosmos of the imagination he has built and dwelt in all his life,
what else exists? Nothing—'unless I be relieved by prayer'. Both
Caliban and Shakespeare 'seek for grace'.

Cymbeline

With two collaborative plays still to come, *The Tempest* was not
quite Shakespeare's farewell to dramatic writing. We assume that
Cymbeline had been written earlier, but its date is in fact
uncertain and it is not inconceivable that it was written after *The
Tempest*. It too is a kind of farewell play. It was not wholly a
mistake to put it among the tragedies in the Folio; but it could
have been put among the histories, or among the comedies. Its
extremely long and intricate happy ending is a happy ending to *all*
the plays: Othello and Desdemona reunited and Iago penitent;
Britain promised 'peace and plenty' with conqueror and con-
quered reconciled; and the happiness of a comedy's ending
ratified by Jupiter himself.

Imogen is the least submissive of the brilliant trio of calumniated wives of which with Hermione and Desdemona she is a
member. Her indignant carriage in response to the news that
Posthumus believes her false is superb.

PISANIO.   O gracious lady,
  Since I received command to do this business,
  I have not slept one wink.
IMOGEN.   Do't, and to bed then.

(III. iv. 98–100)

Her presence overawes Iachimo, not merely defeating his plan to
possess her but arousing in him the totally unexpected resource of
poetry in which he extols her beauty as she sleeps (II. ii. 11–50).
Her cool attitude to autarky is put in strong contrast with the
blustering patriotism of the Queen and Cloten.

Hath Britain all the sun that shines? Day, night,
Are they not but in Britain? I' th' world's volume
Our Britain seems as of it but not in it,
In a great pool a swan's nest. Prithee think
There's livers out of Britain.

(III. iv. 136–40)

Yet this heroine of tragedy must slip into boy's clothes and wander into a pastoral play where by an extraordinary coincidence she comes face to face (without knowing it) with her princely brothers who were stolen from court in infancy and are being brought up in the wilds of Wales. The wilds of Wales, however, are nothing like the forest of Arden. Cloten is the ugliest villain in Shakespeare, a stupid, malevolent, sadistic brute proposing to rape Imogen while he's wearing Posthumus' garments. He is killed and beheaded by the princes (one of the few deaths in the tragicomedies and the only violent one), and then—that incredible, gratuitous, bizarre, gross, inexplicable incident— Imogen wakens from drugged sleep to find herself by the headless body of one who by his clothes she takes to be her husband.

From this grim pastoral we move to a war play, tiny Britain against powerful Rome. The confusion of these scenes seems near to frenzy, and it is difficult not to accept the view that Shakespeare created them in order to lead up to the complex ingenuity of the final unravelling. The establishment of peace between Britain and Rome is but one element in a virtuoso scene of revelations, explanations, repentances, and forgiveness. But the peace is extremely important. Though *The Tempest* is a political play it is not a 'history-play'. In *Cymbeline* the histories, which have often seemed to be heading for tragicomedy, are brought within its healing embrace. Once Britain has asserted its independence and strength by defeating Rome, it submits to Rome, and Rome accepts the new alliance in words that look forward to the ideal partnerships of an imagined British empire of the future.

A conclusion

Such tricks hath strong imagination,
That if it would but apprehend some joy,
It comprehends some bringer of that joy.
(*A Midsummer Night's Dream*, v. i. 18–20)

Shakespeare's tragicomedies are deeply concerned with the power of the imagination. They demonstrate its power, unquestionably, in the splendid vitality of character, language, and incident. Then they stand back to query what it is that has been demonstrated. By narrative links which make fun of the story's credibility, by presentations of the gods in which the human carpentry is made embarrassingly visible, by the ostentatious use of magic and folktale devices, Shakespeare lays siege to the status of the conflicts which are so vividly enacted. The later plays are so candid about their make-believe that they dissolve the discomfort which the awkward manœuvrings of the middle tragicomedies tend to cause. We don't feel cheated, because the contract between us and the dramatist is so plainly before us. But the problem remains. On the one hand we have the strong enactment of problems which are recognizably real; on the other we have what might seem thoroughgoing satire of the way in which art lays hold of these problems and solves them. Can these aesthetic transactions that we call tragicomedies offer themselves *in any way* as an order of truth? Or do they serve more humbly as fabrications of the imagination, forswearing all claims beyond the insistence that if art is insubstantial, so is life?

There is no doubt at all that the tragicomedies point more directly than the early comedies do towards the life we actually live. They know about misery and joy, betrayal and contrition, love and hate, kindness and cruelty. But in contrast with the tragedies they more or less abandon faith in being able to perceive and comprehend the dynamics by which people move from one condition to another. For all the mystery about the meaning of life which invests great tragedy, the action of tragedy is above all things sequential, with each new incident and configuration of characters depending on what has gone before and seeming to be its irresistible consequence. The sense of inevitability so essential to tragedy is absent from Shakespeare's tragicomedy. Towards explaining origin, process, and outcome, it makes only gestures which often look ironic. Its procedures are so obviously manufactured that they are a disclaimer. Tragicomedy says with Ophelia: 'We know what we are: but we know not what we may be. God be at your table!'

The religious colouring of the tragicomedies is one of their most striking features. Yet religion is always in questionable company; nearly always proffered to us in a context of faking. In the tragedies, as we have seen, the obscure conviction that man is not on his own in the universe and that good and evil are not simply his own invention is often expressed in rather crude and enigmatic images of divine intervention or satanic interference. The crudeness of the metaphysical emblems is defensive; not too much is claimed. The intimations of divine presence and guidance in the tragicomedies, being so beset with irony and mockery, are even more hesitant. Is anything claimed at all? Before we answer no, we should reflect that Shakespeare may be mocking us with his mockery. You never quite know when he might be being serious. I think we have quite misunderstood the last plays in taking them as determined parables of divine protection and rescue. But they do not rule out and reject the idea of providence as (for example) it is naïvely but movingly expressed by Gonzalo towards the end of *The Tempest*.

> Look down, you gods,
> And on this couple drop a blessed crown;
> For it is you that have chalked forth the way
> Which brought us hither.

(v. i. 201–4)

It was common in Reformation controversy to hold that *other* people's ideas of God and His purposes were 'vain imaginations'; fancied, and therefore not real. Shakespeare would not perhaps disallow such a description of what he offers to us in his tragicomic versions of God's workings. But with him it is always an unanswered question how vain the imagination is. 'The best in this kind are but shadows.' The most convincing parts of the tragicomedies are no less fictional than the least convincing. Shakespearian tragicomedy doesn't in the end deny that imaginative fiction may be an avenue to knowledge, but it asserts (and it is all that it asserts) that it is imagination and not knowledge.

Epilogue

'He was not of an age, but for all time,' prophesied Ben Jonson in his First Folio eulogy. Great mountains can be quite badly damaged by the endless trekking of boots over their surface; that Shakespeare has survived the attention he has received and continues to receive is perhaps the greatest possible testimony of the power of his art. John Dover Wilson once said that the only thing that brought Shakespeare to mind during one of the 'Birthday' celebrations at Stratford-upon-Avon was the cattle market on his way back to the railway station. That was just after the Second World War. Since then the journals, the conferences, the congresses, the festivals, the institutes, the libraries, the theatres, the books devoted to Shakespeare and his plays have burgeoned, and not only in the English-speaking world. In view of such institutionalization, which cannot be entirely a benefit, it is worth remembering that the progress of Shakespeare's unique world-wide reputation has always been attended by reservations and hesitations. Milton was deeply appreciative of Shakespeare, as a reading of *Comus* shows, and the epitaph he wrote for 'my Shakespeare' prefixed to the Second Folio of 1632 is a moving poem. But those lines in 'L'Allegro' are the archetypal left-handed compliment.

> Then to the well-trod stage anon,
> If Jonson's learned sock be on,
> Or sweetest Shakespeare, fancy's child,
> Warble his native wood-notes wild . . .

The idea of Shakespeare as an untutored and largely unconscious genius died hard. Dryden's handsome encomium was in terms of Shakespeare not *needing* learning—'he was naturally learned'—and was accompanied by heavy disparagement: 'many times flat, insipid,' 'swelling into bombast,' 'his whole style is so pestered with figurative expressions that it is as affected as it is obscure.' Samuel Johnson's *Preface to Shakespeare* (1765) is a major document of literary criticism, and the praise given to Shakespeare as 'the mirror of life' in an age that, while producing edition

after edition of the plays, found them sadly wanting in correct-
ness and refinement, was generous, shrewd, and courageous. But
Johnson disliked the perpetual word-play of Shakespeare's language ('A quibble was to him the fatal Cleopatra for which he lost
the world ...') and he thought that Shakespeare's excellence
appeared only in scenes, not in whole plays; not one play of his,
he said, if written by a contemporary, 'would be heard to the
conclusion'. And, he was 'so much more careful to please than to
instruct, that he seems to write without any moral purpose'. In
defending Shakespeare against finicky neo-classicism, Johnson
was answering Voltaire, who found Shakespeare a very rough
diamond, a genius, the barbaric irregularity of whose works
could only be tolerated in a country like England. The enthusiasm
of European romanticism for the soul and the energy of Shakespearian drama, praising its form as organic rather than artificial
and seeing it as a model for every national drama, did not stop
Matthew Arnold from returning to the old complaints. 'Shakespeare is divinely strong, rich, and attractive. But sureness of
perfect style Shakespeare himself did not possess.' He complained
of his 'over-curiousness of expression' and quoted approvingly a
saying of Guizot which he seems to have made up himself:
Shakespeare 'tried all styles except that of simplicity'.

Bernard Shaw's denigration of Shakespeare may seem all part
of the Shavian act. His knowledge of Shakespeare was profound,
and his concern for fidelity to the plays in the theatre shows itself
in his marvellous letters to Ellen Terry about acting Imogen, and
in getting Forbes Robertson to restore Fortinbras to *Hamlet*,
from which he had been missing for nearly two hundred years.
But 'Bardolatry'—his own word—seemed to him a real cultural
danger when a new Ibsenite drama was looking for recognition. It
is very noticeable that his attacks on Shakespeare repeat the
burden of centuries, that (in Ben Jonson's phrase) 'Shakespeare
wanted art', and that his work was deficient in its moral philosophy. In 1905 he gave it as his opinion:

That Shakespeare's power lies in his enormous command of word-music,
which gives fascination to his most blackguardly repartees and sublimity
to his hollowest platitudes.

That Shakespeare's weakness lies in his complete deficiency in that
highest sphere of thought, in which poetry embraces religion,

philosophy, morality, and the bearing of these on communities, which is sociology. That his characters have no religion, no politics, no conscience, no hope, no convictions of any sort.

This is just one year away from the publication of Tolstoy's extraordinary attack on Shakespeare in 1906. This strove to free the people of the world from 'the false glorification of Shakespeare' by giving a ludicrously reductive running commentary on *King Lear*. It is an absolute denial of the viewpoint of Dryden and Johnson that for all his faults Shakespeare was true to life. Tolstoy found in him nothing but exaggeration. 'We do not believe either in the events or in the actions or in the suffering of the characters.'

The history of Shakespeare is a fascinating subject of enormous proportions, embracing the vicissitudes of his plays (and their adaptations) on the stage, the varying popularity of different plays in different countries and cultures, his importance for political movements, his influence on painters and composers, and above all his impact on major European minds like Goethe, Freud, and Tolstoy and on poets and writers of the English language—Keats, Coleridge, Yeats, Joyce for example. I have mentioned in this epilogue a few well-known reservations about Shakespeare because institutionalized adulation may ossify the spirit of Shakespeare, and, as Shakespeare's plays teach us, dissentient voices are essential for life. What I have just quoted from Bernard Shaw is in my opinion absolute rubbish. But at least he is not approaching the plays as though they were an international shrine. Shakespeare's plays ought to be a challenge to us, and everyone has to work out for himself or herself whether they are important and in what way they are important. If this book has given any help in that I shall be more than satisfied, because in adding to the vast volume of Shakespeare criticism it is difficult not to feel the force of the remark with which Hazlitt concluded his essay on 'The Ignorance of the Learned':

If we wish to know the force of human genius, we should read Shakespeare. If we wish to see the insignificance of human learning, we may study his commentators.

A note on Shakespeare criticism

No one in his senses would go to 'the criticism' to get the correct interpretation of a Shakespeare play, because a very slight acquaintance with it demonstrates that the range of perfectly legitimate readings is extremely wide. The possibilities within these unfathomable and inexhaustible works become clearer if we look at the criticism historically. It is obvious that, as each generation takes over the task of interpreting Shakespeare and repudiates the findings of the past, it is not really getting nearer to ultimate meaning but only shifting the point of view and the angle of approach. So far as one can see, the capacity of Shakespeare's plays to yield quite different harvests to the critics of different periods of time and different intellectual environments is endless. In studying Shakespeare criticism we are studying its authors and their times as much as Shakespeare's work, and it is no good insisting that x is wrong and y is right because they disagree.

But given this inescapable relativism—which with Shakespeare is not a matter of critical theory but empirical fact—we are not to think that we are in a situation where anything goes and that there is nothing either good or bad but thinking makes it so. Discrimination is essential. If it is naïve to distinguish between right and wrong readings it is very necessary to distinguish between faithful and false readings. By false readings I mean those realizations, on the stage as well as in print, resulting from ignorance, carelessness, narrow-mindedness, doctrinal zeal, desire for promotion, ill will, and self-love. Every age produces a wealth of these, but every age has its smaller quota of realizations whose hallmark is honesty towards Shakespeare and fidelity to his word. These are the ones which will help each individual to reach his own best understanding of what Shakespeare has to say.

In what follows, I give first an outline historical sketch of criticism, followed by a list of some important general works, before proceeding to a selection of works relevant to the successive chapters of this book.

Historical

The Shakespeare criticism of the seventeenth and eighteenth centuries is very fully presented by Brian Vickers in *Shakespeare: The Critical Heritage* (6 volumes, 1974–81). John Dryden's comments can be found in *Of Dramatic Poesy and Other Writings*, ed. G. Watson (1962). Samuel Johnson's Shakespeare criticism has been collected by W. Raleigh (1908), W. K. Wimsatt (1960), and A. Sherbo (1968). Maurice Morgann's remarkable forensic 'Essay on the Dramatic Character of Sir John Falstaff' (1777) appears with other important items in D. Nichol Smith's *Eighteenth-century Essays on Shakespeare* (1903, 1963). There is also an exhaustive edition by D. Fineman (1972).

Of the major English critics of the Romantic period, Coleridge's work on Shakespeare has been collected by T. M. Raysor (1930, 1960) and T. Hawkes (1959, 1969). The lectures of 1811–12 have been re-edited by R. A. Foakes (1971). Hazlitt's criticism is chiefly in *Characters of Shakespeare's Plays* (1817), *Lectures on the English Poets* (1818), and *Lectures on the English Comic Writers* (1819). All these are in the *Collected Works*, ed. P. P. Howe (1930–4). De Quincey's 'On the Knocking at the Gate in *Macbeth*' (1823) appears in D. Nichol Smith's *Shakespeare Criticism: A Selection* (1916). Keats's informal comments are in the *Letters*, ed. H. E. Rollins (1958).

A general anthology of European Shakespeare criticism, *Shakespeare in Europe*, ed. O. LeWinter (1963), is an introduction to the vast contribution made to the study of Shakespeare in Germany in the eighteenth and nineteenth centuries by Herder, Lessing, Goethe, Schiller, A. W. Schlegel, Hegel, and many others. Specialist studies of this include R. Pascal, *Shakespeare in Germany 1740–1815* (1937). The size and quality of the ever-growing commentary on Shakespeare in the nineteenth century in all parts of the world can be judged from the volumes of the great 'New Variorum' edition which H. H. Furness began to publish in Philadelphia in 1871.

Influential contributions of the later nineteenth century were Edward Dowden, *Shakspere: A Critical Study of his Mind and Art* (1874), A. C. Swinburne, *A Study of Shakespeare* (1880), and R. G. Moulton, *Shakespeare as a Dramatic Artist* (1885). The counter-contributions of Shaw and Tolstoy (see pp. 183–4) are available respectively in *Shaw on Shakespeare*, ed. E. Wilson (1961) and *Shakespeare in Europe* (see above).

The twentieth century begins with the traditionalist approach of A. C. Bradley, whose *Shakespearian Tragedy* (1904) remains, in spite of all derision and abuse, one of the greatest books ever written about Shakespeare. Harley Granville Barker's *Prefaces to Shakespeare* (1927, etc.) reflect a new consciousness of Shakespeare as a writer for the theatre, and in particular the Elizabethan theatre. M. C. Bradbrook's *Elizabethan Stage Conditions* (1932) shows the application of a growing knowledge of the theatre to the plays. Elmer Edgar Stoll's *Art and Artifice in Shakespeare* (1933) finds Elizabethan theatrical conventions more important than psychology in the shaping of the plays.

The ideas of the late Renaissance are waywardly but brilliantly applied to the plays in Wyndham Lewis's *The Lion and the Fox* (1927). Shakespeare was pre-eminently a man of the Renaissance for both W. B. Yeats and T. S. Eliot. Yeats's Shakespeare criticism is best approached through P. Ure's essay, 'W. B. Yeats and the Shakespearian Moment' (in Ure's *Yeats and Anglo-Irish Literature*, ed. C. J. Rawson, 1974). Eliot's essays on Shakespeare are in *Selected Essays* (1932) and *Elizabethan Essays* (1934).

The mid-century attempt to wrest Shakespearian meaning from the climate of thought of his time is illustrated in three very different works: J. Dover Wilson's *What Happens in 'Hamlet'* (1935), Theodore Spencer's *Shakespeare and the Nature of Man* (1942), and E. M. W. Tillyard's *Shakespeare's History Plays* (1944).

The 1920s and 1930s were also insisting on the plays as poems. The Cambridge new criticism did not produce George Wilson Knight, who is *sui generis*, but his work has strong links with its approach to poetry. *The Wheel of Fire* (1930) carried an introduction by T. S. Eliot, and the conception that each play was a visionary whole, 'an expanded metaphor' generated by poetic symbolism, was praised by L. C. Knights in 'How Many Children Had Lady Macbeth?' (1933, reprinted in *Explorations*, 1946). William Empson's brilliant worrying of Shakespeare's words in *Seven Types of Ambiguity* (1930) and *The Structure of Complex Words* (1952) has been immensely influential. Early books on imagery were Caroline Spurgeon's *Shakespeare's Imagery and What it Tells Us* (1935) and Wolfgang Clemen's *Shakespeares*

Bilder (1936). Across the Atlantic, Cleanth Brooks included a famous essay on the imagery of *Macbeth* in *The Well-Wrought Urn* (1947). A pioneer full-length study of meaning-through-imagery in a single play was R. B. Heilman's book on *King Lear, This Great Stage* (1948).

Shakespeare was not central in F. R. Leavis's work, but his essay on *Othello*, 'Diabolic Intellect and the Noble Hero' (1937; reprinted in *The Common Pursuit*, 1952), is a notable document in twentieth-century anti-heroism. D. A. Traversi's work, beginning with *Approach to Shakespeare* (1938), emanates from the *Scrutiny* school. Psychoanalytic criticism begins with Ernest Jones's essay on *Hamlet* of 1910, which developed into *Hamlet and Oedipus* (1944). There is some remarkable early use of comparative religion and anthropology in Colin Still's *Shakespeare's Mystery Play: A Study of 'The Tempest'* (1921). Marxism was not a strong element in Shakespeare criticism until quite recently: Shakespeare hardly features in Christopher Caudwell's *Illusion and Reality* (1937). Indeed, immediately after the Second World War it could be said that Shakespeare criticism was markedly Christian in tone: S. L. Bethell's *The Winter's Tale: A Study* (1947) is an example.

In the 1950s and 1960s two notable influences were Northrop Frye and Jan Kott. Frye's *Anatomy of Criticism* (1957) brought some of his earlier work into a general book which showed the different genres of Shakespeare expressing the archetypal myths by which humanity holds on to life. Jan Kott's *Shakespeare Our Contemporary* (1964) is a much slighter book, but it struck absolutely the right note for its time, and on stage and in the classroom for years afterwards the Shakespeare of meaningless repetitive power-struggles and despair held sway.

And at that decent distance it is safer to leave this sketch. Important scholarly work of recent years and representative work of current critical schools is mentioned under the various headings below.

General

Facsimiles of Shakespeare's works as originally printed are available in *The First Folio of Shakespeare* (The Norton Facsimile), ed. C. Hinman (1968) and *Shakespeare's Plays in Quarto,* ed. M. J. B. Allen and K. Muir (1981). Individual plays in quarto have been issued by Oxford University Press. The best outline of the problems of establishing Shakespeare's text is in W. W. Greg's two books, *The Editorial Problem in Shakespeare* (1942; 3rd edition 1954) and *The First Folio of Shakespeare* (1955), and in F. T. Bowers, *On Editing Shakespeare* (1955; revised edition 1966). The standard one-volume edition of the works, without annotation, by P. Alexander (1951), which superseded the Globe edition (1864), is itself growing a little elderly. The most convenient one-volume annotated editions are *The Complete Signet Classic Shakespeare*, general editor S. Barnet (1972) and *The Pelican Shakespeare*, general editor A. Harbage (1969; now available in three volumes). *The Riverside Shakespeare*, general editor G. B. Evans (1974) provides a library of information as well as a meticulous text; but it is a heavy book to carry about.

The standard annotated editions of individual plays are those in 'The Arden Shakespeare' (Methuen; from 1951, under revision), and two new series, one from Oxford University Press, commencing 1982, and one from Cambridge University Press, commencing 1984. With rather less annotation, but very sound and scholarly, are the volumes of 'The New Penguin Shakespeare', general editors T. J. B. Spencer and S. Wells (1967, in progress).

The sources of Shakespeare's plays are available with introductory material in the eight volumes of G. Bullough's *Narrative and Dramatic Sources of Shakespeare* (1957–75). K. Muir's *The Sources of Shakespeare's Plays* (1977) is a one-volume survey.

In spite of the wealth of annotated editions, the student of Shakespeare soon graduates to exploring the possibilities of Shakespeare's language for himself, and for this a concordance and a glossary are indispensable. The 'hand-made' concordance by J. Bartlett (1894) has been superseded by M. Spevack's computerized *Harvard Concordance to Shakespeare* (1975), based on an eight-volume *Systematic Concordance* (1968–75). The *Oxford Shakespeare Concordances*, by T. H. Howard-Hill, devote a single volume to each main text (1968–72). Among glossaries, there is no substitute for the outstanding *Shakespeare Lexicon* of Alexander Schmidt (1874–5, with later revisions), though it must be used in conjunction with the full *Oxford English Dictionary*, which had not begun to appear while Schmidt was at work. C. T. Onions's briefer *A Shakespeare Glossary* (1911, with later revisions) incorporates the material on Shakespeare's vocabulary from the *Oxford English Dictionary*. The standard bibliographies of writings about Shakespeare are by W. Ebisch and L. L. Schücking, *A Shakespeare Bibliography* (1931) with *Supplement* (1937), and G. R. Smith, *A Classified Shakespeare Bibliography 1936–1958* (1963). A useful *Select Bibliographical Guide* was edited by S. Wells (1973). Current work on Shakespeare is listed in the journal *Shakespeare Quarterly* and the annual volumes of *Shakespeare Survey, The Year's Work in English Studies* (The English Association), and *The Annual Bibliography of English Language and Literature* (Modern Humanities Research Association). The Garland Shakespeare Bibliographies (general editor W. Godshalk), providing annotated bibliographies of individual plays (mostly since 1940), began publication with *King Lear* in 1980.

Chapter 1. A career in the theatre

The standard biography of Shakespeare is E. K. Chambers, *William Shakespeare: A Study of Facts and Problems* (1930). Later findings are included in *Shakespeare: A Documentary Life* (1975) by S. Schoenbaum, who also has an entertaining account of the growth of Shakespeare's biography in *Shakespeare's Lives* (1970). E. I. Fripp's fascinating but not very orderly *Shakespeare Man and Artist* (1938) should not be overlooked. Shakespeare's hypothetical education is exhaustively analysed in T. W. Baldwin's *William Shakspere's Petty School* (1943) and *William Shakspere's Small Latine and Lesse Greeke* (1944).

For the theatre of Shakespeare's day, the standard work is again by E. K. Chambers: *The Elizabethan Stage* (1923). A. Gurr's useful and compact work, *The Shakespearean Stage 1574–1642*, is based on Chambers's great study. There is a detailed account of the playhouses themselves by R. Hosley in Volume III of *The Revels History of Drama in English* (1975); this might be supplemented by W. Hodges's engaging picture-book, *Shakespeare's Theatre* (1964). Theatrical conditions are surveyed in a number of M. C. Bradbrook's works, especially *The Rise of the Common Player* (1962). G. E. Bentley's *The Profession of*

Dramatist in Shakespeare's Time (1971) is a standard work. See also M. Hattaway, *Elizabethan Popular Theatre: Plays in Performance* (1982).

Chapter 2. Relationship

There are very interesting if individual views about personal relationships in L. A. Fiedler's *The Stranger in Shakespeare* (1972). C. L. Barber's contrast between love and sex in the earlier and later comedies, in ' "Thou that beget'st him that did thee beget" ' (*Shakespeare Survey* 22, (1969)) is brief but imaginative. Love, sex, and the family are naturally a main concern of the large body of recent writings about women in Shakespeare, e.g. J. Dusinberre, *Shakespeare and the Nature of Women* (1975), and C. R. S. Lenz, G. Greene and C. T. Neely, *The Woman's Part: Feminist Criticism of Shakespeare* (1980). L. Jardine's *Still Harping on Daughters* (1983) reviews the earlier literature in a provocative and acerbic study. See also M. Garber, *Coming of Age in Shakespeare* (1981).

Opinions of Shakespeare's views on society and authority are of course to be found in all work on the histories (see below) and the more political tragedies. And the vexed question of the 'self' is fundamental in most critical discussion. I reviewed some trends in the debate on this matter in 'Person and Office in Shakespeare's Plays' (British Academy Lecture, 1970). There is a good wide-ranging account in Jonathan Dollimore's *Radical Tragedy* (1984). S. Greenblatt's *Renaissance Self-Fashioning* (1980) is essential reading, though I can't respond with any enthusiasm to his view of the malleable self cringing under the power-structures and ideologies of the time.

Chapter 3. Poems and poetry

The poems are discussed in the context of Ovidian erotic narrative, the sonnet sequence, and Elizabethan poetry generally in Hallett Smith's *Elizabethan Poetry* (1952) and M. C. Bradbrook's *Shakespeare and Elizabethan Poetry* (1951). There is an introductory essay by J. W. Lever on 'Shakespeare's Narrative Poems' in *A New Companion to Shakespeare Studies*, ed. K. Muir and

S. Schoenbaum (1971). C. Kahn has a psychoanalytic study of *Venus and Adonis* in *Man's Estate* (1981).

The best discussions of the sonnets are in essays and chapters rather than full-length studies, e.g. P. Cruttwell's chapter in *The Shakespearean Moment* (1954). *The Riddle of Shakespeare's Sonnets*, ed. E. Hubler (1962), brings together stimulating essays by R. P. Blackmur, Northrop Frye, and L. Fiedler. W. H. Auden's fine introductory essay to the Signet edition (1964) should not be missed. J. B. Leishman's *Themes and Variations in Shakespeare's Sonnets* places the sonnets in the European literary tradition. S. Booth followed his *Essay on Shakespeare's Sonnets* (1969) with a vast commentary in his edition of 1977, which, for all its merits, tends to strangle the individual sonnets in a superfluity of meanings while obscuring the genuine equivocations on which they depend. K. Muir's *Shakespeare's Sonnets* (1979) examines the sonnets in relation to the rest of Shakespeare's work and provides a guide to critical opinion.

For music and song, see F. W. Sternfeld, *Music in Shakespearean Tragedy* (1963) and P. J. Seng, *Vocal Songs in the Plays of Shakespeare* (1967).

The relationship of Shakespeare's writing to the rhetorical teaching of his time is discussed by M. Joseph, *Shakespeare's Use of the Arts of Language* (1947), B. Vickers, 'Shakespeare's Use of Rhetoric' in *A New Companion to Shakespeare Studies* (1971) and M. Trousdale, *Shakespeare and the Rhetoricians* (1982). Vickers also has a book on *The Artistry of Shakespeare's Prose* (1968).

The best book on Shakespeare's English, W. Franz, *Die Sprache Shakespeare* (1939), superseding E. A. Abbott's *Shakespearian Grammar* (1869), has never been translated.

W. Empson's *Structure of Complex Words* (1952) was mentioned earlier. M. M. Mahood's *Shakespeare's Wordplay* is a sensitive and stimulating book which includes a chapter on the sonnets. Some of the problems in analysing Shakespeare's 'imagery' were discussed in an early essay by R. A. Foakes, 'Suggestions for a New Approach to Shakespeare's Imagery' in *Shakespeare Survey* 5 (1952). A novel contribution on the 'image cluster' was made by an ornithologist, E. A. Armstrong, in *Shakespeare's Imagination* (1946). H. Hulme's *Explorations in Shakespeare's Language* (1962) is an original and tenacious enquiry into 'some problems of lexical meaning'. *Shakespeare's Styles*, ed. P. Edwards,

I-S. Ewbank, and G. K. Hunter, is a collection of essays on Shakespeare's language and his attitude to language by critics including L. C. Knights, G. K. Hunter, A. Barton, Wilson Knight, I-S. Ewbank, and R. A. Foakes.

Chapter 4. Comedy

The most influential of modern studies is C. L. Barber's *Shakespeare's Festive Comedy: A Study of Dramatic Form and its Relation to Social Custom* (1959). A wide European context is provided by L. G. Salingar in *Shakespeare and the Traditions of Comedy* (1974). Much of N. Frye's seminal essay, 'The Argument of Comedy' (English Institute Essays, 1948), reappeared in *The Anatomy of Criticism* (1957). The approaches of both Barber and Frye are rejected as too abstract by Elliot Krieger in *A Marxist Study of Shakespeare's Comedies* (1979). A. Leggatt's *Shakespeare's Comedy of Love* (1974) is a judicious survey.

The best essays on individual comedies usually reappear in the various 'casebooks' published from time to time. Special collections include *Shakespearian Comedy*, ed. M. Bradbury and D. Palmer (1972) which has a number of important essays. Introductions to editions like the New Penguin Shakespeare are often more helpful, being less cluttered by hobby-horses and King Charles's heads, than articles in the specialist journals. A. Barton's prefaces in the Riverside Shakespeare are particularly good. Her earlier work, *Shakespeare and the Idea of the Play* (1962), includes material on the comedies.

Chapter 5. History

My views on Shakespeare's histories and their relation to the work of other dramatists and to the national life are represented in more extended form in my book, *Threshold of a Nation* (1979).

E. M. W. Tillyard's *Shakespeare's History Plays* (1944), along with L. B. Campbell's *Shakespeare's 'Histories': Mirrors of Elizabethan Policy* (1947) and J. Dover Wilson's *Fortunes of Falstaff* (1943), established a view of the histories as concordant with a monolithic Elizabethan view of political theory and English history. That Tudor views on history were in fact discordant was demonstrated by H. A. Kelly in *Divine Providence in the England of Shakespeare's Histories* (1970). Among the many works arguing that the histories are not conformist are A. P. Rossiter, *Angel With Horns* (1961), W. Sanders, *The Dramatist and the Received Idea* (1968), and J. Wilders, *The Lost Garden* (1978). A major contribution to the understanding of kingship in Shakespeare's plays was E. F. Kantorowicz, *The King's Two Bodies* (1957).

H. Jenkins's work on the pattern of the *Henry IV* plays (mentioned in the text) is *The Structural Problem in Shakespeare's 'Henry the Fourth'* (1956).

Chapter 6. Tragedy

In spite of a wealth of good writing on individual tragedies, there is no single book on Shakespearian tragedy which serves as a coherent synthesis for our time as Bradley's was for his. It is not surprising; the criticism of the age has been too Christian, too Marxist, too moralistic, or too anti-heroic to *want* the woe and wonder of true tragic comprehension. It is understandable that K. Muir in his *Shakespeare's Tragic Sequence* (1972) should make the assertion that 'There is no such thing as Shakespearian Tragedy; there are only Shakespearian tragedies.' The next logical step is the demolition of the individual tragedies, which might be said to be the darker purpose of John Bayley's *Shakespeare and Tragedy* (1981), which saw the need to extricate and rescue Shakespeare from the clutches of his chosen dramatic forms. Is it futile to hope that someone will come along to demonstrate again that there *is* such a thing as Shakespearian tragedy?

Some writings with very different objectives which I have found helpful on the tragedies are: N. Brooke, *Shakespeare's Early Tragedies* (1968), U. Ellis-Fermor, *The Frontiers of Drama* (1945), W. R. Elton, *'King Lear' and the Gods* (1966), J. Holloway, *The Story of the Night* (1961), G. K. Hunter, *Dramatic Identities and Cultural Tradition* (1978), E. Jones, *Scenic Form in Shakespeare* (1971), M. Mack, 'The World of *Hamlet*' (Yale Review, 1952) and *'King Lear' in Our Time* (1965), A. Sewell, *Character and Society in Shakespeare* (1951), B. Spivack, *Shakespeare and the Allegory of Evil* (1958), E. M. Waith, *The Herculean Hero* (1962).

There continues to be a wide choice of books devoted to the tragedies. I have selected some recent examples which provide a variety of approaches. R. A. Brower, *Hero and Saint: Shakespeare and the Graeco-Roman Heroic Tradition* (1971), B. Evans, *Shakespeare's Tragic Practice* (1979), E. A. J. Honigmann, *Shakespeare: Seven Tragedies* (1976), R. Nevo, *Tragic Form in Shakespeare* (1972), J. L. Simmons, *Shakespeare's Pagan World: The Roman Tragedies* (1973), S. Snyder, *The Comic Matrix of Shakespeare's Tragedies* (1979).

Chapter 7. Tragicomedy

The two earlier tragicomedies are discussed in an important early book, W. W. Lawrence, *Shakespeare's Problem Comedies* (1931) and in E. M. W. Tillyard, *Shakespeare's Problem Plays* (1950). Their relationship with Italian tragicomedy was examined by G. K. Hunter in 'Italian Tragicomedy and the English Stage' in *Dramatic Identities and Cultural Tradition* (1978). *Measure for Measure* has a particularly rich and interesting mid-century critical history, with essays by Wilson Knight, R. W. Chambers, F. R. Leavis, M. C. Bradbrook, L. C. Knights, Clifford Leech, Mary Lascelles, and others. See *Shakespeare: Select Bibliographical Guides*, ed. S. Wells (1973).

I gave a detailed analysis of criticism of the late tragicomedies in 'Shakespeare's Romances: 1900–1957' (*Shakespeare Survey* 11, 1958. My attitude to these plays in the present book develops from a more general argument on Shakespeare's view of his art expressed in my *Shakespeare and the Confines of Art* (1968).

Some milestones in the criticism of the last plays are: D. G. James, *Scepticism and Poetry* (1937), E. M. W. Tillyard, *Shakespeare's Last Plays* (1938), G. Wilson Knight, *The Crown of Life* (1947), E. C. Pettet, *Shakespeare and the Romance Tradition* (1949), J. F. Danby, *Poets on Fortune's Hill* (1952), D. Traversi, *Shakespeare: The Last Phase* (1954), F. Kermode, *Shakespeare: The Final Plays* (1963).

Other studies of the last plays include books by D. R. C. Marsh (1962), D. L. Peterson (1973), H. Felperin (1972), and Hallett Smith (1972). See also R. G. Hunter, *Shakespeare and the Comedy of Forgiveness* (1965), and the selection of essays in *Shakespeare's Later Comedies*, ed. D. J. Palmer (1971).

A chronology of the plays and poems

There is little certainty about the dates of Shakespeare's plays.
The order of his writings in this list is necessarily conjectural.

1588	*1 Henry VI*	History
	2 Henry VI	History
	3 Henry VI	History
	Titus Andronicus	Tragedy
	The Two Gentlemen of Verona	Comedy
	The Comedy of Errors	Comedy
	The Taming of the Shrew	Comedy
	Love's Labour's Lost	Comedy
	Richard III	History
	Additions to *Sir Thomas More*	
1593	*Venus and Adonis*	Narrative poem
1594	*The Rape of Lucrece*	Narrative poem
	The sonnets	Sonnets
	King John	History
	Romeo and Juliet	Tragedy
	A Midsummer Night's Dream	Comedy
	Richard II	History
	The Merchant of Venice	Comedy
	1 Henry IV	History
	2 Henry IV	History
	Much Ado About Nothing	Comedy
1599	*Henry V*	History
	As You Like It	Comedy
	The Merry Wives of Windsor	Comedy
	Julius Caesar	Tragedy
	Hamlet	Tragedy
1601	'The Phoenix and the Turtle'	Poem
	Twelfth Night	Comedy
	Troilus and Cressida	Tragedy?
	All's Well That Ends Well	Tragicomedy
	Measure for Measure	Tragicomedy

(1604)	*Othello*	Tragedy
	King Lear	Tragedy
	Macbeth	Tragedy
	Antony and Cleopatra	Tragedy
	Coriolanus	Tragedy
	Timon of Athens	Tragedy
(1608)	*Pericles* (with ?)	Tragicomedy
	Cymbeline	Tragicomedy
	The Winter's Tale	Tragicomedy
	The Tempest	Tragicomedy
1613	*Henry VIII* (with Fletcher)	History
	The Two Noble Kinsmen (with Fletcher)	Tragicomedy

'Love's Labour's Won' was listed among Shakespeare's comedies by Francis Meres in 1598 (see p. 17). A scrap of paper which it is hard to dismiss as a forgery has recently surfaced indicating that this play not only existed but actually reached print. See T. W. Baldwin, *Shakspere's Love's Labour's Won* (1957).

For Shakespeare's possible share in *Edward III*, and his possible collaboration with Fletcher in the lost *Cardenio*, see K. Muir, *Shakespeare as Collaborator* (1960).

Index

Shakespeare's plays and poems are listed under his name; page references in heavy type indicate main discussions.

Abbott, E. A., 192
Admiral's men, 7
Aeschylus, 126
Alexander, P., 189
Allen, M. J. B., 189
Alleyn, Edward, 10
Ariosto, Ludovico, *Orlando Furioso*, 161
Aristotle, 83, 126, 139
Armstrong, E. A., 192
Arnold, Matthew, 183
Auden, W. H., 192

Baldwin, T. W., 190, 197
Barber, C. L., 191, 193
Barker, H. Granville, 187
Barnet, S., 189
Bartlett, J., 189
Barton, Anne, 193
Baudelaire, Charles, 86, 102
Bayley, J., 194
Beaumont, Francis, 24, 126
Bentley, G. E., 190
Bethell, S. L., 188
Bible, English, 2
Bishopton (Warwickshire), 25
Blackfriars theatre, *see* theatres, London
Blackmur, R. P., 192
Booth, Stephen, 192
Borromeo, Cardinal Carlo, 3
Bowers, F. T., 189
Bradbrook, M. C., 187, 190, 191, 195
Bradbury, M., 193
Bradley, A. C., 187, 194
Brooke, Nicholas, 194
Brooks, Cleanth, 188
Brower, R. A., 195
Bullough, G., 189
Bunyan, John, 3
Burbage, Richard, 16, 25
Burghley, William Cecil, Lord, 11

Camden, William, 1
Campbell, L. B., 193
Capell, Edward, 117
Caudwell, C., 188
Chamberlain's men, Lord (later King's men), 8, 16, 19, 24
Chambers, E. K., 190
Chambers, R. W., 195
Chapman, George, 126
Chettle, Henry, 11; *Kind Heart's Dream*, 10
Clemen, W., 187
Coleridge, S. T., 184, 186
Combe, Thomas, 25
commedia dell' arte, 9
Condell, Henry, 21, 25, 127, 173
Congreve, William, 86
Constable, Henry, 12
Cottam, John, 2
Cruttwell, P., 192

Danby, J. F., 195
Daniel, Samuel, 10, 12, 105
Davies, Richard, 4
Dekker, Thomas, 11, 78
De Quincy, Thomas, 186
Dollimore, J., 191
Douai, 2
Dowden, Edward, 186
Drayton, Michael, 12
Droeshout, Martin, 25
Dryden, John, 46, 182, 186
Dusinberre, J., 191
Dymoke, Sir Edward, 10

Ebisch, W., 190
Edward III, 197
Eliot, T. S., 187
Elizabeth, Queen, 6, 19, 26
Ellis-Fermor, U., 194
Elton, W. R., 194
Empson, W., 187, 192

Essex, Robert Devereux, Earl of, 19, 125
Euripides, 126
Evans, B., 195
Evans, G. Blakemore, 189
Ewbank, I-S., 193

Felperin, H., 195
Fiedler, L. A., 191, 192
Fineman, D., 186
Fletcher, John, 24, 126, 197; share in *Henry VIII*, 19
Foakes, R. A., 186, 192, 193
Folio, First, 25–6, 27, 127, 167, 182; facsimile, 188
Ford, John, 126
Franz, W., 192
Freud, Sigmund, 184
Fripp, E. I., 190
Frye, Northrop, 28, 188, 192, 193
Furness, H. H., 186

Garber, M., 191
Globe theatre, *see* theatres, London
Godshalk, W., 190
Goethe, J. W. von, 184, 186
Gower, John, 168
Greenblatt, S., 191
Greene, G., 191
Greene, Robert, 5–6, 7, 9, 104; *Groatsworth of Wit*, 5, 10; *Pandosto*, 31, 170
Greg, W. W., 189
Greville, Fulke, 10
Guarini, Giambattista, 161
Guizot, F. P. G., 183
Gurr, A., 190

Hall, Edward, 105
Hall, Dr John, 25
Harbage, A., 189
Harsnett, Bishop Samuel, 155
Harvey, Gabriel, 20
Hathaway, Anne, *see* Shakespeare, Anne
Hattaway, M., 191
Hawkes, T., 186
Hazlitt, William, 184, 186
Hegel, G. W. F., 186
Heilman, R. B., 188
Heminges, John, 21, 25, 127, 173

Henry VII, King, 110
Henslowe, Philip, 8, 10
Herder, J. G., 186
Hinman, C., 188
Hodges, Walter, 190
Holinshed, Raphael, 105
Honigmann, E. A. J., 2, 195
Hosley, R., 190
Howard-Hill, T. H., 189
Howe, P. P., 186
Hubler, E., 192
Hulme, H., 192
Hunt, Simon, 1–2
Hunter, G. K., 193, 194, 195
Hunter, R. G., 195

Ibsen, Henrik, *Ghosts*, 158
Inns of Court, 19

Jaggard, William, 12
James I, King, 19, 26
James, D. G., 195
Jardine, L., 191
Jenkins, Harold, 117, 194
Jenkins, Thomas, 1
Johnson, Samuel, 117; *Preface to Shakespeare*, 182–3
Jones, Emrys, 194
Jones, Ernest, 188
Jonson, Ben, 1–2, 6–7, 11, 26, 78, 97, 183; *Workes*, 21; Folio elegy, 26, 182; on *Pericles*, 168
Joseph, Sister Miriam, 192
Joyce, James, 184

Kahn, C., 192
Kantorowicz, E. F., 194
Keats, John, 184, 186; 'Ode on a Grecian Urn', 34
Kelly, H. A., 193
Kempe, William, 16
Kermode, F., 195
King's men, *see* Chamberlain's men
Knight, G. Wilson, 176, 187, 193, 195
Knights, L. C., 187, 193, 195
Kott, Jan, 188
Krieger, E., 193
Kyd, Thomas, 6–7, 126; *Spanish Tragedy*, 7, 18

Lambarde, William, 19

Lascelles, Mary, 195
Lawrence, W. W., 195
Leavis, F. R., 188, 195
Leech, Clifford, 195
Leggatt, A., 193
Leicester's men, Earl of, 6
Leishman, J. B., 192
Lenz, C. R. S., 191
Lessing, G. E., 186
Lever, J. W., 191
LeWinter, O., 186
Lewis, Wyndham, 187
Lyly, John, 6; *Galathea*, 53

Machiavelli, Niccolò, *Il Principe*, 115
Mack, M., 194
Mahood, M. M., 192
Malone, Edmond, 3, 117
Marlowe, Christopher, 1, 6–7, 8, 78, 126; *Tamburlaine*, 7; *Edward II*, 7, 113; *Jew of Malta*, 101
Marston, John, 78
Massinger, Philip, 126
Meres, Francis, *Palladis Tamia*, 12, 17, 197
Middleton, Thomas, 126
Milton, John, 182
Montaigne, Michel de, 175; 'On Friendship', 35
More, Thomas, *Utopia*, 48
Morgann, Maurice, 186
Moulton, R. G., 186
Mountjoy, Lord, 10
Muir, Kenneth, 189, 191, 192, 194, 197

Nashe, Thomas, 8, 18, 78, 104
Neely, C. T., 191
Nevo, R., 195
Nietzsche, F. W., 126

Onions, C. T., 190
Ovid, 9, 91

Palmer, D., 193, 195
Pascal, R., 186
Passionate Pilgrim, The, 12
Peele, George, 7; *Old Wives Tale*, 7; possible share in *Titus*, 8
Pembroke, Countess of, 10
Pembroke's men, 7

Peterson, D. L., 195
Pettet, E. C., 195
plague (1592–4), 10–11, 16
Plautus, 2, 9, 17
Plutarch, 18, 150
Pope, Alexander, 17, 23, 98

Quiney, Richard, 17
Quiney, Thomas, 25

Ralegh, Sir Walter, 'Ocean to Cynthia', 68
Raleigh, W., 186
Rawson, C. J., 187
Raysor, T. M., 186
Robertson, Forbes, 183
Robin Goodfellow, 98
Roche, Walter, 1
Rollins, H. E., 186
Rose theatre, *see* theatres, London
Rossiter, A. P., 194
Rowe, Nicholas, 15, 164

Salingar, L. G., 193
Sanders, W., 194
Schiller, F., 186
Schlegel, A. W., 186
Schmidt, Alexander, 189
Schoenbaum, S., 190, 192
Schücking, L. L., 190
Scot, Reginald, *Discovery of Witchcraft*, 98, 137
Seneca, 9, 17, 18
Seng, P. J., 192
Sewell, A., 194
Shakespeare, Anne (Hathaway), 4, 25
Shakespeare, Edmund, 25
Shakespeare, Hamnet, 4, 17
Shakespeare, John, 1–4, 18, 25
Shakespeare, Judith, 4, 25
Shakespeare, Mary (Arden), 1, 25
Shakespeare, Susanna, 4, 25
SHAKESPEARE, WILLIAM:
parentage, 1–4; schooling, 1–2; religion, 2–4; theatre companies, 7, 8, 16, 19; handwriting, 8; collaboration, 8; audiences, 8, 10, 14, 20–1, 83; patronage, 11–12; residences, 17, 24; grant of arms, 18; length of plays, 21–2;

SHAKESPEARE, WILLIAM (*cont.*)
publication, 21, 25–6; will, 25;
death, 25
PLAYS:
All's Well That Ends Well, 18, 54,
127, 160, 162, **162–4**; son/father,
30; Helena, 99; bed-trick, 166–7
Antony and Cleopatra, 18, 20, 56,
131, 133, **149–53**; length, 21;
sexual love, 41–2; setting, 88;
dispossession, 154
As You Like It, 9, 17; disguise, 28;
brothers, 29; initial unhappiness,
29, 87; songs, 71; prose, 72;
satire, 86; pastoral setting, 87,
161; love, 92, 94; controlling
forces, 99
Cardenio, 197
Comedy of Errors, 9, 28; family
ties, 28, 32; self, 51; citizen play,
84; sea symbolism, 84;
enchantment, 88; romance
source, 161
Coriolanus, 18, 20, 131, **139–42**;
son/mother, 30; communities, 42;
self, 49; relation with *Timon*, 130
Cymbeline, 14, 43, 124, 160, 162,
173, 175, **178–9**; length, 21;
genre, 27, 127; masque, 70, 176;
dirge, 70; style, 74
Hamlet, 18, 20, 21, 70, 131, **133–6**,
157; length, 21; text, 22;
brothers, 29; sons, 29; son/
mother, 30; father/daughter, 30;
sex guilt, 38; community, 44;
kingship, 47; self, 52–3; songs,
71; Ophelia, 71, 75; rhyme, 71;
prose and verse, 72–3; metaphor,
76–7; distrust of language, 80–1;
link with *Titus*, 127
Henry IV (Parts 1 and 2), 16, 44,
116–21; son/father, 29–30; self,
52; prose, 72; style, 74;
metaphor, 77–8; historical truth,
105; structure, 116–18
Henry V, 16, 19, 44, **120–5**; relation
to *Henry IV*, 116–18
Henry VI, 7, **106–8**; Part 1, 9, 104,
106; authorship, 8; Part 2, 9,
106–7; Part 3, 107–8
Henry VIII, 4, 24, 173;

collaboration, 8, 19, 24
Julius Caesar, 18, 131, **132–3**;
length, 21; authority, 46; song,
71; style, 73, 74; metaphor, 76;
Brutus's language, 81
King John, 4, 16, **110–12**; Bastard,
44–5, 105; descriptive verse, 75–
6; distrust of rhetoric, 78–9;
historical truth, 105
King Lear, 20, 28, 54, 131, **137–8**,
153–7; text, 21; disguise, 28, 53;
brothers, 29; father/daughter,
30–1; sexual guilt, 38–40;
authority, 48; self, 49, 53;
doggerel, 70; Fool, 70, 71;
Dover-cliff speech, 74; distrust of
language, 79–80; foreshadowed
by *Titus*, 127; relation with
Timon, 130; Tolstoy's criticism,
184
Love's Labour's Lost, 9, 10, 11, 19;
celibacy, 33, 90; Berowne, 45;
sonnets, 70; linguistic excess, 80;
Armado, 86; love, 90–2; ending,
95
'Love's Labour's Won', 17, 197
Macbeth, 19, 20, 28, 37, 57, 131,
136–9; length, 21, 22; sexual
imagery, 37; community, 43–4;
self, 50; chanting, 70; metaphor,
76
Measure for Measure, 18, 127, 160,
161, 162, **164–6**; Christian
element, 4; asceticism, 33; views
of sex, 37–8; community, 43;
authority, 47; self, 48–9, 53–4;
disguise, 53–4; octosyllabics, 70;
song, 71; bed-trick, 166–7
Merchant of Venice, 28, 70, **100–3**;
source, 33; Venetian society, 44;
romance/realism, 84; sea
symbolism, 84; alternating
setting, 88; controlling forces, 99
Merry Wives of Windsor, 18, 19,
84, 117; prose, 72
Midsummer Night's Dream, 9, 7,
19; father/daughter, 30; celibacy,
33; rhyme, 72; illusion-breaking,
85, 169; initial unhappiness, 87;
bewilderment, 87; structure, 88;
Bottom's transformation, 89;

love, 90, 92–3; ending, 95; controlling forces, 97–8

Much Ado About Nothing, 17; brothers, 29; deceit, 54, 98–9; song, 71; prose, 72; metaphor, 77; Benedick and Beatrice, 86, 89, 98–9; structure, 99

Othello, 20, 57, 131, **144–9**; length, 21; Venetian society, 44; self, 49; song, 71; rhyme, 71–2; prose, 72; Iago, 101

Pericles, 26, 160, **167–70**, 173; collaboration, 8; father/daughter, 31, 32, 36; chastity, 33; venereal disease, 40

Richard II, **113–16**; influence of Marlowe, 7; Essex's rebellion, 19; as tragedy, 27, 154; image of England, 43; kingship, 47; self, 49–50; rhyme, 72; distrust of rhetoric, 78; alteration of sources, 105; dispossession, 154

Richard III, 54, **108–10**, 125; influence of Marlowe, 7; length, 21; as tragedy, 27; death of Clarence, 74–5; historical truth, 105

Romeo and Juliet, 16, 28, 92, 131, **142–4**; father/daughter, 30; attitude to sex, 41; rhyme, 72; distrust of language, 79

Sir Thomas More, 8

Taming of the Shrew, 10; source, 33; self, 50, 51, 89; verse, 75; Sly as audience, 83; financial element, 84; love, 91; ending, 95, 97

Tempest, 4, 23, 54, 160, 162, **173–8**, 181; epilogue, 16; brothers, 29, 32; father/daughter, 32; masque, 32; chastity, 32–3; community, 43; music, 69, 70

Timon of Athens, 15, 20, **130–1**; length, 21; venereal disease, 40; images of society, 42; dispossession, 154

Titus Andronicus, 9, 18, 54, **127**; sources, 1; authorship, 8; length, 21

Troilus and Cressida, 15, 18, 19, **127–30**, 158; epistle, 20; genre, 27–8; 'degree', 46; prose and verse, 73; metaphor, 78

Twelfth Night, 4, 18; family relations, 28; source, 33; self, 50–1, 89; music, 70; Feste, 70–1; sea symbolism, 84; illusion-breaking, 85; structure, 88; love, 91, 93–4; ending, 96

Two Gentlemen of Verona, 9; ending, 35–6, 96–7; self, 51–2; prose, 72; pastoral element, 84, 88; love, 90

Two Noble Kinsmen, 26, 160, 167, 173; collaboration, 8, 24; address to Venus, 34; friendship, 34–5

Winter's Tale, 23, 54, 160, 161–2, **170–3**; influence of Lyly, 7; sources, 9, 31; father/daughter, 31, 36; friendship, 35; self, 53

POEMS:

'Phoenix and the Turtle, The', 15, **57–8**

Sonnets, 23, 54, **58–69**; rival poet, 7; autobiographical element, 12–16; date, 14; friendship/sex, 36–7

Rape of Lucrece, 10–12, 37, 55, **56–7**

Venus and Adonis, 10–12, 41, **55–6**; descriptions of animals, 75

Shaw, G. Bernard, 183–4, 186–7

Sherbo, A., 186

Shottery (Warwickshire), 17

Sidney, Sir Philip, 78; *Astrophil and Stella*, 12; *Apology for Poetry*, 85–6, 168–9; *Arcadia*, 92, 161

Simmons, J. L., 195

Smith, D. Nichol, 186

Smith, G. R., 190

Smith, Hallett, 191, 195

Snyder, S., 195

Sophocles, 126; *Oedipus Rex*, 158

Southampton, Henry Wriothesley, 3rd Earl of, 11–12, 14, 15, 19

Spencer, T. J. B., 189

Spencer, Theodore, 187

Spenser, Edmund, 12; *Faerie Queene*, 161

Spevack, M., 189

Spivack, B., 194

Spurgeon, C., 187

Sternfeld, F. W., 192

Still, Colin, 188
Stoll, E. E., 187
Strachey, Lytton, 24
Strange's men, 7
Stratford, Old, 25
Stratford-upon-Avon, 1–4, 17–18, 24–5, 182
Sturley, Abraham, 17
Swift, Jonathan, 129
Swinburne, A. C., 186

Terence, 2
Terry, Ellen, 183
theatres, London, 6, 8, 16; Rose, 8; Globe, 18, 20, 25; Blackfriars, 24, 25
Thorpe, Thomas, 12
Tillyard, E. M. W., 187, 193, 195
Tolstoy, Leo, 184, 186–7
Tourneur, Cyril, 126
Traversi, D. A., 188, 195
Troublesome Reign of King John, 111
Trousdale, M., 192

Ure, Peter, 187

venereal disease, 40
Venice, 44
Vere, Elizabeth de, 11
Vickers, Brian, 186, 192
Voltaire, 183

Waith, E. M., 194
Watson, George, 186
Webster, John, 126
Welcombe (Warwickshire), 25
Wells, Stanley, 189, 190, 195
Westminster School, 1
Wilde, Oscar, 86
Wilders, J., 194
Wilson, J. Dover, 182, 187, 193
Wimsatt, W. K., 186
Wordsworth, William, 159
Wriothesley, Henry, *see* Southampton, Earl of
Wyatt, Sir Thomas, 'Whoso list to hunt', 73

Yeats, W. B., 147, 157, 184, 187